Feminism and Social Justice in Education: International Perspectives

Feminism and Social Justice in Education: International Perspectives

Edited by

Madeleine Arnot and Kathleen Weiler

The Falmer Press
(A member of the Taylor & Francis Group)
London • Washington, D.C.

UK The Falmer Press, 4 John Street, London, WC1N 2ET
USA The Falmer Press, Taylor & Francis Inc., 1900 Frost Road, Suite 101, Bristol, PA 19007

First published 1993

A catalogue record for this book is available from the British Library

Library of Congress Cataloging-in-Publication Data are available on request

ISBN 0 750 70 101 3 cased
ISBN 0 750 70 102 1 paper

Jacket design by Caroline Archer

Typeset in 10/13pt Bembo
by Graphicraft Typesetters Ltd., Hong Kong.

Printed in Great Britain by Burgess Science Press, Basingstoke on paper which has a specified pH value on final paper manufacture of not less than 7.5 and is therefore 'acid free'.

Contents

Introduction

Madeleine Arnot

This collection offers a unique opportunity to host an international forum on contemporary feminist theory and practice in education. The book gathers together contributions from leading feminist educators in five different countries. Each author examines contemporary feminist theory, politics and/or practice in their own national context. After more than twenty years of feminist education research, policy development and innovative school practice, it seems appropriate to make some attempt to evaluate the impact and significance of this worldwide struggle for social justice. At the same time, the recent restructuring of educational provision (whether in the name of sex equality of the ideologies of the New Right) also requires a considered response from those committed to promoting greater social equality. The work of each of the authors represents therefore both an evaluation of the past and a contribution to the continuing transformation of feminist educational agendas which are suited to the political and economic conditions which prevail in the 1990s.

The condition which allowed this collection to be put together was the willingness on the part of the contributors to share their current thinking and concerns outside of the national frameworks in which we are all located. Each has contributed substantially to the development of gender and educational research in her own country. Indeed some of us have spent most of our academic careers working in the field of gender and education. We are well versed in the now extensive literature which represents the field of feminist studies in education, albeit affected by different biographical influences and different perspectives. Yet feminist studies of education (as one can see from the sources used) has managed to cross its national boundaries and has, in some senses, constructed a common agenda for the English speaking academic world (in, for example New Zealand, Australia, the United Kingdom, the United States of America and Canada). Feminist education research as currently constituted has allowed those of us worldwide, who speak the English language, to share another language — the concepts, terms and grammar of a common field of study. And, as can be seen in many of the chapters represented in the collection, that language and set of shared understandings has helped us learn from each others' experiences and the experiences of women within different but often historically related educational systems. Feminist educational theorizing and practice now provides, as Sue Middleton argues in her chapter, many of the 'domain assumptions' we use in talking about gender issues in education.

At the same time, there is increasing awareness of the limits and constraints of that common academic agenda. The commonalities of women's experiences of schooling across different societies are now being actively questioned and the ways in which white Western feminist thought has channelled and colonized indigenous national concerns and have sustained particular power relations between women (especially between white and black women) are clearly on the agenda. What is also noticeable therefore when reading the chapters in this book is the commitment on the part of the authors to continually and actively assess the appropriateness of the theoretical frameworks in which we work. Feminist theorizing is clearly both the condition for a recognition of our unity across national boundaries but also the condition for recognizing our diversity, between nations and within nations.

The idea to put together a book on feminism and social justice in education was a result of two converging trends. On the one hand it seemed appropriate to ask leading educational feminists to respond to new currents of thinking, particularly in light of the development of, for example, black feminist scholarship and post-modernist feminism. For some, these developments had already had considerable influence. Secondly economic recession and the emergence of free market philosophies in a range of countries had generated a crisis in education and a new pattern of educational reform. How should feminist educational theory respond to such events? The annual American Educational Research Association conference in 1991 in Chicago provided an excellent opportunity to bring together leading feminist academics to discuss the struggles for social justice in education in various countries. A number of the chapters in this collection therefore were presented at this meeting and later modified. Others were directly commissioned in order to ensure a greater range of contributors and a broader perspective on feminist agendas in education. We recognized the need to document both the specificity and similarity of feminist concerns internationally in these industrialized, white dominated, Anglophone settings.

Although hard to classify, the range of theoretical perspectives adopted by the different authors in the book were purposively selected because (despite their diverse interests) they seemed to take a similar stance in relation to gender equality. The approach adopted in this collection could be described as that of *critical feminism*. The authors quite clearly search for the deeper levels of explanation rather than accept the taken-for-granted world of daily life. Whilst concerned to give voice to women's concerns, the various contributors point to the necessity of linking individual and group experiences to their material conditions and the power relations inherent in them. The tensions between concepts of structure and agency, between ideology and subject, between discourse and power (whether structuralist, post-structuralist or post-modern) which has framed our academic writing over the last fifteen years can be found in the various contributions. The necessity of including contexts is integral to our analyses of education.

This critical feminist approach contributed to a commitment to social change which went further than the politics of equal access. What the symposium, and now this book, seeks to do is to re-establish the presence, albeit in new form, of what in the United Kingdom we call 'the egalitarian traditions' — traditions such as those of radical feminism, socialist feminism and black feminism which seeks to transform social relations. What these traditions retain is a belief in the necessity of continuing the struggle for social justice (in terms of class, race and gender), even within increasingly hostile political environments.

Such egalitarian traditions grapple with the thorny problem of relating gendered education to the development of modern capitalism and its class and race formations. They address challenging questions about the relationship between social class, race and gender and the ways these articulate with feminist educational praxis. Such traditions are significant for their commitment to extending, promoting and developing a coherent and scholarly body of theory which would address key political concerns in contemporary society. It is noticeable, therefore, how seriously the authors represented here address the shifting concerns of feminism and how they are not shy to expose the limitations of current feminist theorizing and research. Common to all is an engagement with both feminist theory and contemporary political practice.

The chapters in this volume signal the different ways in which feminists working in the state educational system have struggled or are struggling to democratize education, not only in favour of girls, but also in favour of social justice for all. Other goals therefore have linked to that project — the analyses show how the struggle for gender equality has been part of wider movements for social change. Thus we find discussion of the impact of black feminism, social democratic reforms, and teachers' resistance to state control. Such diverse policies as desegregation of schooling in the United States, the promotion of Maori culture in schools in New Zealand, debates about the teaching of history in the United Kingdom, the conceptualization of equality in the family also can be seen to impinge on women's struggles for justice through education.

Reassessing feminist politics in relation to education therefore clearly involves a complex narrative. It involves identifying different feminist visions, different strategies and tactics, and different types of research. But it also involves, as the contributors make very clear, understanding specificities. Historical and political specificities emerge in these accounts precisely because of their different national settings. So for example, the concepts of equity, equality, egalitarianism and equality of opportunity are defined differently in different social settings. They are hard to extract from the conditions of their existence — the discourses of political and educational life. Similarly feminist educational theories, although often produced within the ivory tower of academia, are, nevertheless, also clearly framed within state discourses and structures.

A number of contributors in this collection make clear too their concerns about the authorship of feminist theory and the promoters of educational reforms in the name of gender equality, be they white or black feminists, women from different social classes, women with different sexualities. Increasingly the reflexivity encouraged by the recent studies of official discourses is evident in the awareness of how feminists themselves have constructed particular world views and not others. Increasingly we, as feminist educationalists, are becoming aware of the complex construction of our own work, our own struggles and our subjectivity. Increasingly we are able to reassess work on equality projects which we ourselves were engaged in and to consider critically the impact of that work.

On the whole, as academics mainly working within institutions of higher education, our own contribution is likely to have been more theoretical than practical so far as schooling was concerned. Most of the authors in this collection teach on courses within sociology, women's studies or education departments. The frameworks we use and the questions we chose to prioritize, quite naturally, have been shaped by a concern with the development of the academic study of women in education. There is a commitment to reveal girls', young women's and adult women's experiences as students and increasingly as teachers within the educational system to those unaccustomed to consider anything other than male experiences and world views. We inflect our work with a desire to challenge and expose the limitations of orthodox academic accounts of education. For all of the authors of this book, the critique of existing male, ethnocentred academic discourses is an essential ingredient of our own political practice.

Chapter 1 by Miriam David provides a good example of precisely this approach. In her review of the theories of the family developed in the last twenty to thirty years, one begins to see the limitations and political consequences of particular conceptions of gender relations. In a climate where the New Right has promoted particular explanations about the breakdown of the family and emphasized the role of parental power, it is significant that feminist and non-feminist social scientific theories of the family have not offered viable alternatives. In particular there is little feminist analysis of the educational relationship between mothers and fathers and their children, and between families and schooling.

Miriam David's call for a more comprehensive study of gender and generation within the family sets an appropriate context for Heidi Safia Mirza's important chapter on the educational achievement of young Afro-Caribbean women. The construction of black motherhood, prevalent in the United States but also to be found in the United Kingdom, suggests a dominance of the mother-daughter relationship and the lack of a male presence in black families. Whilst white feminism has failed to address issues of race, black feminism, she argues, has, it seems, fallen into the trap of constructing artificial notions of black womanhood and family life. The search for explanations of educational 'failure' and success clearly cannot be found in cultural universalisms. Feminist theory must address the concrete social relations which shape educational experiences. As Heidi Safia Mirza argues, we need to understand the different effects of industrial capitalism on different sets of gender relations and different groups of pupils. In this context, we can understand the expectations and values of young Afro-Caribbean girls who strive to achieve a certain 'relative autonomy' in their lives.

A common theme which links the experiences of young Afro-Caribbean women (discussed in chapter 2) with those of Black teachers in New Zealand (chapter 3) and in the United States (chapter 5) is the use of what Heidi Safia Mirza calls 'cultural resources' and 'inner strengths'. In chapter 3, Linda Tuhiwai Smith gives an account, drawn from her personal experiences, of the struggle which Maori women in New Zealand engaged in, to resist colonization. In order to maintain their own cultural identity and authenticity, Maori women in the community and women teachers campaigned to establish a Mana Wahine (a cultural complex) in a state school. The school was used to resist the dominant oppressive culture which constituted Maori as an underclass ethnic minority.

Using the school as a site of struggle is a strategy with which most feminist educationalists are familiar. Women as a majority of the teaching profession have waged campaign after campaign to ensure greater equality for female students and to improve the conditions and prospects of female teachers. Curriculum reform has provided an important focus too of that struggle — not least because of the increased awareness of the ideological influences involved in the selection and organization of school knowledge. The campaigns, however, around the curriculum and teaching have changed, particularly in the United Kingdom where teachers had in the past were encouraged to appreciate classroom autonomy. The impact of the New Right has promoted a new set of priorities and retrieved others. As Gaby Weiner argues in chapter 4, the New Right has created the conditions for what Stuart Hall called 'regressive modernism'. The effects of such educational values can be found in subjects such as school history. The context for developing 'woman centred' history has been made that much more difficult. Nevertheless Weiner urges feminist teachers to begin the task of constructing a counter educational hegemony by analyzing educational policy for themselves and by challenging the forms of teaching now being promoted.

Developing an alternative vision of education in the current crisis can take different forms. Gaby Weiner suggests the importance of reviewing pedagogy and the hidden curriculum of schooling. In chapter 5, Michèle Foster describes some of the ways in which black American women teachers challenge a hostile educational system and respond to the contemporary crisis in education. Her fascinating account of these teachers' educational philosophies reveals their 'connectedness' to their communities and how they perceive the centrality of human relationships within teaching and learning. Like the teachers described in Linda Tuhiwai Smith's account, the struggle for equality was articulated through an emphasis on cultural identity and alternative meanings. Such black voices, Michèle Foster argues, are unlikely to be heard within a policy community that is committed to the values of economic and technical expertise. Yet they have much to offer to those looking for a different way forward towards social justice.

The impact of educational policies on teachers' work is a theme which is shared by a number of other authors in the book. Sue Middleton (in chapter 6) perhaps speaks to all of the authors in the book when she calls for a reflexive analysis of the development of feminist studies of education. She uses, in a novel way, the methodology of post-modernism to consider how, on the one hand, educational policies, particularly in the post-war period in New Zealand, shaped the institutional settings in which feminism developed and, on the other, how feminists themselves were 'positioned inside' their own theories. Aware in particular of the effects of economic conditions but also of the effects of dominant discourses of colonization, Sue Middleton argues for the development of the sociology of women's education which promotes an indigenous culture and which utilizes a 'post-modern critical feminist pedagogy' which challenges such dominance.

Sue Middleton's biographical account raises important questions about how we conceptualize our own position in higher education. Despite the considerable body of literature on the relationship between schooling and capitalism, there is little critical research on the nature of higher education. In the United Kingdom, the dearth of feminist theory on the nature of women teachers' experiences in the tertiary sector has held back the advancement of appropriate policies and reforms. Sandra Acker in chapter 7 provides a useful exploration of what such feminist theory might offer by way of explanation and strategy. By using different feminist frameworks, she explores the variety of ways in which the positioning of women academics could be understood and tackled. The United Kingdom and Canada are used to providing interesting indicators on how cultural specificities have an impact on academic women's lives.

Lyn Yates' chapter on 'Feminism and Australian State Policy' (chapter 8) and my own chapter on British feminist educational politics also have much in common despite their national concerns. Both seek in their own way to interpret the role of the state in relation to gender politics. Increasingly new interest is being shown in the relationship between feminist educational reforms and government initiatives on equal opportunities. In what ways, for example, have feminist educational theorizing and campaigning been shaped by state control of education and party politics? Conversely what impact, if any, have feminist educational movements had upon government policy? Have feminists changed political agendas, and if so, how?

Lyn Yates's chapter of Australian educational reforms offers a particularly interesting insight into the nature of government policy which explicitly addressed the issue of girls' education and sex equality through a sequence of curriculum reports. Her textual analysis reveals not just the implicit framing of the 'problem', but also the historical shifts from a policy discourse around equality to that of 'difference'. Key questions are also identified about the ways in which feminist theory has been used and reinterpreted to construct new policy agendas by the Australian Labour government.

Like Sue Middleton, Lyn Yates uses post-modernism to generate an understanding of policy as discourse and to focus upon 'the silences' within such discourses. Yet at the same time, she identifies the structural conditions which allowed certain feminist ideas to be taken up by the Australian state. In similar fashion, I am also concerned to link the generation of feminist educational politics in the United Kingdom with dominant political discourses and the structure of educational provision. In a context in which teachers were granted classroom autonomy, where central government devolved financial and political powers to local government, feminist teachers found spaces to campaign for social justice. In chapter 9, I argue that such was the success of feminist research and theory that many of the principles of the post-war period came under sustained attack. The principles of universalism which had framed the welfare state, the concepts of freedom of choice and meritocracy, the ideals of co-education and even child-centred philosophies were scrutinized by feminists and were identified as highly problematic. By the mid-1980s feminism had, I argue, generated a crisis of legimitation in patriarchal relations, comparable to that of the crisis in capitalism. The response of the New Right must therefore be interpreted as more than a restoration of class relations in favour of the property-owning classes. Its educational reforms can be interpreted as part of state regulation of gender relations. In this context, the 'modernizing' of gender relations we are currently seeing is a response to feminist educational politics in the last two decades.

A number of key issues for those working within the field of feminist studies of education are raised by authors in this book. This introduction has only hinted at some of those issues. Kathleen Weiler, as the original discussant at the American Educational Research Association conference, drew out some key themes from the set of conference papers. The task, needless to say, proved challenging. In the concluding chapter of this book, she extended that original discussion by locating many of the concerns identified in this introduction in a much broader social context than that of feminism. Drawing her perspective from the experience and issues affecting the United States, Kathleen Weiler usefully contextualizes feminist educational theory and the struggles for social justice in education in the wider political and economic trends of the 1990s. In this sense, the book itself is positioned within its social context — a context which has seen, for example, the rapid growth of worldwide corporate capitalist economic systems, the resurgence of the right wing, the fragmentation of the Eastern Block and the 'collapse of socialism', the emergence of nationalism, and growing social inequality both between different countries and within seemingly advanced economies.

We are reminded in Kathleen Weiler's conclusion that the struggle for sex equality is but one part of a much larger struggle for democracy and education in the modern world. Feminist educational theory and practice contributes to the struggles not merely over how female children should be educated, but how all children should be educated. If the chapters in this book say one thing in common, it is that feminist struggle is an integral part of political struggle over education, and in particular over state education. The context for the successes of the movement lay in the particular conditions of the post-war period and perhaps within the relative economic affluence of Western nations. In this context, the concept of right of citizenship and the ideals of welfarism exposed some of the damaging individual and collective effects of capitalist economic formations and gave sufficient space for women to wage their own struggle. Also in this context, the imposition of patriarchal and race relations, historically embedded within national institutions, also seemed not just outmoded but extraordinarily and consistently oppressive. The challenge for feminists, from different social classes, from different ethnic cultures was to learn how to struggle on so many fronts at once.

The chapters in this collection bear witness to the complexity of issues involved in attempting to democratize educational systems within advanced industrial economies. Struggles for social justice cover the structure as well as the shape and content of education. Framed within dominant political discourses, positioned within feminist discourses, located within higher educational institutions or within schools, feminist educationalists (such as the contributors to this book) have struggled to identify and shape alternative visions of education. It is those alternative visions which provide the reason and the method of our work.

Chapter 1

Theories of Family Change, Motherhood and Education

Miriam E. David

Introduction: Theories of the Family Versus Debates about Families and Education

In this chapter I shall review various theories of the family that have been developed, especially those by feminists, in the last twenty to thirty years, largely in Britain but also where relevant drawing on research from the United States. I am concerned to consider their appropriateness and adequacy in respect to current political debates about the relationship of families to the education system. Current education reforms are based upon giving power to the family and to parents to decide about their children's schools. Although there have been extensive debates in feminist circles about the family and motherhood, as there have been by anti-feminist New Right writers, they tend not to bear on these public policy debates and proposed reforms. The education reforms, giving parents power to make educational choices, have been based instead on social scientific non-feminist evidence.

It is my aim to show the relevance of feminist theories of motherhood and the family to the political debates and social scientific evidence around families and education reform. Feminists have been at the forefront of debates about social justice and equal opportunities in terms of gender and education. Applying their theories to these current education reforms and the family, would demonstrate that such reforms would have serious effects, especially on *mothers*' lives.

My argument is that very few theories of the family, whether feminist or not, have had any bearing on political debates about education, educational policy or the organization of the system of schooling. Indeed, it is also the case that theories of the family, particularly those by feminists, tend not to have had any major effects upon broader policy issues of children's care and social development, even though they may have some bearing upon particular issues in relation to aspects of child care in the context of domestic violence, abuse against women and wider questions of women's fertility or infertility.

Most theories of the family, whether feminist, anti-feminist or non-feminist, tend to focus on either the relationships between the sexes or between the private world of the family and the public world, either of paid employment or broader issues of political life. In feminist and anti-feminist theories the focus is more on gender than generation, and in non-feminist theories, more on the relations between the public and the private worlds.

However, there is a plethora of theories, debates and discussions about the relationships between the family and education. Most of them are specifically applied to policy debates about parents and education or the home and the school. On the whole they have emerged from the social scientific research that developed from the education policy evaluations that began in the 1960s, focussing on how to implement equality of educational opportunity. The taken-for-granted assumptions of the current period, given that past research and education reforms, are that there should be a close and intimate relationship between families and education or between home and school in order to achieve effective, if not equal, schooling.

These kinds of discussions or theories are based upon assumptions about the nature and characteristics of the family that fail to address either gender or race. They assume a particular constant form of traditional family life, in which relationships between the sexes and the generations are relatively unproblematic. It is assumed that there is a sexual division of labour in the traditional and 'national' family whereby fathers/husbands are the main 'breadwinners' and mothers/wives care for the family in the privacy of their own homes and in relation to public institutions such as school. They are not linked either to the theories or practices of contemporary family life, in which there have been major changes in women's roles as wives and mothers, especially through increases in divorce or separation and maternal employment.

In this chapter I want to explore the inadequacies of feminist, anti-feminist and non-feminist theories of the family for understanding the dynamics of family-education relationships. I also want to reveal the inadequacy of contemporary social scientific theories of education over the relationship with families and parents, given that they are not gendered. I will use the insights of feminist theories of the family to highlight the ways in which new perspectives could be brought to bear on family-school relationships, by pinpointing gender and generational issues and those to do with race and/or ethnicity. In other words, I aim to bring together feminist theories of the family and non-feminist social scientific theories of the relation between families and schooling, in order to bring out new perspectives on education and gendered parenthood, specifically motherhood.

Feminist Theories of the Family and/or Motherhood

Snitow (1992) has usefully reviewed the ways in which feminists have considered theories of the family, particularly motherhood. She has identified three periods in the development of feminist theories of *motherhood*, mainly reviewing the literature from the United States, although she attempts to incorporate British material. In so doing she reveals both her own biases and those of the literature that she selects. Admittedly, she herself points out her own and other feminists' predilections. She is not concerned with motherhood in relation either to child-care or to more formal issues of education, but rather with feminist theories over questions of fertility. Nevertheless the three periods that she identifies are useful for a general review of feminist theories and their limitations. They are 1963–75, 1976–79 and 1980 to the present. I shall discuss these periods, drawing on her ideas about how such theories developed in relation to academic women's studies and political movements.

Snitow argues that the early feminist texts between 1963 and 1975 were 'trying to pull away from the known and, like all utopian thinking, they can sound thin, absurd, undigested. But mother-hating? No'. She adds that

> in my search for early feminist mother-hating . . . there are *hardly any articles on any aspect of mothering*. Nothing strange, really, about this blindness. The mouse had only just started down the python; most of the writers were young. (*ibid*, p. 37) (my emphasis)

Her second period 1976–79 is brief, since she argues that

> in these years the feminist work of exploring motherhood took off, and books central to feminist thinking in this wave were written, both about the daily experience of being a mother and about motherhood's most far-reaching implications. (*ibid*, p. 38)

She shows how this kind of writing became central to feminist theories, which were, in fact, not about the family, child care or education, but rather about women's general position in society and in relation to men.

In the 1980s, as Snitow points out, there was a blossoming of feminist theories, in particular as a result of the development of academic women's studies, which came out of the activities of the women's movement. Many of these theories bore on motherhood and the family in a particular fashion. They were concerned with the relationships between men and women both within the privacy of the family and in the public worlds of paid employment and civic or political life. Indeed, the relationships between public and private life were critical to the development of these theories.

Snitow has argued that the political situation in the US in the 1980s was a difficult one for feminists and that 'my line doesn't work outside the US' (*ibid*, p. 41). Moves to the Right clearly limited the development of feminist strategies. She states:

> My time-line for the eighties is a record of frustration, retrenchment, defeat and sorrow . . . Broad societal events like the steady rise of divorce and women's increasing work place participation collide with women's failure to get day care, child support, fair enough custody laws, changes in the structure of a work day and a typical work life and finally any reliable, ongoing support from men. Our discouragement is, in my view, the sub-text of most of what we have written about motherhood in the past decade. I think women are heartbroken. Never has the baby been so delicious. We are — in this period of reaction — elaborating, extending, reinstitutionalizing this relation for ourselves . . . A feminist theorist tells me she is more proud of her new baby than of all her books. (*ibid*)

Feminist thinking in the US in the 1980s, according to Snitow, became more fragmented, more frustrated and more cynical. Moreover, the term 'family' increasingly replaced the more gendered concepts that had been common in the early periods. The association between motherhood and the family was a constant pressure given New Right thinking and its anti-feminist backlash. Faludi (1992) has made similar comments about how the anti-feminist backlash affected feminist writing and political action. Feminists, in other words, became more defensive, less assertive about the possibilities and about alternatives. Nevertheless, their focus remained that of the power dynamics entirely in terms of gender rather than generation. Although Snitow is more despondent about the US than other countries, I think there have been very similar trends in British feminist thinking on the family, also related to the broader political situation.

Rosalind Coward (1992) has also argued that women, especially feminist women, have retreated from engagement in political and public struggles in Britain in favour of family life and motherhood. Part of her argument relates this to the political context of the moves to the Right; another part relates the changes in feminist strategies and political action to how women feel about their lives in relation to their family backgrounds and personal rather than work circumstances. In other words, Coward provides a psychoanalytic explanation, relating changes to the female psyche. Her interviews with about 150 women seem to confirm these conclusions. Yet this kind of analysis is very new, and rather defeatist and fatalistic, withdrawing from wider concerns about political change in favour of psychoanalytic conclusions.

A central tenet in theories of what feminists had, by the 1970s, termed 'women's oppression' was the idea and ideology of the family (Barrett, 1981). However, the issue of women's oppression was seen to be crucially related to the nature of women's 'unpaid work' within the family and its relationship to men's paid work outside the family. It had much less association, in feminist theories, with the nature or 'real' characteristics of women's familial roles as wives, mothers, daughters. Indeed, the extent to which this kind of 'unpaid work' was seen as on a continuum of 'care' and had developmental aspects to it in terms of child care and children's upbringing remained relatively untheorized by feminists. It was not the central concern of feminists, given that they espoused a stronger interest in power relationships between the sexes. The power dynamics in family life, between both gender and generation or mothers and fathers, sons and daughters, was marginalized.

With the expansion and development of feminist theories of the family, the focus remained stubbornly upon theories of relationships between the sexes than on the wider consideration of the triangular pattern of relationships in the family. From an early concern with the family as a site of women's oppression through women's confinement to domestic and caring activities, feminist theories developed along three rather contrasting lines. One was around the general nature of *caring* as an activity within the family, not specifically in relation to children, but rather in relation to men as husbands and in relation to a range of adult caring responsibilities, such as of elderly or handicapped relatives. This can be seen particularly in the work of Finch and Groves (1983) and Ungerson (1989).

The second and more extensive area of theorizing about these aspects of family life related to issues about women's relationships to men in the context of questions and issues about domestic violence and/or abuse. Latterly these theories about domestic violence have been extended from theories about adult men and women's physical and sexual relationships to a broader consideration of the continuum of forms of physical and sexual abuse between men, women and children. A key theorist in this context has been Liz Kelly (1988). She has considered the similarities and differences of types of violence and abuse, developing theoretical insights across a wide range of issues to do with gender and generational relationships largely within the family.

The third type of feminist theories developed in relation to questions of motherhood and fertility or infertility, including also abortion (Klein, 1989). This is the kind of feminist thinking that Snitow (1992) has addressed and highlighted. These theories were very specific and tended to focus upon women's perspectives and experiences rather than upon women's relationships with children. When they did consider women's relationships it was with respect to men as partners and/or husbands and as fathers or potential fathers of their children (Barrett and McIntosh, 1982). Indeed, the vast majority of this work has been about developing theories of difference between the sexes. In particular, psychoanalytic theories about the differences between men and women have been applied and/or adapted to give consideration to the ways in which the differences between the sexes have social effects or manifestations.

As Snitow, amongst others, has argued some of the most useful feminist theories on the family distinguish motherhood from fatherhood. Nevertheless, these theories remain at the level of abstraction and do not address child care and development as opposed to mothering, the concept and ideology of motherhood and the influences on social organization. As we noted earlier, Snitow did not even draw that distinction in her otherwise careful review of the rather voluminous literature. Similarly, the theories concerned with fertility and its obverse, infertility, focus more on questions of the relationships between men and women and various professional groups than on practices related to children and child care and wider issues of public forms of care and socialization or education (Hamner and Maynard, 1987; Klein, 1989; Stanworth, 1987).

The changing political context in the 1980s towards the Right may go some way to explaining why feminist theories of motherhood and the family, especially amongst white feminists, have developed along these lines. They have not looked at questions of either child care and development or the more formal issues with respect to children's education either informally at home or more formally in schools. Much of the time in the 1980s has been spent by feminists developing arguments against either the confinement of women to roles within the home or the pervasive and suffocating ideology of motherhood, in which women's 'right to choose' becomes largely risible, especially when it is carefully circumscribed, if not denied, with respect to abortion. In other words, feminist theories and thinking have mainly been in dialogue with anti-feminist or New Right theories and policies on the family. Earlier feminist attempts to create alternative visions and roles for women, not simply to do with familial roles, have inevitably become very constrained in this harsh New Right political context.

Feminist Theories of the Family and Education

There are some notable exceptions to the general lack of attention to the relationship of families and education. In particular, Dorothy Smith has concerned herself with developing theories which concentrate on the interaction between mothers and education, especially in terms of the ways in which the formal school system delimits the work of mothers. Given this emphasis it is perhaps surprising that Smith's work has not been taken up by feminists concerned to theorize the family. It was a very early paper of hers, originally published in 1975, that first drew attention to these substantive issues. Entitled 'A Peculiar Eclipsing: Women's Exclusion from Man's Culture', she pointed out how influential both the theories and practices of education were for constricting notions of motherhood. The paper has been reprinted several times, most recently in *The Everyday World as Problematic.* Smith (1988) noted:

> The enormous literature on the relation of family socialization and educational attainment, in which the role of the mother takes on such a prominent part, can be seen also to have its distinctive biases. The treatment of mothering in this literature is in various ways evaluative, critical or instructive with respect to the practices and relations conducive to educational attainment or to the psychosocial well-being of children. Virtually the whole of this literature presupposes a one-way relation between school and family practices, organization, and, in particular, mothering practices are seen as consequential for the child's behaviour at school. The phenomenon of school phobia as it is vulgarly described is one notorious example, whereby the protectiveness of mother is understood as creating a dependence in the child and hence the child's fearfulness at school . . . (p. 21)

Smith then questions why this has not been seriously addressed as an issue:

> Who has thought to take up the issue of these relations from the standpoint of women? Might we not then have studies concerned with the consequences of the school and the educational processes for how the child matures in the family and for the family itself? Where are those studies showing the disastrous consequences of the school for the families of immigrants, particularly non-English speaking immigrants . . . Where are the studies telling us anything about the consequences for family organization of societal processes that 'subcontract' educational responsibilities for homework and so forth to the family and in particular to the mother? . . . What are the implications of this role for family relations, particularly relations between mothers and children? (*ibid*)

The majority of educational research, she argues, has been conducted from the standpoint of men:

> In the field of education research itself, our assumptions are those seen from men's position in it. Turn to that classic of our times, Phillippe Aries's *Centuries of Childhood.* Interrogate it seriously from the standpoint of women. Ask, should this book not be retitled *Centuries of Childhood of Men*? Or take Christopher Jencks's influential

> book entitled *Inequality*. Should this not be described as an examination of the educational system with respect to its implications for inequality among men. The very terms in which *inequality* is conceived are based on men's occupations, men's typical patterns of career and advancement.
>
> A work examining the educational system with respect to the inequality of women would be focused quite differently. It would, among other matters, be concerned with the educational system as systematically producing a differential of competence among women and men in almost every educational dimension, including that of physical development. It would focus on inequality between the sexes as a systematically organized product of the educational process. (*ibid*, p. 22)

From these examples, Smith tries to reach a broader theory about women's exclusion from wider social processes. She claims that the examples illustrate the 'outcomes of women's absence'. She also sees them not as 'accidental' but as 'a general organizational feature of our kind of society' (*ibid*). Her analysis has had important repercussions for, and influences on, feminist research methodology. But while Smith has been celebrated as a major feminist thinker, oddly her work has not led to more systematic mapping of the sexist presuppositions in educational research and the policy consequences of such 'absences'.

Feminist writers have, more recently, begun the process of more detailed studies of the educational process. In Britain, there has also been some serious consideration given to these kinds of questions by Valerie Walkerdine, a feminist psychologist, who works from the psychoanalytic tradition but who also emphasizes sociohistorical developments and theories. Walkerdine has attempted to theorize how social expectations about motherhood in relation to early childhood education have come about in a particular sociohistorical and policy context. In a rather polemical text co-authored with Lucey (1989), nicely entitled *Democracy in the Kitchen*, she has considered how the developments in official ideologies and practices around motherhood have grown up in post-war Britain.

Walkerdine and Lucey (1989) started this study by reanalyzing a study of young children's learning both at home and at school. The study was originally conducted by Tizard and Hughes (1984) from a traditional social psychological perspective. Walkerdine and Lucey critically appraise that perspective and reach rather different conclusions about mothers' contributions to children's learning and the general effects on policies and ideologies on future generations of women, especially as mothers. They argue that mothers have been severely circumscribed both by law and governmental policies as well as by social scientists' prescriptions, essentially about their necessary educational 'work' or 'play' with young children. They show the effects, too, of class upon mothers' roles.

Phoenix (1991) and Phoenix, Woollett and Lloyd (1991) have also developed a feminist psychological perspective on mothers in relation to child care and, to some extent, education. Similarly, Gordon (1990) has studied the ways in which mothers who consider themselves to be feminists rear their children in the present climate. She looks at their relationships to schools and the education system. She concludes that, although fraught with difficulties, such women take pleasure in trying to develop alternative styles of family life and child-rearing. However, these two studies are most unusual in taking the mothers' perspectives as central in the education and care of children.

The majority of feminist theorists who concern themselves with education do not address the issues in this way. Rather they have adopted the liberal-social democratic framework which tends to focus on issues about *equal opportunities in education*. The now 'traditional' focus of feminist thinking has been on relationships between men and women. It is this approach that has dominated within the rather extensive feminist literature on education. For example, the very important and critical work of Dale Spender (1989) has looked at the ways in which women and girls have been treated relative to men throughout the education system, focussing especially upon male power and dominance as the reason for women's relatively poor treatment within the education system. This theme of the ways in which the education system itself produces and reproduces gendered people, together with its associations with the labour market, has dominated feminist research. There is now a vast accumulated array of evidence about the differential treatment of boys and girls, from different class and ethnic backgrounds, within and throughout the education system. Perhaps this is best summarized by two collections by Arnot and Weiner (1987) and Weiner and Arnot (1987).

One reason for this kind of approach may be, as Snitow (1992) argued, that the political situation has forced feminists to consider the wider political consequences of their theories. Equal opportunities, having been accepted in legislation even by ostensibly right-wing administrations, become acceptable as a political framework for feminist thinking and action. In any event it is again a matter of some curiosity that most feminists in education have not addressed the issues of the relations of family or motherhood to education. Perhaps the predominance of New Right thinking on the family has provoked a defensive reaction. It is certainly clear that there has been, in the late 1980s, what has variously been called an anti-feminist backlash or reaction to feminism from the Right both in the political and academic arenas. There is now a plethora of anti-feminist and non-feminist theories of the family, especially in relation to changes in family life through both demography and employment.

Anti-Feminist, New Right Theories About the Family and Family Changes

Many of the theories and commentaries about changes in families, especially those from the USA, have imputed the causes of such changes to women, mainly feminists, and have asserted that they have had deleterious effects on children. New Right or conservative thinkers in the USA, including those who are social scientists, have assumed that the changes in family life are 'morally wrong' and have deleterious effects on the affected families. Although educational consequences have not been chief amongst their targets they have been alluded to nevertheless. Their arguments have been specifically anti-feminist and have blamed women for changes in society (Faludi, 1992).

Gilder (1981 and 1983), for example, has pointed to the serious consequences of changes in family life for the traditional structure of society. His concern was in particular for male motivation to work arguing that 'man has been cuckolded by the compassionate State'. He was especially concerned that family or marital breakdown would reduce men's motivation to work hard. He also felt that state social support provided to 'errant' wives and mothers for their child-rearing responsibilities would reduce male economic responsibilities. His strategy was, therefore, to try to change the state's economic and social relationship with women in families, in order to stem the tide of marital breakdown and ensure that women remained within marriages. Although Gilder wanted to try to reinvoke traditional family life, his focus was less on children than on the behaviour of wives. His consideration was on the role that the state played not with respect to education, but to financial maintenance of families. Indeed, his concerns stemmed from his twin interest in social policy and a critique of feminist politics and their effects on public policy (Gilder, 1981 and 1983).

Murray (1984 and 1989), a social and political scientist, has developed similar arguments about the decline of the traditional family. He wrote two texts to popular conservative acclaim. The first, *Losing Ground: American Social Policy 1950–80*, was a re-analysis of the impact and effects of federal and liberal policies to deal with social issues. He was particularly concerned to argue for a reduction in state and social intervention because of their adverse consequences on family and community. In his second text, *In Pursuit of Happiness and Good Government*, he widened his commentary to consider 'happiness' as the most important criterion of successful governmental policies. He demonstrated how liberal and neo-conservative policies had led to the persistence, rather than prevention, of social problems and, in particular, changes in family life. He used a variety of examples to make his point, including that of education:

> To return to the running example of education, the reforms in education during the 1960s and 1970s may be seen as a series of steps that

> 'took some of the trouble' out of educating one's child and to that degree attenuated this important source of satisfaction. Responsibility for decisions about nearly everything — curricula, textbooks, disciplinary standards, rules of attendance and suspension, selection of teachers, testing requirements, the amounts of money to be spent, guidelines for lunch menus — moved outward from the neighbourhood to the state or federal government. The argument here is not about whether these changes were substantively good or bad; rather, it is that *even if* they had been good educationally, they were still bad for parents in that they constrained and depressed the ways in which a parent with a child in public school could take satisfaction from that component of life called 'overseeing the education of one's child'. (Murray, 1988, p. 268)

In other words, Murray was concerned that liberal social policies had, in effect, reduced individuals' personal responsibilities, including and especially those of parents for their children. These policies had generally negative effects on family life.

But Murray was more perturbed about the consequences of the loss of community for the traditional family. His argument essentially focussed on the moral and social consequences of the changes. He saw the effects of such changes as the creation of an 'under-class', largely consisting of black families, who are prone to crime, indolence, and having children illegitimately. Although he did not specify gender differences in the effects of the break-up of the traditional family, he was, in fact, focussing upon women, especially single mothers and particularly black female headed households and their child-rearing responsibilities. He also pin-pointed the role of black, unemployed 'youth' or young men who resorted to crime. However, although Murray raised the question about how children are reared in such circumstances of illegitimacy and poverty, his central remedy was not state education or social policies. Instead, it was to reduce state intervention and reinvoke individual women's parental responsibilities.

Murray's theory was a gloomy prognostication about the future of the family and community. His remedy was limited to the reassertion of a particular set of moral values about the traditional nuclear family, which may not be effective in modern industrial societies. Nevertheless, his analysis points to the problematic future for children of such kinds of family life, without proffering any evidence or alternative positive possibilities.

Murray's arguments became so popular amongst conservative thinkers in Britain that he was asked by the Institute of Economic Affairs, a conservative 'think tank', to give consideration to the applicability of his ideas in Britain. As a result, he wrote a sharply polemical essay entitled 'The emerging British

UNDERCLASS' published, with rejoinders from three British social scientists, in 1990. He argued that similar social problems existed in Britain as a result of similar social policies. He wrote:

> It seems safe to conclude that as of 1989 the British underclass is still small enough not to represent nearly the problem it does in the US . . . The question facing Britain is the same, haunting question facing the United States: how contagious is the disease? . . . In the case of illegitimacy, it is impossible to assume the exponential curve in the trendline since 1970 will continue to steepen — if it were to do so, all British births would be illegitimate by the end of the century. But even if we assume more conservatively that the trend of the past 10 years will continue linearly, more than 40 per cent of births will be to single women by 1999 . . . In both countries, the same humane impulses and the same intellectual fashions drove the reforms in social policy. The attempts to explain away the consequences have been similar . . . . The *central truth . . . . is our powerlessness to deal with an underclass once it exists*. No matter how much money we spend on our cleverest social interventions, we don't know how to turn around the lives of teenagers who have grown up in an underclass culture. Providing educational support opportunities or job opportunities doesn't do it. Training programmes don't reach the people who need them most. *We don't know how to make up for the lack of good parents* — day care doesn't do it, foster homes don't work very well. Most of all, we don't know how to make up for the lack of a community that rewards responsibility and stigmatizes irresponsibility. (pp. 24 and 33)

Despite this agnosticism, Murray jumped to particular solutions and advocated a reduction in the responsibilities of government. He even cited this as an example:

> If people in one neighbourhood think marriage is an outmoded institution, fine, let them run their neighbourhood as they see fit. But make it easy for the couple who thinks otherwise to move into a neighbourhood where two-parent families are valued. (*ibid*, p. 34)

His wider analysis led him to advocate a whole range of private, rather than public, policy solutions such as education vouchers and tuition tax credits. But his solutions remain polemical.

Three major social scientists debated his views in the same pamphlet and pointed variously to problems in the statistical analysis of single mothers and illegitimacy, social policy, crime and 'indolence' and the concept of the underclass itself. Brown (in Murray, 1990), in her response, presented a more careful statistical picture of the characteristics of lone mothers in Britain, pinpointing differences between single, never-married, separated, widowed and divorced mothers and the status of black families. In reply to Murray, she wrote:

> The picture the figures present is of a growing population of one-parent families, mostly fatherless families dependent on benefit to quite a staggering extent. Moreover, while in 1986, 50 per cent of married mothers went out to work to help support their families, only 42 per cent of lone mothers worked, and as few as 25 per cent of single mothers, and half of them part-time only . . . (But) by 1987 . . . 27 per cent of single mothers were (more than five years) on benefit and 37 per cent of divorced mothers . . .
>
> Among women aged 18–49, with and without children, the proportion cohabiting has risen from 9 per cent of single women and 39 per cent of divorced and separated women in 1981 to 20 per cent of single and 52 per cent of divorced and separated women in 1988.
>
> Given these patterns, *pointing a finger at single mothers — but not at divorced or separated wives* — as an especial danger to society makes little sense. If, for a child, being brought up without a father is of key importance, it is hard to see a difference or major social significance between starting life without a father and acquiring one, and starting life with a father and then losing him, even though it might have been better for the child in both cases if there had been a stable union involving both natural parents. (pp. 45–6, my emphasis)

Brown captured a key flaw in Murray's study — that of confusing the effects of changes in family life on child-rearing practices and responsibilities. Yet neither Murray nor Brown gave much consideration to the links between changes in family life and education, a point to which I will return. Other American studies such as Berger and Berger's, in *The War Over The Family* (1984), also point to the debates between the right and the left over the theory and future of families, particularly in the context of rapid social change. As liberals, Berger and Berger were loath to recommend intervention in the privacy of family life. They did, however, recommend a range of public policy strategies to ensure the continuation of the traditional family. They did not choose to address questions of education reform.

This brief review of the American debates over changes in family life and strategies to deal with them, once again illustrates the ways in which these debates about the family have, to a large extent, been pursued independently of education. The same is also true in Britain. Similar arguments to those of Gilder and Murray have been developed by right-wing thinkers in Britain, most particularly Mount (1982) and members of the Institute of Social Affairs (ISA), such as Anderson and Dawson (1986), the Institute of Economic Affairs (IEA), such as Green with Quest (1992), as well as Willetts of the Centre for Policy Studies (CPS). The IEA has pursued most vigorously the arguments, about changes in family life (Green with Quest, 1992). Anderson and Dawson (1986) have denounced the demise of the traditional family and have argued for its resuscitation through moral censure, rather than through government action.

Most of the right-wing British commentaries again do not link their analysis of trends in family life with educational strategies, except in general moral terms. But all of their solutions to the social problems of changes in family life, such as divorce, separation and out-of-wedlock parenthood, have implications for education as well as social policy. Their key argument is that changes in family life have been 'caused' by state interference. In other words, the 'nanny' state has provided excessive social and economic supports to families. A reduction in state intervention and an increase in private, parental responsibilities is the Right's solution to a range of problems, including children's educational development. Murray's arguments chime in well with those of conservative family and educational commentators in Britain such as Sexton (1990), Flew with Green *et al.* (1992), Cox (1991) and Anderson and Dawson (1986).

Durham (1991) has carefully reviewed the construction of conservative arguments about the family and morality in Britain in the 1980s, by contrast with the USA. He has used five case studies of moral crusades, namely sex education, abortion, contraception for under 16-year-old girls, embryo research and 'sex and violence' campaigns. He argues that the British New Right has 'relatively little interest in moral issues' (p. 60).

> A comprehensive account of the New Right would have to acknowledge that it does contain significant moralist strands. But this remains fundamentally different from the situation in the United States. Issues of family and morality were crucial to the rise of the American New Right in the seventies and have remained central to major components since. The British New Right is far less focussed and far more disparate on such issues. (*ibid*)

He also tries to assess the links between the various 'moral' campaigns and the Conservative governments, particularly in 'the Thatcher years'. He concludes:

> If the eighties were the decade of Margaret Thatcher, one of its many effects has been to popularise the term 'Victorian values'. A political project which was committed to privatisation . . . and the restoration of Britain's standing on the world stage was also committed to a

> revival of discipline and standards . . . When sex education is placed in 'a moral framework' . . . and government begins to show concern over single parent families, then moral campaigners can believe their time has come. But on key issues the government proved to be a disappointment or even an antagonist rather than an ally, and many of the social indices which outrage campaigners — the abortion rate, the divorce rate, the illegitimacy rate — have risen and are continuing to rise . . . . But what we . . . are not likely to see in the nineties, is the coming together of the political right and the moral lobby and a shift from a rarely implemented government rhetoric to a sustained 'moral majority' stance. (*ibid*, p. 179)

Durham does not fully review the conservative government's policies but instead focusses on the moral crusaders on family matters. In fact, had he reviewed the strategies, he would have noted their lack of effectiveness. As Murray pointed out, New Right politicians, in government, have not pursued effective social strategies to reverse the changes in family life, such as the rate of divorce, separation and maternal employment. Nevertheless, the rhetoric has been strong. This rhetoric can be seen as well in the work of Dawson who has raised the issue of the connection between changes in family life and children's educational performance as a basis for adding vigour to arguments about policies for families and education. Citing Halsey's works, he claims that the evidence of the poorer educational performance of children from single parent families is now incontrovertible.

Indeed, it has been the case that left perspectives on the relation between parents and education has not necessarily been any less 'traditional' than those of the 'moral' or the new right. A similar rhetoric about the negative effects of changes in the family have often been employed by left researchers. Arguments about the family from left-wing commentators have not, however, centred crucially on the links with education. In particular, Lasch's arguments, although couched in Marxian language, are redolent of those of the New Right. Faludi (1992) links him with other anti-feminist arguments. His *Haven in a Heartless World* and its sequel also mourn the passing of the traditional family, without developing notions about its effects or how to deal with it (Barrett and McIntosh, 1982).

Non-Feminist Social Scientific Theories of Families, Change and Education

In Britain much of the evidence about changes in the family does not touch on its effects on educational performance. However, it would not be fair to argue that this work is anti-feminist. Indeed, the most recent publications from the relatively newly established left-wing policy 'think-tank' — the Institute for Public Policy Research (IPPR) — considered issues about the family without reference to educational effects or strategies (Coote *et al*, 1990). At approximately the same time the IPRR also published a pamphlet on education without reference to the links with the family, despite its public policy agenda (Coote *et al*, 1990; Miliband, 1991). In other words, the public policy debate on the left about changes in family life has rarely been related to that of educational reforms. Family changes are mourned without reference to the possibility of either creating positive effects or noting their complexity.

Most of the work by social scientists concerned with understanding family change, such as Bradshaw and Millar (1991) have only documented the changes and their financial and social consequences rather than their educational implications. But some social scientists have developed a broader perspective on changes in family life. In particular, there has been documentation to the extent of, and type of changes with respect to, the gender and/or race or ethnicity of parents.

A critical perspective has been applied to notions originally developed in the USA about 'the feminization of poverty'. The argument developed in the USA was essentially about the extent to which the growth and development of female headed households with dependent children had led to their dependence on state welfare and support. 'Welfare mothers' — women rearing children alone on state support — were deemed to be a new category of the poor. (Eisenstein, 1982; Scott, 1984). Indeed, for the most part they were also seen to be disproportionately women from racial or ethnic minorities, particularly black.

However, evidence for Britain suggests that 'family poverty' as a social category and term has been a mask for considerable poverty amongst women as *mothers*, whether or not they are dependent upon husbands or the state (Land and Ward, 1986). Changing family patterns, such as marital break-up and the creation of lone parent households consisting predominantly of mothers with dependent and often school-age children, makes for different patterns of female poverty and social dependence. Glendenning and Millar (1987 and 1991) have variously pointed to the characteristics and social needs of lone parents. Whilst lone parenthood is not only the prerogative of those who are disadvantaged or in poverty, it certainly has important social repercussions for those who do become dependent upon state support (Bradshaw and Millar, 1991). Lone parenthood amongst the middle classes has different effects and consequences, including those of education.

Changes in family life, away from the apparently 'traditional' family composed of two natural parents, with dependent children being reared in the privacy of their own homes, evoke a range of political responses. However, the majority of responses focus on women's changing role especially as *mothers*.

On the one hand, mothers have been blamed for the family changes and their effects, especially on both men and children. On the other hand, feminists have tried with difficulty to argue that these changes are not the fault of women but of wider social processes and that strategies should be developed to transform social relationships both inside and outside the home.

Despite this range of theorizing on the family and motherhood by feminists and non-feminists alike, educational reformers or educational researchers have tended to ignore the debates. From both left and right perspectives it has been assumed that a strong and positive relationship between families and education is necessarily a 'good thing'. No reference is made to the impact or effects of reforms on either children or on women as mothers: they are invisible and ungendered. The literature is replete with both research evidence and prescriptive material about how to develop and maintain a close and positive relationship between home and school, on the general assumption that this will enhance effective schooling. Three examples suffice. Two recent collections by John Bastiani entitled *Parent and Teachers* (1987) refer to the more generally critical social scientific literature but do not raise the question of the *gendered* characteristics of, or processes in families. Similarly, Bastiani's more prescriptive work on home school relations does not address the question of the differences between working with mothers or fathers. Alastair Macbeth, who has also written widely on the issues of parents and schools in Britain, especially Scotland, and in the European context, fails to question gendered parenthood or the gender or generational processes within families. This is despite an extremely thorough review of the issues in his most recent textbook entitled *Involving Parents: Effective Parent-Teacher Relations* (Macbeth, 1989). Thirdly, a major research study conducted for the Policy Studies Institute by Smith and Tomlinson (1989) investigated the characteristics of effective schools in multicultural settings. Controlling for ethnic and racial differences, they found that the most effective schools were those with a particular *ethos*. They did not question the characteristics of the families but assumed the necessity of close liaison between home and school.

These examples are from the perspective of the left. But it is also true of the recent voluminous literature on parental choice that different types of parents or families are rarely acknowledged. On the one hand, commentators from the right such as Chubb and Moe (1990) from the USA or Flew with Green *et al* (1992) and Macleod (1989) in Britain debate the issues without an eye to gender questions. Even Glenn (1989) in his seven-nation survey for the US government did not question gender although he raised issues about race, religion and/or ethnicity. British writers, developing critical appraisals of recent policies on parents and schools, such as Ball (1991), Walford (1990) and Johnson (1990) also discuss theories about parents and education without addressing gender *or* changes in family life.

Two American theorists in education have, however, noted the dissonance in these theories, taking up Smith's point without her feminist perspective. Epstein (1990), reviewing research about families and education in the USA, concluded that the two issues have developed separately and in parallel rather than together. Her particular focus, however, is on how to integrate the two approaches to ensure an emphasis on improved relations or partnerships in the interests of children's education. She writes:

> All the years that children attend school, they also attend home. The simultaneous influence of schools and families on students is undeniable, but too often ignored in research and in practice. In research, social scientists who study one environment rarely give serious attention to another. Sociologists of the family rarely study how family practices affect student success in school, or how school practices affect family attitudes, interactions, and practices. Sociologists of education who study school and classroom organization rarely examine how school practices affect school practices and effects. (p. 90)

She goes on to argue for more research on the issue of changes in family life and their impact on education. To quote her:

> Families are changing. The 'traditional' family of two natural parents with mum working at home is now 'untraditional' (Bureau of the Census, 1984). Most children live in other types of families — one-parent homes, reconstituted or blended families, joint-custody families, foster homes, extended families, relatives as guardians, and other variations. These arrangements cross economic lines and are not indicative of uncaring families. And, all schools and families must understand how they can influence each other to benefit the children they share. A continuing research agenda needs to focus on questions of the effects on students of family and school programs that provide developmental and differentiated experiences for families of children at all grade levels and for the special needs of different families . . . (*ibid*, pp. 116–7)

Lareau (1989) has argued similarly that changes in family structure and family life have been occurring at the same time as the schools have been demanding greater involvement of parents. She has written:

> Indeed, the last few decades have seen substantial changes in the family, notably changes in women's labour force participation, family size and family structure. For example, with the increase in divorce, a

> majority of school-aged children now spend some time in a single-parent family . . . We believe there must be a restructuring of family-school relationships to reflect the changes occurring both within schools and the larger society. Schools and families are in a synergistic combination. Teachers' expectations for parental participation in schooling have escalated in the last few decades, precisely at the same time that changes in family structure have reduced familial resources for participating in schooling. (p. 254)

She wants schools to give greater consideration and respect to these family life changes.

Conclusions: Theories of the Family and its Relation to Education Reform

I have argued here that feminist, anti-feminist and non-feminist theories of the family and motherhood tend to ignore issues of education, whilst theorists and reformers of education, despite arguing for a close relationship between parents or families and schools, do not address changes in family life or theories of the family or motherhood. However, it may be possible to adapt feminist theories of the family and motherhood, on the lines that Smith has argued, to an educational context. This would entail highlighting the implications of changes in family life for the relations between families and schools, pointing up the implications for women's lives not only as parents *per se* but as mothers in particular. It would also address policy prescriptions attempting to involve parents more widely in their children's education. These developments have been manifold, from parental involvement in the pre-school years, to early childhood education, to political participation in decision-making and the ongoing work of the schools, through governing bodies etc., to the apparently 'one-off' event of parental choice of school (David, 1992).

A theory that incorporated gender issues especially a view of gendered parenthood as well as the gender of the children would be capable of differentiating a range of critical implications of these new developments. Moreover, a feminist analysis of the relationship of mothers and education in terms of parental involvement, participation and choice as well as wider issues would also provide the context for understanding the impact of these policy-related issues on women's lives within the privacy of the family. In other words, developing a feminist theory of the relation between family and education would provide evidence of the two-way relation: the impact of changes in educational policy on family life as well as the impact of changes in family life on education. This would, in all probability, reveal quite how complex the patterns of interactions have become, with particular effects on women's lives, especially as *mothers*, both inside the family and in education, on their own behalf as well as on behalf of their children. There is already some interesting evidence largely from feminist case study examples of the impact of changes in women's expectations and roles within the family on their educational as well as occupational lives (Edwards, 1991; Sperling, 1991; David, Edwards, Hughes and Ribbens, forthcoming). Indeed, it has become almost commonplace for some women as mothers to become involved in forms of education whilst their children are either very young or themselves involved in education. These trends, given changes in family life as well as in the wider social and economic context, are likely, like families themselves, to be here to stay.

References

ANDERSON, D. and DAWSON, G. (Eds) (1986) *Family Portraits*, London, Social Affairs Unit.

ARNOT, M. and WEINER, G. (Eds) (1987) *Gender and the Politics of Schooling*, London, Hutchinson.

BALL, S. (1991) *Markets, Morality and Equality*, Hillcole Group Papers No 5, London, Tufnell Press.

BARRETT, M. (1981) *Women's Oppression Today*, London, Verso.

BARRETT, M. and MCINTOSH, M. (1982) *The Anti-Social Family*, London, Verso.

BASTIANI, J. (Ed.) (1987) *Parents and Teachers Vol 1 Perspectives on Home-School Relations*, Windsor, NFER Nelson.

BERGER, P. and BERGER, B. (1984) *The War Over the Family*, Harmondsworth, Penguin.

BRADSHAW, J. and MILLAR, J. (1991) *Lone Parents in the UK*, London, HMSO.

CHUBB, J. and MOE, T. (1990) *Politics, Markets and America's Schools*, Washington, DC, Brookings Institution.

COOTE, A., HARMAN, H. and HEWITT, P. (1990) *The Family Way*, London, IPPR.

COWARD, R. (1992) *Our Treacherous Hearts: Why Women Let Men Get Their Way*, London, Faber and Faber.

COX, C. (1991) 'Review of Chubb and Moe', *British Journal of the Sociology of Education*, **12**, 3, pp. 385–8.

DAVID, M.E. (1993) *Parents, Gender and Education Reform*, Oxford, Polity Press.

DAVID, M.E., EDWARDS, R., HUGHES, M. and RIBBENS, J. (forthcoming) *Mothers and Education: Inside Out? Exploring Family-Education Policy and Experience*, London, Macmillan.

DAWSON, P. (1991) quoted in *The Daily Telegraph*, 9 August, p. 12.

DURHAM, M. (1991) *Sex and Politics: The Family and Morality in the Thatcher Years*, Basingstoke, MacMillan.

EDWARDS, R. (1991) 'Degrees of difference: Mature women students in higher education', unpublished PhD, London, South Bank Polytechnic.

EISENSTEIN, H. (1984) *Contemporary Feminist Thought*, London, Allen and Unwin.

EISENSTEIN, Z. (1982) 'The sexual politics of the New Right', *Signs*, **7**, 3, pp. 567–88.
EPSTEIN, J. (1990) 'School and family connections', *Marriage and Family Review*, **15**, 1–2, pp. 99–126.
FALUDI, S. (1992) *Backlash: The Undeclared War Against Women*, London, Chatto and Windus.
FLEW, A. with GREEN, D. *et al* (1992) *Empowering the Parents: How to Break the Schools Monopoly*, London, IEA.
FINCH, J. and GROVES, D. (Eds) (1983) *A Labour of Love*, London, RKP.
GILDER, G. (1981) *Sexual Suicide*, New York, Basic Books.
GILDER, G. (1983) *Wealth and Poverty*, New York, Basic Books.
GLENDENNING, C. and MILLAR, J. (Eds) (1987) *Women and Poverty*, Hemel Hempstead, Harvester Wheatsheaf.
GLENDENNING, C. and MILLAR, J. (1991) 'Poverty: The forgotten Englishwoman's reconstructing research and policy on poverty' in MACLEAN, M. and GROVES, D. (Eds) *Women's Issues in Social Policy*, London, Routledge.
GLENN, C.L. (1989) *Choice of Schools in Six Nations*, Washington, DC, US Dept of Education.
GORDON, T. (1990) *Feminist Mothers*, Basingstoke, MacMillan.
GREEN, D. and QUEST, C. (Eds) (1992) *Equal Opportunities: A Feminist Fallacy*, London, IEA.
GROVES, D. (Eds) (1983) *A Labour of Love*, London, Routledge.
HAMNER, J. and MAYNARD, M. (Eds) (1987) *Women, Violence and Social Control*, London, Allen & Unwin.
HAMNER, J. *et al* (Eds) (1989) *Women, Policing and Male Violence: International Perspectives*, London, Routledge.
JOHNSON, D. (1990) *Parental Choice in Education*, London, Unwin Hyman.
KELLY, L. (1988) *Surviving Sexual Violence*, Oxford, Polity Press.
KLEIN, R.D. (Ed.) (1989) *Infertility: Women Speak Out About Their Experiences of Reproductive Medicine*, London, Pandora Press.
LAND, H. and WARD, S. (1986) *Women Won't Benefit*, London, NCCL.
LAND, H. (1991) 'Time to care' in MACLEAN, M. and GROVES, D. (Eds) *Women's Issues in Social Policy*, London, Routledge.
LAREAU, A. (1989) *Home Advantage*, London, Falmer Press.
LASCH, C. (1975) *Haven in a Heartless World*, New York, Basic Books.
LASCH, C. (1982) *Haven in a Heartless World*, New York, Basic Books.
MACBETH, A. (1989) *Involving Parents: Effective Parent-Teacher Relations*, Oxford, Heinemann.
MACLEOD, F. (Ed.) (1989) *Parents and School: The Contemporary Challenge*, London, Falmer Press.
MILIBAND, D. (1991) *Learning by Right: The Entitlement to Paid Education and Training*, London, IPPR.
MILLAR, J. and GLENDENNING, C. (1989) 'Gender and poverty', *Journal of Social Policy*, **18**, 3, pp. 363–82.
MOUNT, F. (1982) *The Subversive Family*, Harmondsworth, Penguin.
MURRAY, C. (1984) *Losing Ground: American Social Policy 1950–80*, New York, Basic Books.
MURRAY, C. (1989) *In Pursuit of Happiness and Good Government*, New York, Basic Books.
MURRAY, C. (1990) *The Emerging British UNDERCLASS*, London, IEA Health and Welfare Unit.

Phoenix, A. (1991) *Young Mothers*, Oxford, Polity Press.

Phoenix, A., Woollett, A. and Lloyd, E. (Eds) (1991) *Motherhood: Meanings, Practices and Ideologies*, London, Sage.

Scott, H. (1984) *Working Your Way to the Bottom: The Feminization of Poverty*, London, Pandora Press.

Sexton, S. (1990) 'Reward, responsibility and results, the new 3Rs', *Sunday Times*, **21** October, p. 9.

Smith, D. (1988) *The Everyday World as Problematic*, Milton Keynes, Open University Press.

Smith, D. and Tomlinson, S. (1989) *The School Effect: A Study of Multi-racial Comprehensives*, London, Policy Studies Institute.

Snitow, A. (1992) 'Feminism and motherhood: An American 'reading', *Feminist Review*, **40**, pp. 32–52.

Spender, D. (1989) *Invisible Women: The Schooling Scandal*, London, Women's Press.

Sperling, G. (1991) 'Can the barriers be breached? Mature women's access to higher education', *Gender and Education*, **3**, 2, pp. 199–215.

Stanworth, M. (Ed.) (1987) *Reproductive Technologies: Gender, Motherhood and Medicine*, Cambridge, Polity Press.

Tizard, B. and Hughes, M. (1984) *Young Children Learning*, London, Fontana.

Ungerson, C. (1989) *Policy is Personal, Sex, Gender and Informal Care*, London, Allen & Unwin.

Walford, G. (1990) *Privatization and Privilege in Education*, London, Routledge.

Walkerdine, V. and Lucey, H. (1989) *Democracy in the Kitchen*, London, Virago.

Weiner, G. and Arnot, M. (Eds) (1987) *Gender Under Scrutiny*, London, Hutchinson.

Chapter 2

The Social Construction of Black Womanhood in British Educational Research: Towards a New Understanding

Heidi Safia Mirza

The idea that the educational experiences of young black women of African Caribbean origin are shaped by the demands of their female centred society has remained an uncontested assumption in British educational research. It manifests itself in the pervasive belief that young black women are motivated to succeed in school primarily through their identification with their 'strong black mothers'. However, this idea appears to be the outcome of widespread common-sense idealizing about the matrifocal nature of African Caribbean society rather than qualified academic research.

My argument here is that the construction of black womanhood that the positive female role model entails, despite appearing outwardly progressive, offers an interpretation of African Caribbean culture that is both misleading and problematic. Firstly, it misleads us by promoting the assumption that black men are marginal in the lives of black women. Secondly it is problematic because in its reification of motherhood, the construction of the 'strong black mother' encourages us to focus on the internal cultural dynamics of the family as an explanation of differential black achievement.

My research findings show that while there is a culturally specific form of black femininity among the young African Caribbean women in Britain, it does not appear to be shaped by the demands of a female centred society. In an exploration of what I have called 'relative autonomy between the sexes', an ideology expressed by the young black men and women in the study which emphasizes the effectiveness of the individual regardless of gender, I suggest that we can understand the issue of relative black female success without employing the problematic concept of 'the strong black woman' and her complementary partner, the marginal black male.

Understanding the Construction of the 'Strong Black Mother'

The 'strong black mother' as constructed in educational research is not unlike its better known counterpart, the 'black superwoman', a popular image with the press.[1] Despite its dubious merits, the media myth of the dynamic black superwoman busy outstripping her male partner in terms of achievements in education and work, has been uncritically adopted as a social reality in the public mind.

Employing a similar rationale, the academic notion of the 'strong black mother' suggests that black women possess internal and natural strengths that account for their endurance and ability to overcome the structural racism and sexism they face in the work place and in the home. While on the surface it appears a logical and common-sense interpretation of black female survival and persistence in the face of hardship, if we examine the notion of the strong black woman/mother it offers an inherently contradictory explanation of the black female experience.

It was not until the 1980s that studies began to address the issue of black female education. These 'progressive'[2] studies were characterized by a distinct underlying ideological premise. This premise was the central role of the black mother. Unlike the distinctly pathological explanations of black disadvantage from America in the 1960s, which suggested the matriarchal structure of the black family caused it to be weak and disorganized (Moynihan, 1965 in Rainwater and Yancey, 1967), black female achievement was now being seen as the outcome of the strong and central position of the female in the black family.

Though both the 'pathological' and 'progressive' theoretical positions appeared outwardly to be constructed in opposition to each other, they in effect drew on two similar assumptions; the presumed matriarchal structure of the black family and the marginalization of the black male within that structure.

While the former position regarded the centrality of the females' role as 'seriously retarding the progress of the group as a whole' (Moynihan, 1965 in Rainwater and Yancey, 1967, p. 76), the latter celebratory approach draws on the common-sense myth of the black females' 'tradition of self-reliance' (Phizacklea, 1982).

The analysis of West Indian migrant women in Britain offered by Phizacklea (1982) illustrates some of the many problems engendered by the 'strong black woman' role model. Phizacklea argues that West Indian female workers, because of their gender and race, occupy a doubly subordinate position in the labour market. But while she describes black women structurally as a 'doubly disadvantaged class fraction', she employs the culturalist argument of a black female 'tradition of self-reliance' (p. 115) to account for differences associated with black and white female working class labour. She explains:

> Their subordinate position in economic and politico-legal and ideological relations is to some extent shared by women generally, but is nevertheless distinct. Racial categorisation, and its concrete effects, is the most obvious difference, but socialisation in a culture with a different interpretation of gender roles and in particular 'motherhood' is also highly significant. (*ibid*)

Phizacklea is arguing that black female socialization within their culture helps in their struggle to counteract some of the disadvantages inherent in their 'fractionalized class position'. What appears to be happening is that Phizacklea, while giving an essentially economistic explanation for black female labour market disadvantage on the one hand, uses notions of self-determination and individualism to account for any unexpected findings that are out of character for a doubly disadvantaged class fraction, on the other. In short, her analysis inadvertently employs two seemingly incompatable criteria; external structural economic inequality and internal cultural traits.

It can be argued that within this perspective the dynamic which structures the black female experience is constructed differently from that of other groups in the labour market, be they black men, white women or men. While black women do have traditions of work and marriage that play an important part in understanding their working lives, here it is confused with what is essentially a situation determined by the dynamics of an economy with a sexually differentiated labour force, fundamentally distorted by racism.

Dex (1983) offers a similarly contradictory analysis when she writes that the young West Indian women school leavers in her research were unique in that they:

> were indicating their intention to resist filling a permanent migrant's position in the British economy, drawing where it seemed useful on their West Indian roots . . . (p. 69)

Dex argues that second generation West Indian women benefited from both the positive and negative lessons of their migrant mothers' economic and cultural experiences. For example, she suggests that the shift toward non-manual work among the second generation is a reaction to their mother's undesirable position in the economic hierarchy. Dex concludes on a celebratory note:

> . . . their positive responses, however, learnt through the migration process of their parents and in facing for themselves discrimination in the British labour markets, may provide them with a useful resource with which to be active in facing the future. (p. 70)

At the core of both Phizacklea's and Dex's explanations is the assumption that black females are motivated through identification with their 'strong black mothers'. The female centred family structure, in which motherhood takes on a special meaning, is seen as a resource. It is implied that the maternal role model provides black women with special powers of endurance which especially equip them in their struggle against racism and sexism at home, in school and the work place.

British black women, Bryan, Dadzie and Scafe (1985) explain the shortcomings inherent in such well intentioned efforts of social scientists to understand the black woman:

> They have tended, however, to portray black women in a somewhat romantic light, emphasising our innate capacity to cope with brutality and deprivation, and perpetuating the myth that we are somehow better equipped than others for suffering. While the patient, long-suffering victim of triple oppression may have some heroic appeal, she does not convey our collective experience. (pp. 1–2)

However, in spite of just such a 'romantic' portrayal of black womanhood, the influence of Mary Fuller's study of black girls still persists (Fuller, 1978, 1980 and 1982). Fuller argues that the girls she studied formed a discernible 'subculture' in their London secondary school. Within the context of the school the black female 'subculture' had peculiar characteristics. She claims that it was neither one of resistance nor of conformity to the school.

Fuller argues that the forms of action by the black girls in the school were strategies for trying to effect some control over their present and future lives by proving their own worth through their academic success. Thus the structure of the subculture, she argues, emerged from the girls' positive acceptance of the fact of being both black and female, derived from an identification with their mothers. She ascertains that its 'particular flavour' was the outcome of the girls' critical rejection of the negative connotations with which the categorizations female and black commonly attract.

Fuller's use of the concept of 'cultures of resistance' (Willis, 1977) results in an unrealistic, 'romantic' reappraisal of black girls' actions and decisions. Fuller's belief that these girls were highly politicized about unemployment, racism and sexism during their educational career, and planned their actions as a defiant gesture to the world, does not stand up to closer scrutiny. Research by Ullah (1985) indicated that young black women, at the point of entry into the job market, were the least aware of the groups in his study, of the racism they would encounter in the work place.

Fuller suggests a major influence on the girls feelings of isolation and anger which in turn determines the characteristics of the subculture, is the low value of domestic work in the home and the girls negative relationships with black male peers. However Riley (1985) found that African Caribbean girls looked forward to relationships with men, and reported that the girls in her study felt that parents encouraged boys and girls equally. It was a sense of responsibility, and not the need to establish their self-worth, that Riley suggests gave black girls their stronger commitment to education.

Much of the work on black girls still remains largely influenced by the concept of subculture first employed by Fuller.[3] Thus while academic performance for black girls is explained in terms of sub-cultural resistance, for black boys it is still regarded as the outcome of negative self-concept and the self-fulfilling prophesy (see Stone, 1985): a fundamental inconsistency in the analysis of race and the analysis of gender in education.

Explaining the Persistence of the 'Strong Black Mother'

The persistent use of the myth of the 'strong black mother' appears to be the outcome of inappropriate, ethnocentric theories of female oppression that dominate educational research.

As is so often the case in sociological accounts of inequality, the cultural 'universalism' of theories of gender reproduction are rarely questioned. For example the 'culture of femininity' with its central notion of 'subcultures of resistance' has become the perceived wisdom for explaining the persistence of sexual inequality.

It is argued that the 'culture of femininity' is the means by which working class girls, through their own activity and ideological development, reproduce themselves as a subordinate class (McRobbie, 1978a, 1978b and 1990). It suggests that young women subjectively rationalize and thus freely choose situations such as marriage and childrearing which objectively oppresses them. With its emphasis on subculture and motherhood, this dominant and pervasive explanation on the reproduction of gender disadvantage has offered the ideal framework in which the theory of the strong black female role model could be developed.

That culturally specific theories such as the culture of femininity have remained largely unchallenged in feminist educational research, is due, in part, to the shape and direction of the black feminist discourse in the UK. Concerned with political exclusion and theoretical marginality the small and limited resources of British black feminism have been drawn into a protracted exchange with white feminists about *exclusion.* Issues surrounding invisibility and the various ethnocentric cultural interpretations of 'the family', 'motherhood' and 'marriage' have been the subject of an ongoing black and white socialist feminist debate.[4] As a consequence, the problematic *inclusion* of black women, in the shape of the 'strong black mother', has gone virtually unchecked.

In response to the international black feminist debate on ethnocentrism (see Spelman, 1988; Gunew, 1991; Ramazanoglu, 1989), the attempt of British sociologists to include the celebratory tradition of black women's writing into educational analysis appears, in part, responsible for the popular construction of the 'strong black mother' that we see in the UK. In particular the universally renowned writings of African American women have been inadvertently influential in shaping this construction.

Unlike white women writers who often define themselves in opposition to their mothers, black women writers particularly in America, have, since the 1960s engaged in a celebration of the maternal presence emphasizing the generational continuity between mothers and daughters (Hirsch, 1989).[5] With their powerful narratives and exploration of black womanhood, the novels, essays, and poems of black women, while instrumental in opening up the historically and culturally distinct world of black women have also engendered a sensitivity toward the positive portrayal of the black female. To this end both Carby (1990) and Wallace (1990) offer interesting observations of black women's writing. The former suggests the black female folk tradition established from Alice Walker back through to Zora Neale Hurston has had the effect of marginalizing the important telling of the urban confrontation of race, class and sexuality. Similarly the latter argues that black women writers do reinforce the black superwoman myth in their nostalgic renderings of rural and folk life. However, as Spillers (1990) eloquently demonstrates, the black female literary canon does distance itself from the preoccupations of the 'African-American-Father-Gone' and the 'Black Matriarchate', two themes that appear to dominate the sociological discourse on race and gender.

The sensitivity toward a positive construction of the black woman in the context of her maternal role, has been further compounded in Britain by the virulent ideology of 'anti-racism'. As Gilroy (1990) points out, 'the inflated rhetoric and culturalist orthodoxies of anti-racism . . . have led directly to an extraordinary idealisation of black family forms' (pp. 80–1).

The idealization of black family forms, sanctioned by the essentialist writing of Afrocentric feminism, reifies the role of mothering in its efforts to construct the homogenous black family.[6] However there are significant dangers involved in idealizing and mystifying the certain biological female experience of motherhood and in so doing reviving an identification between femininity and maternity that in the past has not served the interests of women

(Hirsch, 1989; Bleier, 1991). Clearly the notion of 'the strong black mother', as presently constructed in 'progressive' educational research, with its emphasis on the natural links between mother and daughter, is in danger of embracing just such a reactionary idealization.

Towards an Alternative Construction of Black Womanhood

In response to the problems raised by the maternal emphasis in sociological analysis, which is the strong black female and its complementary partner the marginal male, in this final section I investigate the presence of 'relative autonomy between the sexes'. Acknowledging that there is a specific form of black femininity among young black women, characterized by an egalitarian ideology with regard to appropriate male and female roles, allows us to move toward a more satisfactory understanding of black womanhood.

For our purposes of rethinking black womanhood I shall examine the experiences of second generation, African Caribbean women living in Britain. These young women are the British-born daughters of migrants who came to Britain in the 1950s. Encouraged by the British government's recruitment drive for cheap skilled and semi-skilled labour these West Indians came from their newly-emerging post-colonial countries to work mainly in the hotel and catering, transport and hospital services. The recipients of crude anti-immigrant hostility, and later, the more subtle workings of institutional racism, these black migrants and their descendants have experienced many obstacles to their social, economic and political advancement (see Fryer, 1984; Gilroy, 1987; Ramdin, 1987).

The Study[7]

The overall aim of the project was to investigate the complex influences that affect the career aspirations and expectations of young black women. The 62 young black women in this study, who were aged between 15–19 years, attended two averaged sized secondary schools in two of the most disadvantaged inner-city boroughs of South London. The girls and their black and white male and female peers, who numbered 198 in all, and who could be objectively identified as coming from working class homes, answered questionnaires, and were interviewed and observed in their homes and classrooms over a period of eighteen months.

In each school a random sample was drawn from pupils in the fifth and the sixth year of their secondary schooling. All pupils and schools were given fictional names. From St Hilda's, a co-educational Catholic school, 128 (65 per cent) black and white male and female pupils were taken whereas 70 (35 per cent) were taken from St Theresa's, a single sex, Church of England school. Of these, 62 (31 per cent) were African Caribbean young women; 13 (7 per cent) were African Caribbean young men; 77 (39 per cent) were young women from other (mainly white) backgrounds; 46 (23 per cent) were young men from other (mainly white) backgrounds.[8]

This study attempted to combine a longitudinal survey approach, with what can be described as essentially a school-based ethnographic study. Thus both questionnaire data and information derived from a range of participant observation and informal discussions were collected.

The questionnaire endeavoured to place the 'objective' criteria affecting career choice, such as social and family background, culture and economic status, in the context of individual, 'subjective' preferences being made with regard to future occupations. During the academic year spent in the schools, informal interviews were conducted, pupils contributing data of a less 'controlled' nature. Formal interview situations were set up in the two schools. Different groups of pupils were asked questions guided by a detailed, structured interview schedule.

In several respects I shared much in common with my respondents. I was myself young, female, and came from the West Indies. Having left one of the schools six years earlier, I enjoyed a unique insight into the experience of the young black women in the study. It may be assumed that the researcher's close identification with the cohort could lead to complications of 'internal validity'. Any subjective bias arising from my familiarity with the school, the staff and my experiences must to some degree be recognized. However, it was felt that the introduction of bias this situation might encourage was far outweighed by the positive aspects of access and confidentiality that I enjoyed.

The findings discussed in this chapter relate to only one aspect of this research project; that is the cultural construction of gender identity among young women of African Caribbean descent.

The Findings: Reconstructing Black Womanhood

The evidence presented here suggests that the cultural construction of femininity among African Caribbean women fundamentally differs from the forms of femininity found among their white peers.

While a general desire towards economic dependency prevailed among the young white working class women in the sample, there was no evidence that this cultural orientation existed among the young black working class women that were interviewed. While all of the black women responded positively to the prospect of having a full-time career upon leaving school, only 80 per cent of their white female peers said they would. Young black women of all abilities and social backgrounds, with a wide variety of career aspirations, reiterated time and time again their commitment to full-time work and their desire for economic independence. Evidence of this positive ideological orientation was clear in the data:

> I would just like to be an independent lady. Not dependent on any one, especially a man. (Joy, aged 16, aspiration: legal assistant)

> I don't want to rely on anyone. What I want is a good job as I would like my life to be as comfortable as possible, and have a nice environment to live in so my children can grow up with everything they require. (Laurie; aged 16, aspiration: journalist)

On the basis of this evidence alone there is little justification for adopting an analytical framework that emphasizes the centrality of an oppressive form of femininity, which the prevailing theories on the black female experience clearly do.

The key to why this situation of positive orientation and commitment to work should prevail was provided by the girls themselves. The statements they made showed that they expected to work just as their sisters, mothers, aunts and grandmothers had done for generations before them. However, and this is the important point, they expected to do so without the encumbrance of male dissent. This meant the young women did not regard their male relationships, whether within the institution of marriage, or not, as inhibiting their right to work in any way.

This attitude to work, marriage, and motherhood among black women has been misinterpreted by white socialist feminists. While they have argued that for white women, marriage is a 'psychologically and materially oppressive institution' (Barrett and McIntosh, 1982), they state that for the West Indian, marriage is 'no more than a prestige conferring act' (Phizacklea, 1982, p. 100; see also Sharpe, 1987, p. 234). This suggestion appears to imply that black people 'mimic' the social institutions of the dominant white society. The effect of this 'common-sense' assumption has been that marriage, the family, and male relationships in the West Indian context, are dismissed as unimportant in the lives of black women.

However, Caribbean feminists provide evidence to the contrary. For example Powell (1986) suggests that West Indian women are strongly marriage-orientated, though there seems to be little urgency regarding its timing. While conjugal relationships, motherhood and childrearing were important dimensions in the lives of black women, they did not perceive their unions as presenting barriers to the things they wished to do. In support of Powell's findings it was not uncommon to find among the young women in the study statements such as these:

> My sister has moved out, got a nice little flat to herself . . . having your own place . . . a little job not getting married now, just having your boyfriend . . . well living together, . . . no . . . well popping round to see you . . . that what I'd like. (Debra, aged 16, aspiration: designer)

> Work is as equally important in marriage, or your relationship. I don't care if it's marriage or not, whatever, I think it's important. (Floya, aged 16, aspiration: data processor)

However, the young women also stated that while they wanted to work, they did not wish for a repetition of their mothers' experiences. They often spoke of their mothers' work, which was discussed invariably in terms of hardship and sacrifice. They always gave a unanimous 'no' to the question 'would you like to be like your mum and do the same sort of work?'

> My mum has worked hard to give us things, and to bring us up, even if it was shit work. They want to give you all the things they never had . . . I suppose I'll do the same for my children, I mean give them what's right. (Annette, aged 16, aspiration: nurse; mother: cleaner)

When interviewed on the subject of marriage and women's work, the young black women in the study agreed that they should work regardless of child-rearing responsibilities. The following statements were common examples of the sentiments expressed by the girls:

> . . . even if you have kids you have to work. I sometimes feel sorry for my sister's kids. She leaves them with a minder. She works in the council or, I don't know, something like that. They don't even know who their mother is . . . one day I heard Damian call the minder mum. I don't want that for my kids. But it's like this if you don't work what will you do? Stay home and knit? You'll be useless to everybody.

> Its important to work and to bring up your family as best you can. If it is your family I think it is your responsibility.

Anita, one of the girls in the study who became pregnant,[9] spoke of her attitude to marriage:

> I know for sure that one thing is sure, that I don't want to get married . . . he says we should, but I feel we are capable enough to make our own decisions and own plans after all we are adult people, why does everyone else have to interfere so much. If you ignore others you will be alright but in life you can't . . . . marriage no way . . . we've put in for a flat though . . . I'm not rushing into anything.

It was commonplace to find bold and positive statements such as this:

> If I don't work I'll go mad . . . You've got to make something of yourself because in the end no-one cares.

This did not mean as Riley (1985, p. 69) seems to suggest in her analysis of similar types of statements, that young black girls were pursuing a course of aggressive assertion of their femininity (which in the case of black girls is interpreted as female dominance) at the expense of all else, especially permanent male relationships. Nor, as Fuller (1982, p. 96) suggests, was this the manifestation of a 'going it alone' strategy.

In my opinion what the girls were articulating was a much more subtle ideological orientation than either of these two authors suggest. Unlike their white peers, who appear to have inculcated the dominant ideology that women only take on major economic roles when circumstances prevent their menfolk from doing so, the black girls held no such belief about the marginality of their economic participation and commitment to the family. Providing for the children and the household was regarded as a joint responsibility as the following statement illustrates:

> I think it is important for a woman and man to work, to both provide for your family is an important thing to do. (Karen, aged 16, aspiration: computer programmer)

The West Indian boys in the study, had no objections to their future partners working.[10] They were in full support of their womenfolk being gainfully employed, as the following statements illustrate:

> My mum, she's a cook and she looks after me and my brother . . . I think if I got married, I don't see no difference, I don't see it any other way really. (Davis, aged 16, aspiration: armed forces)

> Any woman of mines got to see about herself anyway, it ain't gonna bother me, but I ain't keeping no woman that's for sure. (Maurice, aged 16, aspiration: electrician)

> You must be kidding! . . . of course she's gonna work. If she don't work she don't eat! (laughs) Anyway, I ain't getting married. (Leroy, aged 17, aspiration: plumbing/central heating)

The boyfriend of one of the young black women in the study, Anita who at the age of 16 became pregnant, had a distinctly supportive and encouraging attitude to her moving ahead in her career, as he explained:

> A woman must can and must do all she can . . . but I's believe having children is very important . . . its good to have kids young and enjoy yourself . . . you don't have to take time out to do it or stop nothing . . . Of course she will be set back though, and we have discussed this, I told her to not to stop school, exams are important . . . she can go onto college, you know, yeh, but she got to have 'O' levels or she set right back and she'll have to start from the beginning, I told her not to stop. (Winston, aged 23, games supervisor at the local sports centre.)

The issue of relative economic and social autonomy between the sexes, should not be confused with the matter of the sharing of domestic labour or the permanency of male/female relationships, as is so often the case. That West Indian men do not equally participate in household tasks is well documented, as is the tendency towards instability of consensual relationships (Justus, 1985; Moses, 1985; Powell, 1986). These facts, however, do not impair the matter of joint responsibility toward consanguineous offspring or children within a consensual relationship. Relationships where joint responsibility towards the household within the context of relative autonomy between the sexes are a common feature of West Indian life.[11]

The existence of joint responsibility is more widespread than most sociological commentators of both radical and conservative ideological persuasions care to acknowledge. This can be argued on several counts. Firstly, as evidence of joint economic responsibility, there are almost equal proportions of black men and black women in the labour market, compared to the relatively unequal situation among the white male and female majority (see Brown, 1984; OPCS, 1987).

Secondly, while a high incidence of single motherhood is reported among black families (i.e. relative to white) the numbers are relatively small in comparison to the incidence of stable conjugal unions that do actually exist in the black community. If these figures are considered in their correct context (i.e. not a comparative black-white analysis as is the convention) family stability still remains the overriding norm among black families (i.e. 78 per cent compared to 13 per cent is a significant difference: Brown, 1984). Thus the majority image of most black men as feckless and irresponsible remains largely a product of media stereotyping and academic misrepresentation (see Hoch, 1979; Phoenix, 1988b; Segal, 1990).

The relatively high incidence of single parenthood among, young black women (*vis-à-vis* young white women), can more readily be explained within the ideological framework that stresses the relative autonomy and equality between the sexes in the black community. The existence of this ideology, encourages women to strive for compatibility with their male partner rather than economic security (with its attendant values of duty and loyalty) within relationships.

Colin Brown's evidence (1984, p. 37) that single parenthood is not only common among young West Indians, but also among older West Indians, indicates that single parenthood should be regarded in terms of a life-cycle phenomena, with people moving in and out of relationships seeking compatibility and friendship, and, as Barrow (1986) suggests in the case of women, increased economic autonomy.

The young black women in the study did express a cautious yet positive approach to marriage and relationships:

> Eventually I'd want to get married, but you should be like best friends and live together . . . (another girl shouts out 'you mean platonic . . .' all laugh).

> Well, things have changed now . . . you can have kids but you don't have to be married . . . . my brother's been together for twelve years and got four kids and they just got married. The girls were the bridesmaids and the boy's a page boy.
>
> The thing that worries me about marriage, right, is that the fact you are stuck with that one person for life . . . because a lot of girls rush 'this is the one for me, this is the one for me,' and all that, and rush into it.

> I'll get married when I'm 30 or 35 in the future, after I've done something for myself.

In the study there was no evidence that black men were considered marginal in the lives of young black women. Of West Indian households in the study, to which the girls belonged, 79 per cent had both a male and female adult sharing the parenting role (for white girls 90 per cent belonged to two-parent families). Of the 11 per cent who had only one parent present, 2 per cent were male-headed households, a feature not found among the white families in the study.

Despite the acknowledgment that men in their lives could in the future pose problems, the young black women in the study frequently spoke positively about men and their attitudes. They did so drawing on their own experience and relationships with men, in particular their fathers, male guardians, brothers and uncles.

> I don't think really, looking after children hard if the man behave himself . . . my brothers girlfriend got him under heavy manners right, no back chat, you know, they got three young ones . . . (Janet, aged 16, aspiration: secretary; father: bus conductor)

> Most men do understand the problems faced by women, I think so anyway. I go to my dad whenever I have a problem. (Laurie, aged 16, aspiration: journalist; father: telephonist)

> . . . My dad wouldn't let me work (Saturday job). He says it will interfere with my school work, ask him for pocket money instead. I suppose it is for my own good but I feel he's unfair. (Janice, aged 17, aspiration: social worker; father: painter decorator)

> Since my mum died my dad's brought us up . . . all he cares about is seeing us do well and going to college . . . (April, aged 16, aspiration: art therapist; father: British Rail ticket collector)

Further evidence of black males assisting their partners to stay at work during the crucial and difficult time after the birth of a child is presented in the TCRU Day-Care study (Mirza, 1986). The black relationships in the study provided some of the most unusual and egalitarian forms of partnership. Several men willingly changed shifts to accommodate child care arrangements. One couple agreed upon a complete role reversal so that the wife, who worked in a bank at a more senior level than her husband, would not lose her promotional prospects. However, in some cases the men did not give much physical help (although they were deemed to be a source of emotional support), mostly because as one woman said, 'he's always out doing his own thing'. But in these cases the women stated that despite their partners' frequent absences and the problems this caused, the partners did not obstruct their return to work, and if they failed to provide adequate financial and moral contributions, they did at least show affection for the children.

In short, what the evidence revealed was that it was neither the men's absence or presence that affected the black women's orientation to the labour market.[12] Other factors, specifically the provision of childcare and the accessibility of relatives and the employer, were the crucial variables.

Studies in America, (Moynihan, 1965, in Rainwater and Yancey, 1967), the Caribbean (Smith, 1962), and in Britain (Foner, 1979), have persistently attributed the relatively high proportion of black women in the economy to the absence of a male provider or his inability to fulfil his role. This pathological explanation of the black family — that has come about from the belief that it is 'culturally stripped', essentially a hybrid of Western culture (Frazier, 1966; Little, 1978), has failed to acknowledge that black culture has, evolved an essentially egalitarian ideology with regard to work. An ideology that, as Sutton and Makiesky-Barrow (1977, p. 323) observe, 'emphasizes the effectiveness of the individual regardless of gender'.

Ironically, the dynamic that has produced this equality between the sexes within the black social structure has been the external imposition of oppression and brutality. Davis (1982) documents the evolution of this egalitarian ideology. She argues that under the conditions of slavery egalitarianism characterized the social relations between male and female slaves in their domestic quarters. Here the sexual division of labour did not appear to be hierarchically organized. Both male and female tasks, whether cooking or hunting, were deemed equally necessary and therefore considered neither inferior or superior to each other.

It therefore appears that African Caribbean societies in the Caribbean and in industrialized capitalist settings have not simply replicated the Western pattern of sexual stratification. Like their parents and grandparents, the young black women in the study had not adopted the dominant Eurocentric ideology: an ideology in which gender is regarded as the basis for the opposition of roles and values. These young black women had, instead, a very different concept of masculinity and femininity than their white peers. In the black female definition, as their statements revealed, few distinctions were made between male and female abilities and attributes with regard to work and the labour market. As to why this particular definition of masculinity and femininity should result in greater female participation in the labour market is explained by Sutton and Makiesky-Barrow who write:

> . . . the distinct qualities of masculine and feminine sexual and reproductive abilities are not viewed by either sex as a basis for different male and female social capacities. And unlike the self-limiting negative sexual identities the Euro-American women have had to struggle with, female identity in Endeavour (a town in Barbados) is associated with highly valued cultural attributes. Because the women are assumed to be bright strong and competent, nothing in the definitions of appropriate sex role behaviour systematically excludes them from areas of economic and social achievement. (p. 320)

The argument that the cultural construction of femininity among African Caribbean women fundamentally differs from the forms of femininity found among their white peers is further supported by evidence of black female labour market participation. The proportion of black women in the labour market relative to their white female counterparts, is far greater, a fact that is true for the UK and the USA. Though it is often suggested that high black male unemployment determines increased black female labour market participation this argument cannot be upheld; it is a theory based more on a 'commonsense' assumption than fact. Black male unemployment is only slightly higher than black female unemployment. In the 25–35 age group in the UK 17 per cent of black women are unemployed, as are 18 per cent of black men. In other age ranges the proportion is even greater for black females (see Brown 1984, p. 190). The fact that men and women are concentrated in different sectors of the labour market and so have access to different employment (and educational) prospects is not a consequence of choice but rather due to the dynamics of a sexually segregated labour market (see Farley and Bianchi, 1985).

The study revealed a notable lack of sexual distinctions about work among second generation, West Indian youth. Many girls said that they did not see any difference between themselves and their male counterparts in terms of their capacity to work and the type of work they were capable of.

> I think men and women have the same opportunities, it is just up to you to take it.

> Of course women should do the same jobs that men do. If they feel you can't . . . them stupid . . whose to say anyway, it makes me sick it does.

> Men should do the jobs women do and women the jobs that men do. There's nothing wrong with men midwives, I think all men should find out what it is like to have a child, its the nearest they can get to it.

Young black women living in the West Indies expressed a similar point of view with regard to women's work, as one girl illustrated when she stated:

> I think what is good for a woman is good for a man, there's no difference between men and women when it comes to work.

Further evidence of this trend to refuse to regard certain types of work as the sole preserve of men was shown in the results of the study. Black girls were far more likely to express their desire to do non-gendered work than their white female peers.

There is a common assumption that young black women 'naturally' gravitate toward non-traditional female work (Griffin, 1985). Their desire for woodwork and other conventionally-defined 'male' subjects at school is often cited as evidence of this uniquely black female tendency (Riley, 1985). Their relatively higher uptake and enrolment on 'trade' and access courses, leading to plumbing, electrical and carpentry training, is also used to indicate this trend (Cockburn, 1987). To date the explanation for this 'phenomenon' has centered around an argument which suggests that this willingness is a form of resistance; a conscious statement of 'blackwomanhood'. However, in my opinion, the willingness of young black women to undertake traditionally male work is the outcome of two aspects that are related to their orientation to work.

Firstly, there was no evidence of any cultural constraint that inhibited a woman from aspiring to any occupation that she felt competent to train and undertake. Secondly, it would appear that young black women are primarily motivated in their career aspirations by the prospect of upward mobility. A job, therefore is an expression of the desire to move ahead by means of the educational process. The belief in the promise of a meritocracy and the rewards of credentialism spur black women on to take up whatever opportunities that may become available and accessible to them, especially opportunities that entail a chance to increase their further educational qualifications.

Therefore, non-gendered work expectations do not appear to be the outcome of a female orientated ideology as is so often been suggested. If it were the result of a female-centred ideology, then it would be difficult to account for the obvious need many young black women expressed for emotional dependency, as one young Trinidadian woman explained:

> You need emotional support and strength from a man. You like to feel he rules, even if he don't.

The young black women in the study, both in the West Indies and in Britain, often commented on the desire for male companionship. This, and the fact that many women treat men as 'guests in the house' (Justus, 1985), has been interpreted as evidence of a male centred ideology in the West Indian family structure. The description of the black family as having a 'male centred' ideology is based largely on the evidence of black male non-participation in the domestic sphere.[13]

It is important to note, at this point that there seems to be a contradictory state of affairs with regard to research on the status of the woman in the black family, which can result in a great deal of confusion. On the one hand, it has been argued that what exists is a matrifocal, female dominated structure (Fuller, 1982), and on the other hand the family ideological orientation is often described as 'male centred' (Justus, 1985; Moses, 1985).

These two fundamentally divergent theoretical interpretations of the ideological dynamics of the black family have evolved as a consequence of the confused interpretation of the two essentially different aspects of family life: relative autonomy between the sexes and non-male participation in domestic affairs. In effect what we are observing in this study is an ideological orientation governed, not by male bias or female bias, but by the notion of relative economic and social autonomy between the sexes.

In home visits to the parents of the girls in the study, the statements by wives and husbands illustrated the existence of a measure of independence between the sexes, as well as joint responsibility towards the family. They frequently related stories and anecdotes that told of their independent, but equal, work roles.

One such example was the case of Mr and Mrs Burgess who had come to the UK twenty-four years ago. Between them they had brought up five children, the eldest being the child of a previous relationship of Mrs Burgess. They had both always worked and had an evident pride in their childrens' achievements (one daughter was a computer programmer, another a social worker, while the others who were still at school were doing well). They lived on a bleak, run-down, post-war council estate in Brixton. She enjoyed, and got a great deal of satisfaction from her job as a canteen assistant, he found his work 'on the buses' less interesting. Both wages jointly contributed to the family income, although each wage went towards different aspects of family expenditure. He explained in his broad Grenadian accent how he regarded the relationship:

> She does she work, she go in every day, come home every day. She do she own thing really. Half de time I ain't know what she get up to, always going out spending she money on Bingo or some thing so. I don't min once she leave me alone . . . I's like to do me own thing too . . . ya know . . .

Mrs Burgess had her own comments to make, in her equally broad Dominican dialect:

> He so lazy, girl, He could sit there all day an complain . . . Nothing good enough, well just sit there then. I does go alone if I want to do anything . . . I does pick up myself . . . even go by self to de carnival . . . I's have me work, I's like me work mind.

The indifference in attitude they now expressed towards each other after many years of marriage should not obscure the relative autonomy each partner enjoyed with regard to their own work and social activities. Despite their disagreements on other matters, neither partner interfered with the other's right to work. For Mrs Burgess her work was, and always had been, a source of pride and achievement, a realm of experience quite apart from her life at home. She enjoyed talking about her battles and victories in the work place:

> When I first came to England dere was so many jobs. I move from one to another. It took me four weeks to find my first job. I work for Lyons. Two pounds fifty I got . . . I tell you them days a shilling a lot . . . now I'm the only coloured face at work, but I put them in their place, I stands up for myself, I ain't gone to leave because of them few. Me an the Italian woman wer's the only outsiders so they want us out. They don like me because I'm better than them, I've got better qualifications them and they's know it, especially that supervisor that how I got the work. She wanted to get rid of me always shouting at me, but now I've got my friends we get on well, laugh and thing, have a good time, like at de Christmas party . . .

Considerable independence between the sexes does not presuppose the shedding of social attachments as it can do in other cultural contexts, rather, it necessitates and increases the involvement of both partners in the lives of their families. In spite of their separate economic and social experiences, Mr and Mrs Burgess jointly contributed to the family budget and participated in the upbringing of their children. However, just as each income financed a separate aspect of the household expenditure (see Stone, 1983) so too did each partner perform a different parenting role.

They both agreed that 'life hard [*sic*] for the children nowadays', and that it is up to the parents to see that the children do not 'go astray' and were not out roaming the streets, and if they failed and the children were 'bad', then it was the parents who were at fault. They had, especially Mr Burgess, a strong disciplinarian approach towards their children which, it became quite obvious, had alienated the children to some degree.

Conclusion

In a reassessment of the cultural construction of gender among young African Caribbean women, there was little evidence to support the dominant and established explanations for black female motivation — that is the strong role model of the mother figure and in particular their 'unique' orientation to motherhood. Though on the surface the notion of intergenerational maternal support appears a logical and positive interpretation of black female motivation, it nevertheless presents many problems for the development of educational and social policy with regard to black women.

Because black women are seen able to motivate themselves by drawing on their inner strengths and cultural resources it engenders a complacency toward them. Young black women, who are seen as the beneficiaries of special maternal encouragement, and enjoy the advantage of positive role models, are considered part of a privileged and select club. In contrast young black men, whom it is deemed are marginal within the family structure, and therefore do not receive any special maternal support, remain subject to the injustices of racism and discrimination.

The positive intention of this account of differential achievement, however, has conservative implications. Our attention is subtly turned away from the importance of racial and sexual discrimination, highlighting instead cultural determinants to economic success or failure. Wilson's (1987) study of the black condition in America is just such an example of this cultural redirection. He argues that public policy initiatives aimed at stemming the tide of the growing black 'underclass', should be directed towards displacing the female-headed household by restoring the economically successful, self-assured, black, male breadwinner.

However, there is little evidence to suggest that black women succeed at the expense of their male partners. The asymetrical pattern of attainment in education and the labour market is not a reflection of cultural favouritism within the family. The findings of this study suggest that among young black men and women a situation of relative autonomy between the sexes prevailed. Within this particular definition of masculinity and femininity few distinctions were made between male and female abilities and attributes with regard to work and the labour market. It was this, and not the positive role model of the strong black mother, that has resulted in the positive female orientation to work and education. Because nothing in the definitions of appropriate sex-role behaviour excluded young women from areas of social and economic achievement they expected to, and indeed participated equally, in the world of work.

In conclusion our findings suggest that when we examine the presence of differential achievement, what we are in effect observing is the outcome of the dynamics of a racially and sexually segregated labour market. The black female work force in the inner city is locked into a different occupational sector from that of black men. In London 53 per cent of black women are to be found in non-manual occupations, compared to 20 per cent of black men. In contrast black men are employed mainly as skilled and semi-skilled workers (Brown, 1984; *Employment Gazette*, 1991). That young black men are confined to racially limited areas of the labour market where there is less opportunity for educational mobility than those open to black women is significant. Clearly it is this social reality more than any other that impinges upon the educational orientation of working class young black men and women, who in their aspirations and attainment carefully rationalize their limited educational and labour market opportunities.

Notes

1 The media has taken a particular interest in the subject of the 'black superwoman' ('Flying Colours', *Guardian*, 12 June 1991; 'Black Men: Losers in a One-Sided Sexcess Story', *Voice*, 18 June 1991; 'Sisters are Doing it for Themselves', *Times*, 31 March 1992; 'Race Relationships', *Sunday Times*, 24 May 1992). Offering a sensational interpretation of the 1991 Labour Force statistics (*Employment Gazette*, 1991), these newspapers mischievously suggest that black women are more successful than their male counterparts. But as I have argued (*Guardian*, 12 May 1992), black women are not more successful than black men. This is a divisive representation of a simple fact: black men are locked into racially limited areas of the labour market, where there is less opportunity for educational mobility than in those open to black women.

2 'Progressive studies' collectively refers to both feminist studies (Fuller, 1982; Phizacklea, 1982 and 1983; Dex, 1983; Sharpe, 1987 (1976)), and the liberal tradition of race and education research (Driver, 1980; Rutter *et al*, 1982; Verma, 1986; Eggleston *et al*, 1986).

3 See Griffin, 1985; Riley, 1985; Wright, 1987; Mac an Ghaill, 1988; Wulff, 1988; Coultas, 1989; Reid, 1989.

4 For black British women writers see, Carby, 1982; Anthias and Yuval-Davis, 1983; Amos and Parmar, 1984; Bhavnani and Coulson, 1986; Ramazanoglu, Kazi, Lees and Mirza, 1986; Phoenix, 1987; Parmar, 1989; Brah, 1992; Knowles and Mercer, 1992; Mama, 1992. For White British women see, Bourne 1983; Barrett and Macintosh, 1985; Ramazanoglu, 1989.

5 See Washington, 1984; Willis, 1987; Hirsch, 1989; Wall, 1990; Nasta, 1991; Bell-Scott, 1991.

6 For a discussion on the conservative implications of Afrocentric feminism see Higginbotham (1992) and Frances White (1990). For an Afrocentric analysis of multiple mothering in African American families see Collins (1987, 1990).

7 For a more detailed description of methodology and findings see my book *Young Female and Black*, Routledge, 1992.

8 In addition thirty young women from a school in Trinidad aged between 16–18 years participated in semi-structured interviews concerning their career choices and attitudes to marriage and relationships. Sixteen young women from youth clubs and community centres in South London also participated in the study. Informal discussions and exchanges with these women, aged 18+ provided additional information on the African Caribbean, British, female post-school leaver attitudes to and experience of the labour market.

9 See Phoenix (1988a; 1990) for a detailed discussion of early pregnancy among black and white young women.

10 Eggleston *et al* (1986, p. 95) show African Caribbean boys least likely of all ethnic and white groups to want their wives to stay at home upon having a child. Similar research in the USA has shown that black husbands have a 'permissive' attitude to their wives working (Landry and Jendrek, 1978).

11 (For the West Indies see Sutton and Maikesky-Barrow, 1977, pp. 311–2; Dann, 1987, pp. 25–30; Thorogood, 1987; Barrow, 1988; Mohammed, 1988). It is also a common feature of black American life. The literature on the black condition in the USA describes what in essence are male/female relationships of relative autonomy and independence between the sexes (Billingsley, 1968; Gutman, 1976; Ladner, 1981; Stack, 1982 (1975); Jones, 1985; Wilson, 1987). However such relationships are often misunderstood and thus deemed 'pathological' and thus negative.

12 Research in the USA suggests that among black working wives the husbands approval did not affect their satisfaction with work (Harrison and Minor, 1978).

13 Sutton and Makiesky-Barrow (1977, p. 317) suggest that while much of the literature on sex-roles views the domestic sphere as an area of confinement that is associated with women and their dependent status, for the slave population, the domestic area was the one area of life that for both sexes was associated with human freedom and autonomy. See also Davis, 1982; Mathurin Mair, 1986; Wiltshire-Brodber, 1988; Bush, 1990.

References

AMOS, V. and PARMAR, P. (1981) 'Resistances and responses: Experiences of black girls in Britain' in MCROBBIE, A. and MCCABE, T. (Eds) *Feminism for Girls: An Adventure Story*. London, Routledge and Kegan Paul.

AMOS, V. and PARMAR, P. (1984) 'Challenging imperial feminism', *Feminist Review*, Special Issue: Many Voices One Chant, Black Feminist Perspectives, **17**, autumn.

ANTHIAS, F. and YUVAL-DAVIS, N. (1983) 'Contextualizing feminism: Gender, ethnic and class divisions', *Feminist Review*, **15**, winter.

BARRETT, M. and MCINTOSH, M. (1982) *The Anti-social Family*, London, Verso.

BARRETT, M. and MCINTOSH, M. (1985) 'Ethnocentrism and socialist-feminist theory', *Feminist Review*, **20**, summer.

BARROW, C. (1986) 'Finding support: Strategies for survival', *Social and Economic Studies*, Special Number: J. MASSIAH (Ed.) Women in the Caribbean (Part 1): Institute of Social and Economic Research, University of the West Indies, **35**, 2.

BARROW, C. (1988) 'Anthropology, The family and women in the Caribbean' in MOHAMMED, P. and SHEPHERD, C. (Eds) *Gender in Caribbean Development*, Women and Development Studies Project. St. Augustine, Trinidad, University of the West Indies.

BELL-SCOTT, P. (Ed.) (1991) *Double Stitch: Black Women Write about Mothers and Daughters*, Boston, MA, Beacon Press.

BHAVNANI, K. and COULSON, M. (1986) 'Transforming socialist feminism: The challenge of racism', *Feminist Review*, **23**, pp. 81–92.

BILLINGSLEY, A. (1968) *Black Families in White America*, Englewood Cliffs, NJ, Prentice Hall.

BLEIER, R. (1991) 'Science and gender' in GUNEW, S. (Ed.) *A Reader in Feminist Knowledge*, London, Routledge.

BOURNE, J. (1983) 'Towards an anti-racist feminism', *Race and Class*, **25**, 1.

BRAH, A. (1992) 'Difference, diversity and differentiation' in DONALD, J. and RATTANSI, A. (Ed.) *'Race', Culture and Difference*, London, Sage.

BROWN, C. (1984) *Black and White in Britain. The Third PSI Survey*. London, Heinemann.

Bryan, B., Dadzie, S. and Scafe, S. (1985) *The Heart of the Race: Black Women's Lives in Britain*, London, Virago.

Bush, B. (1990) *Slave Women in Caribbean Society 1650–1838*, London, James Currey.

Carby, H.V. (1982) 'White woman listen! Black feminism and the boundaries of sisterhood' in CCCS (Eds) *The Empire Strikes Back: Race and Racism in 70s Britain*, London, Hutchinson.

Carby, H.V. (1990) 'The quicksands of representation: Rethinking black cultural politics' in Gates, Jr. H.L. (Ed.) *Reading Black Reading Feminist: A Critical Anthology*. New York, Penguin Books.

Cockburn, C. (1987) *Two Track Training*, London, Tavistock.

Collins, P. (1987) 'The meaning of motherhood in black culture and black mother/daughter relationships', *Sage: A Scholarly Journal on Black Women*, **4**, 2, Fall.

Collins, P. (1990) *Black Feminist Thought*. London, Unwin Hyman.

Coultas, V. (1989) 'Black girls and self-esteem', *Gender and Education*: Special Issue: Race, Gender and Education, **1**, 3.

Dann, G. (1987) *The Barbadian Male: Sexual Attitudes and Practice*, London, Macmillan.

Davis, A. (1982) *Women, Race and Class*, London, The Women's Press.

Dex, S. (1982) 'West Indians, further education and labour markets', *New Community*, **10**, 2, winter, pp. 191–205.

Dex, S. (1983) 'The second generation: West Indian female school leavers' in Phizacklea, A. (Ed.) *One Way Ticket*, London, Routledge & Kegan Paul.

Driver, G. (1980) *Beyond Underachievement: Case Studies of English, West Indian and Asian School Leavers at Sixteen Plus*. London, CRE.

Eggleston, J., Dunn, D., Anjali, M. and Wright, C. (1986) *Education for Some. The Educational and Vocational Experiences of 15–18 year old Members of Minority Ethnic Groups*, Stoke-on-Trent, Trentham.

Employment Gazette (1991) 'Ethnic Origins and the Labour Market.' London, Department of Employment, (Feb.) HMSO.

Farley, R. and Bianchi, S.M. (1985) 'Social class polarization: Is it occurring among the blacks?' in Leggon, M. *Research in Race and Ethnic Relations*, **4**, pp. 1–31.

Foner, N. (1979) *Jamaica Farewell, Jamaican Migrants in London*, London, Routledge & Kegan Paul.

Frances, White, E. (1990) 'Africa on my mind: Gender, counter discourse and African-American nationalism', *Journal of Women's History*, **2**, spring.

Fryer, P. (1984) *Staying Power: The History of Black People in Britain*, London, Pluto.

Fuller, M. (1978) 'Dimensions of gender in a school', unpublished PhD, University of Bristol.

Fuller, M. (1980) 'Black girls in a London comprehensive school' in Deem, R. (Ed.) *Schooling for Womens' Work*. London, Routledge and Kegan Paul.

Fuller, M. (1982) 'Young, female and black' in Cashmore, E. and Troyna, B. (Eds) *Black Youth in Crisis*, London, George Allen & Unwin.

Frazier, E.F. (1966) *The Negro Family in the United States*, Chicago, IL, University of Chicago.

Gilroy, P. (1987) *There Ain't No Black In the Union Jack*, London, Hutchinson.

Gilroy, P. (1990) 'The end of anti-racism', *New Community*, **17**, 1, October.

Griffin, C. (1985) *Typical Girls? Young Women from School to the Job Market*, London, Routledge and Kegan Paul.

Gunew, S. (Ed.) (1991) *A Reader in Feminist Knowledge*, London, Routledge.

Gutman, H. (1976) *The Black Family in Slavery and Freedom 1750–1925*, New York, Vintage Books.

HARRISON, A. and MINOR, J. (1978) 'Interrole conflict, coping strategies, and satisfaction among black working wives', *Journal of Marriage and the Family*, November.

HIGGINBOTHAM, E.B. (1992) 'African American women's history and the metalanguage of race', *Signs*, **17**, 2, winter.

HIRSCH, M. (1989) *The Mother/Daughter Plot*. Bloomington, IN, Indiana University Press.

HOCH, P. (1979) *White Hero, Black Beast*, London, Pluto.

JONES, J. (1985) *Labour of Love, Labour of Sorrow: Black Women, Work and the Family, from Slavery to the Present Day*, New York, Vintage Books.

JUSTUS, J.B. (1985) 'Women's role in West Indian society' in STEADY, F.C. (Ed.) *The Black Woman Cross-Culturally*, Cambridge, MA, Schenkman Books.

KNOWLES, C. and MERCER, S. (1992) 'Feminism and antiracism: An exploration of the political possibilities' in DONALD, J. and RATTANSI, A. *'Race', Culture and Difference*, London, Sage.

LADNER, J.A. (1981) 'Racism and tradition: Black womanhood in historical perspective' in STEADY, F. (Ed.) *The Black Woman Cross-Culturally*, Cambridge, MA, Schenkman Books.

LANDRY, B. and JENDREK, M. (1978) 'The employment of wives from black middle class families', *Journal of Marriage and the Family*, November.

LITTLE, A. (1978) 'Schools and race', *In Five Views of Multi-Racial Britain*. London, CRE.

MAC AN GHAILL, M. (1988) *Young, Gifted and Black: Student Teacher Relations in the Schooling of Black Youth*, Milton Keynes, Open University Press.

MCROBBIE, A. (1978a) 'Jackie: An Ideology of Adolescent Femininity', stencilled paper, CCCS, University of Birmingham.

MCROBBIE, A. (1978b) 'Working class girls: The culture of femininity' in Women's Studies Group, Centre for Contemporary Cultural Studies (Eds) *Women Take Issue*, London, Hutchinson.

MCROBBIE, A. (1990) *Feminism and Youth Culture*, London, Macmillan Education.

MAMA, A. (1992) 'Black women and the British state: Race, class and gender analysis for the 1990s' in BRAHAM, P. *et al.* (Eds) *Racism and Antiracism: Inequalities, Opportunities and Policies*, London, Sage.

MATHURIN MAIR, L. (1986) *Women Field Workers in Jamaica During Slavery: The 1986 Elsa Goveia Memorial Lecture*, Mona Jamaica, Department of History, University of the West Indies.

MIRZA, H.S. (1986) 'The material circumstances facilitating and/or constraining a woman's return to work after the birth of a child', unpublished report, TCRU, Institute of Education, University of London.

MIRZA, H.S. (1992) *Young, Female and Black*, London, Routledge.

MOHAMMED, P. (1988) 'The Caribbean family revisited' in MOHAMMED, P. and SHEPHERD, C. (Eds) *Gender in Caribbean Development*. Women and Development Studies Project, St. Augustine, Trinidad, University of the West Indies.

MOSES, Y.T. (1985) 'Female status, the family, and male dominance in a West Indian community', in STEADY, F. (Ed.) *The Black Woman Cross Culturally*, Cambridge, MA, Schenkman Books.

NASTA, S. (Ed.) (1991) *Motherlands: Black Women's Writing from Africa, the Caribbean and South Asia*, London, The Women's Press.

OFFICE OF POPULATION AND CENSUSES AND SURVEYS (1987) *The Labour Force Survey 1985*, Series LFS No. **5**, OPCS, HMSO.

PARMAR, P. (1989) 'Other kinds of dreams', *Feminist Review*, Special Issue, Twenty Years Of Feminism, **31**.

PHIZACKLEA, A. (1982) 'Migrant women and wage labour: The case of West Indian women in Britain' in WEST, J. (Ed.) *Work, Women and the Labour Market*, London, Routledge & Kegan Paul.

PHIZACKLEA, A. (1983) 'In the front line' in PHIZACKLEA, A. (Ed.) *One Way Ticket*, London, Routledge & Kegan Paul.

PHOENIX, A. (1987) 'Theories of gender and black families' in WEINER, G. and ARNOT, M. (Eds) *Gender Under Scrutiny*, London, Hutchinson and the Open University Press.

PHOENIX, A. (1988a) 'Narrow definitions of culture, The case of early motherhood' in WESTWOOD, S. and BHACHU, P. (Eds) *Enterprising Women: Ethnicity, Economy and Gender Relations*, London, Routledge.

PHOENIX, A. (1988b) 'The Afro-Caribbean myth', *New Society*, 4 March.

PHOENIX, A. (1990) *Young Mothers*? London, Polity Press.

POWELL, D. (1986) 'Caribbean women and their response to familial experiences', *Social and Economic Studies*, Special Number: J. MASSIAH (Ed.) *Women in the Caribbean* (Part 1), Institute of Social and Economic Research, University of the West Indies, **35**, 2.

RAINWATER, L. and YANCEY, W.L. (1967) *The Moynihan Report and the Politics of Controversy*, Cambridge, MA, MIT Press.

RAMAZANOGLU, C. (1989) *Feminism and the Contradictions of Oppression*, London, Routledge.

RAMAZANOGLU, C., KAZI, H., LEES, S. and MIRZA, H.S. (1986) 'Feedback: Feminism and racism', *Feminist Review*, **22**, spring.

RAMDIN, R. (1987) *The Making of the Black Working Class in Britain*, Aldershot, Wildwood House.

REID, E. (1989) 'Black girls talking', *Gender and Education*: Special Issue: Race, Gender and Education, **1**, 3.

RILEY, K. (1985) 'Black girls speak for themselves' in WEINER, G. (Ed.) *Just a Bunch of Girls*, Milton Keynes, Open University Press.

RUTTER, M., GRAY, G., MAUGHAN, B. and SMITH, A. (1982) 'School experiences and the first year of employment', unpublished report to the DES.

SEGAL, L. (1990) *Slow Motion: Changing Masculinities, Changing Men*, London, Virago.

SHARPE, S. (1987) *Just Like a Girl: How Girls Learn to be Women*, Harmondsworth, Penguin.

SMITH, M.G. (1962) *West Indian Family Structure*, Seattle, WA, University of Washington Press.

SPELMAN, E.V. (1988) *Inessential Woman: The Problems of Exclusion in Feminist Thought*, Boston, MA, Beacon Press.

SPILLERS, H. (1990) 'The permanent obliquity of an in(pha)llibility straight: In the time of our daughters and fathers' in WALL, C. (Ed.) *Changing Our Own Words*, London, Routledge.

STACK, C. (1982) *All Our Kin: Strategies for Survival in a Black Community*, New York, Harper and Row.

STONE, K. (1983) 'Motherhood and waged work: West Indian, Asian and white mothers compared' in PHIZACKLEA, A. (Ed.) *One Way Ticket*, London, Routledge and Kegan Paul.

STONE, M. (1985) *The Education of the Black Child: The Myth of Multi-Cultural Education*, London, Fontana Press.

SUTTON, C. and MAKIESKY-BARROW, S. (1977) 'Social inequality and sexual status in

Barbados' in Schlegel, A. (Ed.) *Sexual Stratification: A Cross-Cultural View*, New York, Columbia University Press.

Thorogood, N. (1987) 'Race, class and gender: The politics of housework' in Brannen, J. and Wilson, G. (Ed.) *Give and Take in Families*, London, Allen and Unwin.

Ullah, P. (1985) 'Disaffected black and white youth: The role of unemployment duration and perceived job discrimination', *Ethnic and Racial Studies*, **8**, 2, April.

Verma, G.K. (1986) *Ethnicity and Educational Achievement in British Schools*, London, Macmillan Press.

Wall, C.A. (Ed.) (1990) *Changing Our Own Words: Essays On Criticism, Theory, and Writing by Black Women*, London, Routledge.

Wallace, M. (1990) 'Variations on negation and the heresy of black feminist creativity' in Gates, H.L. (Ed.) *Reading Black Reading Feminist: A Critical Anthology*, New York, Penguin Books.

Washington, M.H. (1984) 'I sign my mother's name: Alice Walker, Dorothy West, Paule Marshall' in Perry, R. and Watson Brownley, M. (Eds) *Mothering the Mind*, New York, Holmes and Meier.

Willis, P. (1977) *Learning to Labour: How Working Class Kids Get Working Class Jobs*, Farnborough, Saxon House.

Willis, S. (1987) *Specifying: Black American Women Writing The American Experience*, Madison, WI, University of Wisconsin Press.

Wilson, W.J. (1987) *The Truly Disadvantaged: The Inner City, The Under Class, and Public Policy*, Chicago, IL, University of Chicago Press.

Wiltshire-Brodber, R. (1988) 'Gender, race and class in the Caribbean' in Mohammed, P. and Shepherd, C. (Eds) *Gender in Caribbean Development*, Women and Development Studies Project, St. Augustine, Trinidad, University of the West Indies.

Wright, C. (1987) 'The relations between teachers and Afro-Caribbean pupils: Observing multicultural classrooms' in Weiner, G. and Arnot, M. (Eds) *Gender Under Scrutiny*, London, Hutchinson in association with Open University.

Wulff, H. (1988) *Twenty Girls: Growing Up, Ethnicity and Excitement in a South London Microculture*, Stockholm Studies in Anthropology, 21, Stockholm: University of Stockholm.

Chapter 3

Getting Out From Down Under: Maori Women, Education and the Struggles for Mana Wahine

Linda Tuhiwai Smith

This chapter critically examines the educational and schooling processes within which Maori women, the indigenous women of New Zealand struggle to resist colonization and maintain cultural authenticity. Schools are important sites of resistance for Maori people. Maori issues in education are contested by the media, by politicians, by educational experts and by Maori people themselves. Maori women who play a critical role in education have been active in keeping Maori educational issues on the national agenda. They have also been active in their attempts to work out viable solutions to the crisis in Maori education. It is this latter role in particular which this chapter will examine.

Maori people have provided a classic example of the failure of schools to deliver equal educational opportunities. Although they have been used to support the critiques of state education from both the radical left and the conservative right, there has been a massive failure by educationalists and political reformers to address the needs of Maori people generally.[1] It is primarily because of this failure that Maori people have become committed to seeking alternative solutions to mainstream schooling.

Maori women have been at the cutting edge of these attempts. Maori feminist struggles are grounded in the world views and language of Maori people. One commonly used Maori term for these struggles is Mana Wahine Maori. The following discussion is located in a specific case-study example of the establishment of a *marae* (a Maori cultural complex) in a single-sex, predominantly white or Pakeha[2] girls' secondary school. It contextualizes the multiple tensions which underpin the struggles for Mana Wahine Maori and the attempts by Maori women to use cultural institutions and frameworks as sites of resistance. It also illustrates specific ways in which education can be used to give new space for Maori women within their own culture and within the dominant white or Pakeha culture.

The Legacy of Colonization

New Zealand is a former British colony and British modes of colonization, including schooling, have had a powerful influence over the ways in which Maori people have been structured out of their 'tino rangatiratanga' or status as sovereign people and into a Pakeha New Zealand society as an underclass, ethnic minority. State schools have been significant sites of struggle for Maori people because of the clear intentions of colonial administrators to use education as an instrument of colonization and cultural annihilation. Suppression of Maori language, knowledge and culture was regarded as a necessary condition for becoming civilized.

Schooling for Maori children was viewed by the more liberal politicians of the nineteenth century as an efficient and humanitarian way for bringing civilization and social control to a population of indigenous people who still had the audacity to believe in the 1860s that they were a sovereign people. It was thought by one proponent of Maori education that it was in fact cheaper to 'civilize Maori than to exterminate them' (NZPD, 1867). That audacity has remained an important feature of Maori resistance to the ways in which colonization structured a new British society in the Pacific and to the racist ideological trappings which were used to justify attempts to destroy indigenous, Maori society (Simon, 1990).

Maori society still remains a culturally distinct society which has its own ways of defining itself, its members and its universe. Maori women belong to different tribal groupings. Their status and roles differ according to tribe, to age, to genealogical relationships and to individual talents. Specific contexts determine the importance or lack of importance of their gender (Mahuika, 1975). The interweaving of ancient and contemporary, kinship and non-kinship, traditional and post-colonial, rural and urban, religious and political threads all contribute to a rich and complex pattern of tensions, positions and relationships between Maori women. When these are placed within the wider context of New Zealand Pakeha society this pattern is complicated further. Relationships between Maori women and Pakeha women are equally problematic.

For Maori girls and women the persistent failure of education to deliver equality of opportunity has had far reaching implications for a wider socio-economic crisis in which Maori women often see themselves as 'being at the bottom of the heap' (Nepe, 1989). Maori girls (and Maori boys) leave schools in disproportionate numbers without any school qualifications, many 'leave school' before the legal leaving age is reached and others never really get to school at all. Maori truancy rates are high and rates for expulsion and suspension are also disproportionately greater for Maori than for other groups of children. Others stay at school to go through the cycle of poor results in national examinations and restricted access into tertiary education. School achievement patterns show a wide gap between the rates for Maori and those for Pakeha.[3]

Maori women have high and increasing levels of unemployment. They have one of the highest rates of lung cancer in the world and have high levels of morbidity and mortality with other forms of cancer, heart and respiratory diseases. Suicide rates, admissions to psychiatric hospitals, accident rates and levels of poverty all place Maori women in a marginal position. Similar rates for Maori men are equally disturbing with the exception that Maori women are more likely to be the sole care-givers of children. In the current economic climate where state welfare benefits have been cut back severely and extreme fundamentalist attitudes have been used to justify these measures Maori women are structured even deeper into poverty.

In schools Maori girls are often regarded as presenting serious behavioural problems, many are labelled at an early age as being lazy, recalcitrant and 'too smart for their own good'. Being 'too smart' is usually a reference to girls who have the ability to assert their own will in a classroom, who argue with teachers and who 'defy the authority' of the school. Because a greater proportion of Maori students are streamed or grouped in the lower ranks of their classes at secondary school they are frequently regarded as being troublesome and difficult to teach. Generations of Maori students have left school feeling alienated and 'dumb'. The powerful role of the peer group has been targeted by some educationalists as an explanation for Maori students who do show early signs of success eventually succumbing to the pattern of underachievement. This explanation is simply one of a number of reasons advanced by educationalists and politicians for the failure of schools to deliver educational achievement. Many of these explanations are still driven by notions of cultural deprivation and linguistic and experiential deficits. This victim-blaming ideology is hotly contested by Maori people who accuse schools of failing to educate Maori children and of perpetrating systematic violence against these children through racist policies and practices (Walker, 1984).

Educational and social policies based on a platform of multiculturalism, for example, were dismissed by Maori interests as a ploy for denying difference by denying the historical context in which the legitimacy for Pakeha control was acquired through the illegitimate processes of colonization. Multicultural policies were viewed by Maori as a continuation of the 'divide and rule' strategies of colonization and represented a further attempt to maintain Pakeha domination over social and economic structures by forcing minority groups under the guise of 'multiculturalism' to compete amongst each other for crumbs. Maori people have argued, for example, that in the New Zealand context biculturalism must be a prior step towards multiculturalism. Other than Maori people the most significant 'brown' ethnic minorities are people from various Pacific nations who share in the same polynesian traditions as Maori. New Zealand's past immigration policies have consistently limited the access of non-British and especially non-white minorities. In most socioeconomic indices it is Maori people who consistently appear as the most disadvantaged and oppressed group in New Zealand society.

It is within this context that Maori women have struggled to escape from the 'down under' of New Zealand society. Maori women have tended to articulate the issues within their own cultural framework. Cultural institutions such as the whanau or extended family and the marae are sites of struggle in which Maori interests are continually reshaped and from which Maori interests contest the ideological dominance of Pakeha society. The work of Pakeha feminists have often been regarded with deep suspicion by Maori women although some feminist groups have actively promoted the issues of Maori women. Maori women have argued, for example, that Pakeha women are as much the beneficiaries of colonization as Pakeha men. Others use the 'bottom of the heap' metaphor to argue that Maori women are on their own and that alliances with other groups such as Maori men, Pakeha women and Pakeha men will always be problematic (Awatere, 1984).

There are tensions between the ways in which Maori women view their realities and their struggles and the ways in which Pakeha feminists have defined feminist projects. This tension is sharply delineated over such issues as Maori male violence or dealing with sexual abuse within Maori families. When attempts are made by Pakeha women to blame Maori men or Maori 'culture' for such issues, Maori women are quick to challenge such remarks as being founded on racist ideologies. Donna Awatere, one of the few Maori women who has written in this area has accused Pakeha women of seeking to 'set Maori women against Maori men' (*ibid*). Maori women claim the right to define such issues on the basis that in the end it is Maori women who are left to pick up the pieces of a colonized society.

The current term used by Maori women to explain what it means to be Maori women in a Pakeha society and to be women in a Maori society is *Mana Wahine Maori*. *Wahine* means woman. *Mana* is a concept related to notions of power, strength, status and collective acknowledgment of merit. The *Mana Wahine Maori* term is broad enough to embrace a wide range of womens' activities and perspectives. It is a strong cultural concept which situates Maori women in relation to each other and upholds their *mana* as women of particular genealogical groupings. It also situates Maori women in relation to the outside world and reaffirms their *mana* as Maori, indigenous women. Mana Wahine Maori is the preferred Maori label for what counts as Maori feminism.

It is a term which addresses both the issues of race and gender as well as locates the struggle for Maori women within two distinct societies.

Mana Wahine Maori and Education

One site where these multiple interests and tensions, positions and relationships intersect each other is state education and schooling. The impact of schooling was experienced by generations of Maori children across all tribal and regional boundaries. There is a shared memory of these experiences and the impact this has had on Maori knowledge, language and culture. As one woman writes, 'I passionately, passionately hated that school' (Te Awekotuku, 1988) and another one writes, 'We have to speak English. Kui, you must not speak Maori to me again. I will get the strap if I am caught speaking Maori' (Edwards, 1990, p. 33). There is a shared anger and suspicion of schools.

Although increasing numbers of Maori women are involved in education as teachers they are still under-represented in all sectors. There are only three Maori women who hold doctorate of philosophy degrees and there are no Maori women professors in New Zealand universities. In comparison there are at least fifteen Maori men with doctorate degrees and four Maori men are professors. Very few Maori women are principals of either primary or secondary schools and very few are on career tracks which will qualify them to be principals (Taylor, 1991). Where Maori women do have a presence in the educational bureaucracy their effectiveness is always problematic and their scope to work for the interests of Maori women is often limited (Smith, 1990).

In an article expressing her frustrations as a teacher Maiki Marks (1984) has written:

> If the teacher is given any extra role in the school by the principal, that role is likely to be to hand on gimmicks and tricks to her Pakeha colleagues on how to control Maori kids. (p. 14)

Marks also comments on the frustrations which occur for Maori teachers when they are part of a system they are unable to change. In her eyes the Maori teacher 'every day faces the victims of the system . . . the Maori girls'. She calls them the 'saddest victims' who come to school with their 'selves battered and bruised after eight years in the system . . . They have little confidence. Their behaviour often reflects pain and confusion' (*ibid*). This hurt, pain and confusion which confronts Maori teachers in their classrooms absorbs them into a wider system in which they too are powerless. There is a contradiction for Maori teachers between supporting Maori students and at the same time supporting the very structures which turn Maori students into 'victims'. Since the early 1980s recognition of this contradiction has helped politicize Maori teachers into making greater demands on schools and on their own respective teacher unions. They have been very strong in their support of alternative educational options for Maori students and have come together with other Maori activist groups to demand recognition of Treaty rights and 'tino rangatiratanga' self-determination.[4]

Multiple Roles and Multiple Struggles: The Development of a *Marae* in a Girls' School

The Marae as a Representation of Difference

It is difficult to generalize about the range of frustrations which Maori women face as educators in state schools. What many of them express in terms of frustration, anger or exhaustion is symptomatic of the deeper structural relations in which Maori women are situated. Maori women have multiple roles not just as women who may be teachers, mothers, partners, daughters and grandmothers, but also as women who are descendents of tribal ancestries, women who may also be expert weavers, healers, kaikaranga (callers), kaiwaiata (singers), women who may be the only member of their community or family with skills to negotiate with the police, the doctor, the nurse or the school principal, women who may also be major caregivers of their children, their nieces and nephews, their grandchildren and other peoples' children. The following case-study provides one example of how these multiple roles, tensions and struggles are played out in a particular context. It was a project in which I was involved as a Maori woman staff member.

The *marae* is one of the few Maori institutions to have survived into this century. It is a complex of buildings and grounds used as a forum for collective rituals and practices. It is where the 'systems of tribal (*iwi*), sub-tribal (*hapu*) and extended family (*whanau*) are expressed' and where some of the patterns of behaviours which maintain these systems can be observed (Salmond, 1976). On a *marae* there is usually a meeting house or *whare* which is often carved in traditional style and in which people gather to talk, to sing, to debate, to mourn, to celebrate and to sleep. The *marae* is an expression of collective identity and a site where this identity is often contested and recreated. It is one place where the Maori language is still likely to be heard. As a surviving pre-European institution the *marae* is a powerful representation of Maori identity. It is a forum for public debate and one in which *mana* is defended and claimed.

The School, the Marae and One Maori Woman

The school in this study is a large, urban school which had a roll of 1200 students. It had an ethnically diverse mix of students. The staff at the school consisted almost entirely of Pakeha women.[5] Although there was general support from staff for developing a *marae* at the school the underlying significance of such a project contested some fundamental beliefs held by staff about schooling and about this school in particular. Some staff, for example, held strong beliefs about the importance of school traditions and viewed changes to the school's physical appearance or its operations as challenging the very foundations of the school and undermining educational standards. Some staff saw an absolute distinction between schooling as a site for the learning of 'real knowledge' and schooling as a site of cultural struggle. These staff denied that the school was itself a product and a producer of cultural meanings and argued for the school as a neutral site which should not be used by Maori interests or any other ethnic interests to teach 'culture'. In these arguments Pakeha culture was represented as being non-existent and therefore not present in the school at all.

Staff resistance to the idea was not openly debated.[6] Rather there was an underground debate among certain groupings of staff. The sole Maori staff member at the time felt alienated and marginalized by a debate which she knew was going on but from which she was excluded. Heated discussions and snide comments took place in the staffroom when she had her morning tea and during informal meetings of staff. There were clearly several groupings of opinion amongst the Pakeha women and conflicting submissions being made to the Principal and School Board. As the single 'representative' of Maori people this staff member provided a focus for the debate but was a non-participant in it. This was partly because the debate was carried out around her but not with her and partly because she actively resisted attempts to draw her into a discussion in which she was expected to justify and defend her own belief system.

In these initial stages the struggle over the validity of the *marae* took place primarily within the group of Pakeha women staff members. This group of women were setting the parameters of the discussion and defining the relevant issues. This process was seen as being highly problematic by the Principal and she made several attempts to appoint more Maori staff and give them greater control over the development. I was appointed in 1984 as a guidance counsellor but also had a special brief for developing the idea of the *whare* (the meeting house) by converting a humble, downright ugly classroom into a fine cultural institution. There would now be two Maori women on a staff of about sixty women.

The School, the Marae and Two Maori Women

The Maori woman already on the staff was older than I. She was from a tribal confederation who could rightly claim to have the school within its area. She was a fluent and beautiful speaker of Maori language and had been a teacher at the school for sixteen years. She was the Maori language teacher and was a member of the 'foreign' languages department. She held no seniority but was expected over the years to teach and be responsible for all the troublesome Maori students in the school. I was younger, my tribal links were quite different, I was not a first language speaker of Maori. I was also an 'old-girl' of the school and an example for the older teachers (some of whom taught me) of how good the school really was 'if only other Maori girls were motivated'. Also I had been appointed to a senior management position which gave me more pay and status. It was assumed that the two Maori staff would know each other and would 'naturally' get along with each other. But we did not know each other and it took time and effort for us to become good allies and friends.

As a younger Maori woman I have been educated to respect age even when I think my elders are wrong. As a woman from another tribe I have to maintain my tribal mana but respect the tribal mana of the other woman. As a woman whose tribes are from outside the area I am a visitor and have a separate status from those who belong in the area regardless of how long I have lived there. This would be the case even if I had married into the tribe.[7] With my restricted ability in Maori language my ability to negotiate many of the cultural issues was limited. As a younger Maori woman I was in the position of having more seniority and pay than an older Maori woman, a woman who in the Maori world had the same status as my *whaea* or mother. All of these differences between us needed to be recognized and worked through. We could never be simply two Maori women on the teaching staff.

Although I was appointed as a school counsellor I was also given the brief to develop the marae project further. My first task in this area was to work out a relationship with my Maori colleague. As the younger woman I had to go to her and wait for her to give me support. This turned out not to be so difficult. The other teacher had become so thoroughly disillusioned with the project and the politics involved that she was more than happy to support me. The struggle over the *marae* shifted focus with my arrival from one which involved and was shaped by the interests of the Pakeha women staff to one in which my colleague and I tried to negotiate the wider cultural issues related to having a *marae* in a single-sex, girls' school.

The collective unit for a traditional *marae* is a genealogical unit such as an extended family, a sub-tribe or a tribe. This means that there are always elders and young, men and women, orators and singers and talkers present to support a marae. It is a collective enterprise intended to meet the spiritual, physical and social needs of the people who meet there. The *mana* of the genealogical unit depends on the ability of the unit to carry out its roles in an authentic way, to be hospitable to guests, to defend its group knowledge and traditions.

Locating a *marae* therefore in a school which is owned by the state, which is predominantly of one generation, where its members are not related, where there is only one gender group and where Maori people do not possess *tino rangatiratanga* or autonomy over the concept was just as problematic for Maori people as it was for the Pakeha school staff.

There were issues in which the concerns of some Pakeha women and some Maori women did coincide. One of the hopes, for example, of some of the feminist staff at the school was that the *marae atea*, (the area in front of the actual building) would provide an opportunity for the girls to speak in the fashion of Maori oratory. This was seen by these women as a way of liberating Maori girls from patriarchal structures because many tribes do not allow women to speak during the welcoming rituals which take place on a marae. The fact that in most tribes men do all the talking during this particular ritual is regarded by many women, Maori and Pakeha as a symbol of patriarchal power relations and an example of the co-option of Maori men by Pakeha patriarchal structures (Irwin, 1992).

I have two different tribal affiliations. One of these tribes has had renowned women speakers, the other one has no women speakers. It was thought that at least given one of my tribal backgrounds I would be influential in setting a *kawa (protocol)* which would facilitate women speaking. However, as already outlined the constraints of age, my lack of skill in Maori language and my status as a *manuhiri* or guest in the area did not give me any authority to set *kawa*. Nor did the other Maori women who were part of the community support for the *marae* feel that they had the mana to do such a thing themselves.

The most that I could do was ensure that it was on the agenda and open for discussion. There was no consensus however, among the women and the community people concerned. The women who wanted speaking rights were ones who themselves could not speak Maori.[8] One very influential Maori woman who was herself a former teacher at the school fully supported the idea of women speaking on the *marae*. When she came to talk to the *marae* committee she stated that this was her hope and that possibly she would be able to do this herself one day. Her support was very important but, on its own it was not enough.

The issue of *tino rangatiratanga* or control over how the space was to be used, who could visit, who could agree to visits became increasingly problematic. Teachers wanted to use the room to run life skills discussion groups, others wanted to invite guest speakers to it rather than their own classrooms because 'the room was more comfortable'. The school was seen by the Maori staff and Maori students as intruding more and more into a position where it was beginning to determine its own protocols for the *marae* and was making its own selection of Maori cultural practices and behaviours. This was interpreted as trying to gain the 'warm fuzzies' of Maori cultural practices rather than the more significant practices. In saying 'no' to some groups there was always the danger of being accused of excluding Pakeha groups and maintaining a 'separatist' policy.

The School, the Marae, Maori Women, Pakeha Women: Time-out For a Redefinition

The tension between the boundaries of Maori cultural values and the school became more obvious as demands for the use of the building grew. A major crisis occurred when a group of top women civil servants arrived for a visit. It was thought by someone, not the Maori teachers, that it would be appropriate to welcome this group of very important women at the *whare*. They were greeted with a formal Maori *powhiri* by the Principal, the Maori language teacher and her class. The ignorance and arrogance of a number of these women towards Maori cultural practices shocked the Principal, the staff who were present and the girls who had performed. Here was a small group of Maori women welcoming a larger group of white women who were cold and unsmiling, who did not seem to know or care to know what it was they were being given. One or two refused to *hongi* (traditional touching of noses) and several of them ignored the girls in the greetings. This experience was so clearly offensive to Maori women and Maori girls that a stronger policy was developed by the *marae* committee to exert more control over the ways in which the *whare* was used by outside groups.

As the pressure from groups to use the *whare* mounted some of the younger women who had formed the initial steering group for this project became impatient that the project was becoming bigger and taking longer than they had intended. They felt that the focus had shifted from the Maori staff and students to the whole staff, many of whom were regarded by these former students as being antagonistic to the Maori students in the school and to Maori values and practices. They were particularly concerned that the *whare* might become bound up in the very school rules which alienated Maori girls from school in the first place. This group of young Maori women were quietly persistent that the *whare* be primarily a safe haven for Maori girls.

One of my tasks was to consult with a wide range of Maori interest groups. While these groups could see the merit of a special cultural presence in the school they were almost all uniformly cautious about a *marae*. For example many people avoided even using the word 'marae' and would select another Maori word such as *whare*. It became very clear that among the people who had given most support to the school including the local tribe there was no overt support for a *marae* project. There were too many complex issues which had not been resolved at a tribal level and there was a general feeling that the school context was not the best one in which these ideological issues could be discussed or resolved. There seemed to be a consensus among most of the Maori interests that until the school proved itself capable of defending Maori values there was no room for a *marae*.

The silence of the major Maori supporters led to a downplaying of a *marae concept* and a shift towards the development of a simple *whare*. A *whare* is a generic name for a building or house. This did not remove the pressures coming from other interests but it did clarify the different Maori positions and as a simple act of redefinition it gave the two of us on staff a clearer direction about where the boundaries of Maori interests and school interests lay. The cultural message was to abandon any notion of a school *marae* and concentrate on something more achievable and by implication less risky. This resolution allowed us to continue with other tasks. These included the preparation of the Maori girls and fund-raising activities.

We began with a series of group practices in *waiata* (songs and chants). The girls from the local tribes were excused from class to attend *waananga* or learning sessions on their own history and the protocols they would need as the host tribe. Other girls were involved in various supporting activities such as providing the hospitality support for visitors. The girls had started to claim their space in the *whare* at lunchtimes and took some pride in looking after it although they had to be reminded frequently that the rule prohibiting food also prohibited chewing gum. The group of former Maori students who had instigated the project made frequent visits to school to talk to the current students. They had become important role models who would listen to the girls' problems and provide suggestions for dealing with teachers, parents, sisters and boyfriends. Both seniors and juniors would go to the *whare* at lunchtime to talk or sleep or play cards. They would remove their shoes as they would in a meeting house and were beginning to establish the kinds of rules used in more traditional meeting houses. All of this was a major turn-around for the Maori students at the school.

And Then There Were Two More . . .

At the end of that year my colleague retired and two new Maori women teachers were hired. Both these women came from the local confederation of tribes, were both older and were highly skilled in Maori language and performance. I went on a year's study leave and the two Maori women staff looked after the project. Even though they were linked closely to the local tribe they in fact came from different areas and had very different ways of operating. It was soon apparent that these two disagreed on most things and the other staff had started to see them as a kind of 'good cop, bad cop' combination with the one viewed as being 'good' getting more support from colleagues and the 'bad' one was labelled as being difficult, unreliable and troublesome. Not only was the staff aligned according to how they viewed these teachers but the Maori students and Maori communities had also become split into groups. It was an awkward year.

When I returned to school it was in a new role. Not only was I responsible for apparently difficult Maori students I was also responsible for apparently difficult Maori staff. Various submissions were made to me by Pakeha staff suggesting strategies for dealing with these two women. The tension between the two staff was eventually resolved by one gaining another position elsewhere. Despite their differences they had both been effective in training a group of Maori girls who were not only highly proficient in a range of cultural skills but very proud of themselves.

The *whare* was officially opened with all the protocols and rituals three years after it had been moved as a building onto the site. Respected elders had opened it at dawn with all the appropriate rituals and many important dignitaries came to speak. The *whare* was given a Maori name and was deemed to have an identity and life of its own. It was no longer a *whare* it had taken on a new name by which the school and the Maori girls would be known within the Maori world.

What Does the *Whare* Mean for Mana Wahine Maori?

Many struggles took place around the development of the whare. There were tensions between Maori women and Pakeha women, between the different cultures of school and of Maori society, between the deeper structures of schooling and the interests of Maori and between the different interests and positions of Maori women. These tensions were not merely theoretical constructs but were real enough to the women involved to cause real stress, real pain and at times real excitement.

The relationships between Maori women and Pakeha women were never simple or predictable. The Principal was the most dependable supporter of the Maori women but there were occasions when her political relationships with Maori women outside the school put the whare project in jeopardy basically because she placed herself in the middle of relationships between Maori women. By doing this the Maori staff were caught between their own loyalties to her as the Principal and to their own tribal affiliations or politics. The Principal had a high public profile as a feminist educator and her comments often caused a ripple affect which staff generally had to handle.

With other Pakeha women there were the further complications of curriculum and teaching networks. Maori staff were also members of departments within the school and had to work with other colleagues on various other committees. In formal staff meetings there were always different types of staff alliances. This often puzzled the Maori women because many staff seemed able to situate themselves in a variety of contradictory positions depending on the issue under discussion. In a Maori framework how and where an individual locates themselves publicly is extremely significant and carries with it a number of obligations and responsibilities. As so many Pakeha women appeared to 'jump around' they tended to be viewed as having suspect politics and as being unreliable allies.

The different feminist arguments advanced at various times were also puzzling. Maori issues were frequently caught in the crossfire between differing feminist and non-feminist viewpoints. The whare became a symbol over which feminist perspectives were contested. The more radical feminists on staff were generally supportive of Maori issues. Their support was seen by other women as a very good reason for not supporting the whare. The liberal feminists supported the whare on the condition that it would improve the behaviour and academic performance of Maori students but were less certain about the implications the *whare* might hold for the ways in which the school might reorganize other areas.

The school was clearly a site of struggle over cultural meanings, values and behaviours. The grammar school tradition of the school represented Pakeha culture in particular ways. There were implicit class values which permeated school life. Standards of behaviour were defined according to these values. As a cultural sub-group the staff were highly educated, high earning, middle class Pakeha women. They spoke standard English, had university degrees, were well dressed, drove nice cars, went on overseas trips and lived with equally successful partners. Many staff sent their own daughters to private schools. They represented a culture which for the most part was quite foreign to the families whose daughters attended the school. It was difficult to talk across the divide of class because many staff had absolutely no understanding of how their students lived. Issues such as poverty or sexual abuse were simply problems for classroom teachers because the students could not concentrate on their work.

The whare project challenged the deeper structure of schooling primarily at the ideological level. The debates about the validity of the whare as an 'appropriate' place to have in a school challenged fundamental and taken-for-granted notions of what a school was and what it could be. Simple matters were often the cause of major crises because they challenged long held assumptions and hidden rules. When visitors are hosted at a *whare* for example they must be fed. The school had several kitchens as part of the Home Economics Department. The whole art of Maori hospitality clashed with the culture of the Home Economics Department and this sometimes led to a series of cross-cultural crises. Many of the staff were frightened to go to the whare in case they should offend. They had worked out powerful reasons for avoiding the whare and were able to transmit this to their own students. Pakeha students for example would claim they were 'not allowed' in the whare and that it was 'only for Maoris' and was 'separatist'. It was only possible to intercede in this if the Maori staff were aware of the situation and we were often not aware.

While the development of the *whare* was occurring within the school there was a wider public debate about educational standards. Teaching Taha Maori (selected aspects of Maori culture) was seen by some sections of the community as the major reason for the fall in educational standards. These arguments and other elements of a Pakeha backlash to Maori issues were also present within the school debate. There was a perception, for example, that Maori girls were getting too much attention from the Principal and that this was not only unfair but racism in reverse. Developing the whare provided a specific symbol for a struggle over ideology. Almost everything pertaining to Maori issues within the school and in the wider social context was assembled into arguments over the validity of the whare.

The *whare* is an attempt to provide a solution within the framework of a state school. It is a visual representation of Maori cultural difference and by its presence it challenges the school at the day-to-day level of organization to acknowledge and cater for cultural differences. However, it is limited in its potential to transform the school in more radical ways because its presence is still marginal and dependent on the work of individual Maori staff to promote, contest and struggle for Maori issues to be addressed. Maori people and Maori political organizations generally support the cultural aspirations which the whare embodies but would still argue for a notion of *rangatiratanga* which is independent of Pakeha structures. The more radical Maori view holds that there can never be *rangatiratanga* for Maori within institutions which are located within Pakeha traditions.

Developing a *marae* or a *whare* even in the most ideal conditions is not an easy achievement. It is more usual for projects of this nature to take many years because the process of consensus requires time, negotiation, reflection and further time. Nor is it by any means usual for a group of mainly women to develop a carved house and a supporting unit of people to support that house. This does not mean that Maori women have not been involved in the development of quite impressive traditional *marae* rather that their efforts have often been considered so ordinary and normal compared to the 'extraordinary' efforts of the male carvers that they have gone unnoticed (Te Awekotuku, 1991, p. 10). Most visitors to a carved meeting house see the carvings but do not see the woven panel work traditionally done by women or the invisible support work which has occurred in the background. Some Pakeha feminists, for example, have interpreted the issue of speaking rights as an example of patriarchal power over women's voices, however many Maori women would claim that the definitions of power being used in this example are culturally located and whilst in Pakeha society speaking rights may indicate power and status in Maori contexts, real power is held behind the scenes often by women who sit in the background. Many Maori women cling to a vision of the past which claims that in pre-European society gender roles were complementary and work was a genuinely group effort. This remains problematic because of the wide variation in tribal customs and kawa (Smith, 1992; Irwin, 1992).

The relationships between the Maori women involved in the project were always problematic. The staff had the authority of the school to make decisions. However there were other Maori women involved on the periphery who had to be consulted. These included women from the local tribe, women who were former students and teachers, women who were acknowledged for their expertise in *marae* procedures. These women were from many tribes, were of different generations and had different sets of relationships to each other and to the school. Their advice to the committee was grounded in their own educational experiences. This often meant, for example, that the older women were more conservative and upheld the tradition of the school as a reason for not making changes. Other older women had a more radical analysis of their own schooling experience and wanted a complex which would be totally controlled by the community not by the school. Still other Maori women thought that the school was engaging in a window-dressing exercise and were very cynical about the ability of the school to develop a *whare*. Tribal differences were marked each time Maori women gathered as a group in the *whare* itself. It was never certain as to who would call in the visitors, who would speak and in which order, what songs would be sung. Some women would insist on their tribal protocols and would refuse to speak, others would relish the opportunity. It was my role to negotiate the difficult terrain. There was an almost farcical side to some of these negotiations which often meant that I had to crawl discreetly behind people to deliver messages between certain women while they worked out the procedures for the day.

As an attempt to meet the needs of a group of young Maori women in a large secondary school the establishment of a *whare* represents an innovative approach to the problems faced by ethnic minority children in schools. It is potentially much more than that. The placement of the *whare* in a school provides a stark juxtaposition of unequal power relations. The school is big, the *whare* is small; the front of the school is green and elegant, the front of *whare* is concrete and tar. What is significant is that it is there at all. That fact on its own represents a struggle in which Maori women were active participants rather than passive bystanders. The *whare* has a wider potential to transform the structures by developing alternative pedagogical practices and validating Maori forms of knowledge.

While overt, oppressive gender relations may be absent, other structural and ideological relations of power have to be struggled against even in the context of a single-sex girls school with a predominantly female staff. In a context where Pakeha women were making the decisions there was never a guarantee that those decisions could or would serve the interests of Maori women. Race and class differences tended to struggle against any potentially common interests of gender. The school (as represented by the main body of staff) with its own organizational system and 'the school tradition' was very effective at maintaining control over its own boundaries.

The front lawn was just one example of how school tradition controlled what was on the agenda and what was not. It was one of the few grassed areas in the school grounds and it was very clear that there would never be a building of any kind sited on this patch of grass. The Maori staff would suggest to each other in private that the front lawn was the most appropriate site for a *whare*. When one of the women suggested this idea to the Principal there was absolute silence as if she had broken an unsaid rule which she had of course. The front lawn of this very English grammar school was to remain inviolate.

Another small struggle took place over funding arrangements. Fundraising for the *whare* took place at the same time as the fund-raising for a new centennial hall for the school. The centennial campaign was a very professional campaign which was in sharp contrast to the *whare* fund-raising which involved some projects which raised debts rather than profits and which more often than not involved me as the major fund-raiser going to community meetings to compete with other Maori organizations for small amounts of money. Funds raised were invested by the school and controlled by the school. Although these funds were protected for the use of the *whare*, they were also used as a reason for the school not needing to give any money itself to the project.

To the Maori women involved the *whare* would, when developed, give the school *mana* in the eyes of the Maori community. It was not just for the benefit of Maori girls attending the school but would reach out to benefit the school as a whole. Culturally it is believed that *mana* given should be reciprocated in some way. There were many times when we as Maori women thought the school was getting far more than it deserved. At the same time there were other staff who thought the actual *whare* building was rather unattractive (which it was before the renovations) and that it took up 'valuable' space. *Mana* is contested and struggled for within Maori interests but when it has to be contested with non-Maori interests, the struggle takes on the added dimension of a struggle for *tino rangatiratanga* or autonomy.

Sometimes this tension resulted in the Maori women reacting to what often appeared to the Pakeha women as insignificant incidents. Timetabling decisions often upset the Maori staff because of what was viewed as high-handed assumptions being made about space, time and people. For example in the early days the *whare* was seen by timetablers as a 'space' suitable for classes not as a *whare*. The Maori teacher initially thought this was a good idea until it was realised that several classes would be using the *whare* and that this would limit the cultural activities which could take place in the *whare*. This situation was finally resolved by a counter high-handed decision by myself to get rid of the desks which had been put in the room and to lock the room for two days so that no one could enter.

At the times of greatest stress it seemed to the Maori women that the personal and professional resources we had to do our jobs, to fight the battles, to get the community support, to hold the Maori students together, to raise money, to get along with our colleagues and each other were stretched well beyond their means. There were times when the staffroom became a place of enormous stress with no escape from comments or loud-asides being made about individual Maori students or about Maori issues. This does not deny that other women staff were also under stress but that for Maori women the stress was related not just to their individual workloads but to the very fact that we were Maori women among a larger group of Pakeha women in an institution which reified their knowledge and cultural backgrounds.

The life of a *whare* in the school will always be problematic simply because it represents a different world-view. This world-view celebrates and validates cultural difference. The presence of the whare within the grammar school makes the hidden curriculum of schooling more overt and provides a site from which meaningful resistances by Maori women can be mounted. The visibility of the *whare*, especially in its architectural difference ensures that the struggle over cultural boundaries is explicit and specific to what happens in the school itself. Although the *whare* remains marginal in a physical sense it is a powerful representation of Maori identity and a focus for cultural difference which makes the dangers of co-option by Pakeha structures less likely.

In terms of Mana Wahine Maori, the development of a whare by and for Maori women is significant despite its limitations. Within Maori society, Maori women see the development of powerful male roles through the 'capturing' of *marae kawa* by men as a distortion of the traditional relationships between Maori women and Maori men. Attempts by Maori women to reclaim *mana* are fraught with difficulties (Irwin, 1992). The *whare* project was an opportunity for Maori women to work at a solution in a context where Maori men were not a major influence. As a girls' school with mostly women staff there was space for Maori women to make important decisions about their own culture. It is this participation in the definition of what counts as Maori cultural difference which many Maori women would argue is the major challenge for *Mana Wahine Maori* (*ibid*).

Finally the worth of the project has to be seen in its impact on the Maori girls who attend the school and the Maori staff who work there. As a post-script the *whare* has become the base of a strong Maori language programme. The name of the *whare* has become synonymous in the Maori community with the name of the school. It has given the Maori students at the school and the non-Maori students who participate in Maori activities an identity and has signalled to the wider Maori community that they are serious about their culture. Maori students have also achieved high examination results and Maori staff numbers have been increased. While these last two factors may not be directly attributable to the *whare* on its own, they do suggest that Maori girls and women still have space and *mana* within this school.

Glossary

Note: In attempting to describe and define the world the way we see it, we are caught with a language other than our own with which to communicate across the world. There are some concepts, however, for which English is inadequate. I have tried to use the closest English equivalent immediately after the word when first introduced into the text. The following are further simple dictionary definitions for the Maori words in this article.

p. 63 hapu	Collection of whanau, a sub-tribe, will usually have at least one marae and often several.
p. 67 hongi	A greeting between individuals, in which a person shakes hands and touches both nose and forehead of the other person.
p. 15 hui	Gathering of people.
p. 63 iwi	Tribal group.
p. 61 kaikaranga	Woman who 'calls' people on to a marae. The call generally tells the visitors that they are welcome and often sets out the reasons for the gathering. It is believed that the 'call' is made by women because it is symbolic of the first cry of life when a child is born.
p. 63 kaiwaiata	People who 'sing' or accompany a speaker; the traditional waiata were chants, but a range of waiata both old and new are frequently sung.
p. 66 kawa	The formal behaviours and protocols which determine who speaks, when, how and why. These protocols vary across tribes quite considerably.

p. 61 mana	Power, prestige, status (ref. p. 61).
p. 66 manuhiri	Visitors or guests who must be welcomed formally, i.e. not tangata whenua.
p. 58 Maori	Ordinary, normal, now means a 'native person of New Zealand'.
p. 58 marae	Refer to text p. 63.
p. 66 marae atea	Grass area immediately in front of the whare where formal speech-making occurs, especially where visitors are being received.
p. 58 Pakeha	A non-Maori, often used to describe white non-Maori.
p. 67 powhiri	Rituals for welcoming visitors, these usually consist of a karanga which calls visitors on to the marae atea, speeches of welcome accompanied by chants from hosts and visitors and hongi or touching of nose and forehead.
p. 16 tangata whenua	People of the land, the host group.
p. 59 tino rangatiratanga	Translated to mean shades of sovereignty, self-determination, chieftainship, autonomy. Can be applied to individuals or the collective. This was guaranteed in the Maori version of the Treaty of Waitangi.
p. 14 tipuna	Also tupuna, ancestor, ancestress, one from whom a whanau, hapu or iwi is descended.
p. 68 waananga	Learning sessions, also means knowledge, whare waananga were once formal institutions for training tribal experts.
p. 61 wahine	Woman.
p. 68 waiata	Chants and songs which were composed for many different reasons but which are often heard after a speech is made.
p. 65 whaea	Mother and/or aunt or woman of the same generation as your own mother.
p. 61 whanau	Extended family units.
p. 63 whare	A generic name for a building or room.
p. 16 whare waananga	House of learning ref. p. 16 and note 3.

Notes

1 Maori education has been the subject of several Parliamentary Select Committee Inquiries, Government Reports and submissions by a wide range of organizations.

In the major educational reforms undertaken in 1989 the failure of schools to educate Maori children successfully was used as a rationale for the devolution of state responsibility to local communities. Despite years of reports, research and submissions the participation, retention and achievement rates for Maori students are still significantly behind the rates for Pakeha students.

2 There were several ethnic groups represented at the school and when all the 'others' i.e. non-white groups were added together they represented slightly more than half of the school roll. However, Pakeha students were by far the dominant group and this has been the case since the school opened.

3 New Zealand has national examinations at the end of the third year of secondary school, another set of internally assessed but nationally moderated assessment at the end of the fourth year and national examinations for university bursaries and scholarships at the end of the fifth year of secondary school. As disproportionate numbers of Maori students 'fail' to gain adequate grades in the first set of examinations known as school certificate fewer of them are able to continue at the next levels.

4 One of these Maori groups calls itself Tino Rangatiratanga which is a phrase used in the Treaty of Waitangi which was signed in 1840 between Maori chiefs and a representative of Queen Victoria. In the Maori version of this treaty Maori chiefs were guaranteed their 'tino rangatiratanga' over their lands, forests, fisheries and other 'gifts'. Maori nationalist groups all claim that Maori sovereignty was never ceded to the Crown and that colonial government usurped 'tino rangatiratanga' from Maori people.

5 There was a teaching staff of about sixty women, one full-time male teacher and possibly two more part-time male staff. There was one Maori woman and no staff from any of the other ethnic groups represented in the student body such as Samoan, Tongan, Cook Islands, Niuean, Fijian, Indian or Asian.

6 There were staff meetings which discussed the project but the public nature of this forum restricted the degree to which this issue and many others were debated. It was not a forum in which racist arguments for example were tolerated so these arguments tended to surface in less formal gatherings.

7 A Maori woman retains her genealogical links and these can never be 'owned' by her spouse or vice versa. It also means that a woman from another tribe can not claim descent from her husbands tribe although their children can claim descent from both parents. On death people were expected to be returned to their own tribal area.

8 The marae is one area where a high degree of fluency in Maori language is essential and many second language learners of Maori language still do not have the proficiency to speak in a forum which was and still is the major domain of oral tradition.

References

Awatere, D. (1984) *Maori Sovereignty*, Auckland Broadsheet.

Edwards, M. (1990) *Mihipeka: Early Years*, Auckland, NZ Penguin Books (NZ) Ltd.

Irwin, K. (1992) 'Towards theories of Maori feminism' in Du Plessis, R. (Ed.) *Feminist Voices: Women's Studies Texts in Aotearoa/New Zealand*, Oxford, Oxford University Press, pp. 1–21.

Mahuika, A. (1975) 'Leadership: Inherited and achieved' in King, M. and Longman, P. (Ed.) *Te Ao Hurihuri: The World Moves On*, Auckland, NZ, pp. 62–85.

Marks, M. (1984) 'On the frustrations of being a Maori language teacher' in Walker, R. (Ed.) *Nga Tumanako: Maori Educational Development Conference*, Auckland, Centre for Continuing Education, Auckland University.

Nepe, T. (1989) 'The conscientization and politicization of Maori women', paper presented to Education Department, University of Auckland.

New Zealand Parliamentary Debates, Second Reading on the Native Schools Bill (1867), p. 863.

Salmond, A. (1976) *Hui: A Study of Maori Ceremonial Gatherings*, Auckland, Reed Methuen.

Simon, J. (1990) 'The place of Maori schooling in Maori-Pakeha relations', PhD thesis, Auckland.

Smith, L.T. (1990) *Mana Wahine: Mana Maori*, Report for the Ministry of Education, Wellington.

Smith, L.T. (1992) 'Maori women: Discourses projects and Mana Wahine' in Middleton, S. and Jones, A. (Eds) *Women and Education in Aotearoa*, Wellington, NZ, Bridget Williams Books Ltd, pp. 33–51.

Taylor, M.K. (1991) *Kei Hea Nga Waahine Rangatira?* Research Report, Ministry of Education, Wellington.

Te Awekotuku, N. (1988) 'He Whare Tangata: He Whare Kura? What's happening to our Maori girls?' in Middleton, S. (Ed.) *Women and Education In Aotearoa*, Auckland, Allen & Unwin.

Te Awekotuku, N. (1991) *Mana Wahine Maori*, Auckland, New Womens Press.

Walker, R. (Ed.) (1984) *Nga Tumanako: Maori Educational Development Conference*, Auckland, Turangawaewae Marae, Centre for Continuing Education, University of Auckland.

Chapter 4

Shell-Shock or Sisterhood: English School History and Feminist Practice

Gaby Weiner

In this article, I focus on the possibilities for feminist practice at a time when governments throughout the world are making increasingly prescriptive and conservative interventions in the school curriculum. I consider this in the specific context of debates about school history which emerged with the creation of the English (and Welsh) National Curriculum. While I explore school history in the English National Curriculum as a case-study of the impact of ideology on the school curriculum, I do so in the hope that this study will contribute to a general understanding about curriculum change and its implications for feminist practitioners.

As a starting point, I apply Gramsci's emphasis on the crucial function exercised by *organic intellectuals* to the activities of feminists generally, and in education, in particular. It seems to me that if greater equality is ever to be achieved, the intellectual and political contributions of feminists (and other progressive groups) are vital.

> A human mass does not 'distinguish' itself, does not become independent in its own right without, in the widest sense, organising itself; and there is no organization without intellectuals, that is, without organizers and leaders. (Gramsci, 1971, p. 334)

It seems, therefore, most important that feminist teachers, as organic intellectuals, analyze and understand policy decisions and outcomes so that they can challenge sexist practices and support more effectively girls' and women's interests within school (and other educational) settings.

In fact, feminist teachers in the UK achieved major successes in the early and mid-1980s. As Madeleine Arnot and I pointed out in 1987, teachers were among the first groups of feminists to campaign for change, and reforms initiated by teachers represented a major (if less visible) level of gender policy formation. Feminist teachers were active at many levels. They focussed on removing inequalities at classroom and school level; they were active in lobbying local and central government for policy change; and they often sacrificed career progression and risked 'burn out' in their challenge to the male domination of schooling. Changing the practice of schooling was their main priority: 'The main focus of these teachers was on practical change; how could they help reduce inequalities between the sexes by changing their own perceptions and practice?' (Weiner and Arnot, 1987, p. 355).

By the mid-1980s four strands of feminist teacher activity were evident: teacher initiated changes, usually at local level; action research involving collaboration between external researchers and practitioners; teacher contact and communication networks; and initiatives undertaken by teacher unions (*ibid*). All of these strands are still in existence but are considerably weaker as we enter the 1990s — for some or all of the following reasons:

— The continued hostility (and consequent lack of resources) of central government towards equality issues — which has lasted more than a decade;
— The loss of support of the much weakened local education authorities. This loss of support was particularly noticeable in the case of strong Labour urban administrations such as the Inner London Education Authority (ILEA) which had mounted significant equality initiatives over the past few years;
— The low morale of teachers who have seen their professional status and conditions of service undercut. Further, though they now have responsibility for making the educational changes work, they have been excluded from discussions about how that can best be done;
— The proposed framework for assessing and monitoring the National Curriculum which is bureaucratic, bulky and time-consuming, such that there has been little opportunity for subversion or the pursuit of alternatives.

Feminist teachers might well approach the 1990s with some trepidation. However, I hope in this article, to suggest some possible ways forward.

Recent Curriculum Developments

Curriculum research and innovation in the United Kingdom enjoyed a 'golden age' in the 1960s and early 1970s when government money poured into curriculum development and initiatives explicitly directed at improving the practice and professionalism of teachers — mainly under the auspices of the Schools Council for Curriculum Examinations and Reform (Richards, 1978). I joined this movement rather late in the day when I became involved in two Schools Council Projects, the first on school records in 1976–87 and the second on gender in 1981–82. The latter involved raising awareness among teachers and related educational professionals about the inequities of sex-role typing and sexism in education. (reported in Millman & Weiner, 1985) In the event, in 1981 Keith Joseph, Margaret Thatcher's 'guru' and her second Secretary of State for Education and Science, announced the closure of the Schools Council and the project I had been involved with came to an end.

The closure of the Schools Council marked the end of a particular period of curriculum enquiry in the UK which had jointly involved central government, local government and educational professionals. Throughout the middle and later 1980s, the context altered as an increasingly conservative and confident central government took a more directive stance towards education, particularly in its relationship to local authorities and teachers.

Through the use of targeted (or 'categorical') funding (Harland, 1987), the government increased its power (and diminished that of local authorities and teachers) to implement policies on curriculum, assessment and examinations. The 1988 Education Reform Act (ERA) further centralized the design and control of the curriculum with the inclusion of the framework for a National Curriculum.

According to Maclure (1990), the legislation signalled an expanded authority of central government.

> It increased the powers of the Secretary of State for Education and Science . . . It restored to the central government powers over the curriculum which had been surrendered between the Wars, and set up formal machinery for exercising and enforcing these powers and responsibilities. (p. v)

Significantly, teacher organizations and unions were absent from the nominated membership of the working parties established to develop the details of National Curriculum implementation.

The new legislation, nevertheless, provided a new role for those researchers and academics who had retained their interests in the curriculum beyond the 'golden age'. They (we) now had a new focus — investigation and analysis of the policy implications, contents and working of the National Curriculum. Some (those with external funding) were able to observe and monitor how schools were coping with the changes (for example, Deem, 1990; Gold, Bowe and Ball, 1990). Those who were self-funding were obliged to consider less costly research approaches. A colleague, Leone Burton, and I scrutinized the

National Curriculum documentation with a view to evaluating its impact on equity issues (Burton and Weiner, 1990). I continued the research by investigating efforts to establish a national history curriculum. This extension of the work was undertaken for two reasons: first the contestation of the nature of school knowledge was nowhere more evident than in the heated public discussions about what form school history should take and for what purposes; and second, I had actively campaigned on feminist issues and also carried out some research into feminist history. I was thus interested in strengthening the position of women in school history. Putting the two together has not been easy but similar tasks confront feminist schoolteachers, of history and of other subjects, in struggling to recreate their own practice in these increasingly conservative times.

This article, then, addresses the debate about the nature of school history drawing on two discussions: the role and function of history within the school curriculum and the challenge of feminism to mainstream educational practice. It is divided into three sections: a brief historical account of school history; history in the British National Curriculum; and implications for feminist practice and action.

History as a School Subject

The tradition of school history in England is long-standing and comparatively uncontroversial. History was a feature of the curriculum of most types of schools from the eighteenth century onwards though it was often idiosyncratically taught. At the end of the nineteenth century, the growth of history as a university subject provided a steady supply of enthusiastic specialist teachers who began to staff early twentieth-century secondary schools and who taught mainly political and constitutional history. However, during the 1950s and 1960s the situation changed. At primary level, Piagetian ideas questioned whether young children could adequately conceptualize the historical developments with which they were being confronted. And notions of 'child-centredness' encouraged project work based on the interests of each child rather than coverage of particular historical eras. For older children who could exercise choice, history started to lose its attraction compared with subjects such as science which were deemed more useful and marketable. Hence, by the 1980s, history was perceived as seriously under-represented in the curriculum at all levels of the school system (Little, 1990).

There were also continually changing debates about the purpose and contents of school history. Should it celebrate the triumphs of the British Empire, thereby encouraging patriotism and national pride? Should it portray the developments of Western culture and science, and the achievements of democracy as a motivating force for future achievement? Should it focus on the 'winners', i.e. the rich, successful and powerful, or on the rest (the 'losers'?), i.e. the working class, women, the oppressed? Should it reflect the multiple histories of the culturally diverse population or should it aim for a unified, more nationalistic approach? Or should history teachers concentrate on promoting skills aquisition by fostering understanding of 'the nature of history and its fundamental concepts of time, change and evidence' rather than teaching 'facts'? (*ibid*, p. 323)

When the legislation enabling the establishment of the National Curriculum came into force in 1988, history teaching was at a low point. However, the Education Reform Act resurrected it as one of ten compulsory subjects to be taught to all children in state schools between the ages of 5 and 16 years.[1]

The National Curriculum, government ministers claimed, was founded on principles of accountability and entitlement. It sought to preserve 'important' subjects such as history that were in danger of disappearance or dilution: it was to bring definition and order to others, like English, that had become shapeless: and significantly it promised entitlement for all students — girls as well as boys — to study subjects like science and technology. Thus, it aimed to make public hitherto semi-articulated judgments about curriculum content and pupil performance. How did this strategy affect school history?

History's re-emergence as a fully-fledged subject in its own right was accompanied by the re-emergence of the debate about the nature and purpose of the school curriculum as a whole, and the position of history within it. The 'secret garden of the curriculum' was opened up and, in the case of school history, was found to need substantial improvement. Regardless of political persuasion, historians were united in calling for the reestablishment of history as a key curriculum area, welcoming it back from threatened oblivion.

However, the contestation over the nature of school history representing conflicting political and ideological positions (few historians made claims to historical 'truths') was, as Martin Kettle (1990) identified, 'surrogate for a much wider debate about the cultural legacy of the Thatcher years'. It illuminated the sharp polarization of cultural values and drew attention to the close relationship between politics, culture and schooling. Thus, the tight grip retained by the government on the details of the National Curriculum documentation exemplified, as I shall show, how school knowledge is bound by the perceived needs of government and the state.

From the end of the 1970s, the New Right, in the form of the Centre for Policy Studies, had mounted a sustained attack on a generation of radical and Marxist historians such as E.P. Thompson, Eric Hobsbawm, Christopher Hill and Asa Briggs. These historians were accused of distorting the nation's past and 'denigrating our national history' (Thomas, 1979) and the teachers of history were condemned as having similarly subversive views. The Thatcher administration had an alternative agenda for history. It saw the solution to the economic and social ills of past decades in the values and achievements of Britain's imperialist past. Thus the 'Victorian values' of military and commercial superiority, individualism, self-help etc. were utilized within school history, as we shall see, to arm future generations against the unforeseen challenges of the twenty-first century.

History in the English National Curriculum

In this section, I discuss the documentary research approach that I took to investigate the history curriculum, and then consider its findings in relation to the public debate on school history.

Analyzing documentation as a form of curriculum exploration was chosen for several reasons. First, official documents signal the overt intentions of policy-makers. Also, they constitute a form of *discourse*; that is, they embody both a formal set of linguistic symbols and the social practices which govern their use. It is therefore important to consider the ideas and messages emerging from the text and also their less visible ideological implications. Thus, I attempt to understand the messages embedded within the documents (and the public responses to them) at the same time as treating the texts as ideological and political artifacts, constructed within a specific historical and political context.

First, documentation is, at the time of writing, one of the few forms of data about the National Curriculum currently available — it is still too early to judge how teachers' practice can or will be changed by the legislation or what impact a compulsory curriculum will have on pupils (although as already mentioned, research is currently being undertaken in these areas). Second, the public debate created by the publication of various reports, particularly that of the History Working Group, enables us to explore the 'populist' claims of government and whose interests are perceived as being served. Finally, by comparing documents produced at different historical periods, *shifts* in cultural understandings and educational assumptions may be discerned which are less visible to people living through periods of change.

The research approach adopted involved scrutinizing and making extensive notes of the documentation concerning the development of National Curriculum history. These were then analyzed according to the themes identified in the earlier research (with Leone Burton), i.e. themes of 'regressive modernism', equality issues, continuity/fragmentation of subject areas, emphasis on content, and different conceptions of school knowledge (Burton & Weiner, 1990).

The Power of School History

The debate about school history generated by the interim and final reports[2] of the National Curriculum History Working Group took up more column inches in the educational press than any other comparable working group report, despite school history's second rank status as a foundation, rather than core, subject (the core subjects being English, maths and science and the foundation subjects, art, geography, history, modern language, music, technology and physical education). Is it that the political and ideological debates about the nature of school knowledge, though present in other subject areas, are more visible and accessible in history? Or is history, by definition, a more political subject? In my view, both positions are supportable. Certainly more lay people seem able to engage in discussion, for example, about the importance of certain historical dates compared to others than can hold forth about the value of algebra or probability in the mathematics curriculum.

In fact, the interim report is surprisingly candid about the political nature of school history: '(History) is among the most powerful and effective means of cultural transmission in any society'. It 'helps to give individuals a sense of identity', 'sharpens the mind and fosters intellectual sophistication' and 'has few equals in the particular ways it prepares pupils for adult life' (National Curriculum History Working Group: Interim Report, 1989, pp. 5–6). Despite the dilution of the language on the purposes of school history in the final report — 'cultural transmission' is replaced by '(giving) pupils an understanding of their own cultural roots and shared inheritances' (National Curriculum History Working Group: Final Report, 1990, p. 1) — and the insistence by the New Right on the value of 'facts' and 'dates', the evident passion of the debate has only served to emphasize history's key place in the reforms.

Other emphases in the history documentation also suggest that the government's approach to school history was profoundly political. Pressure to increase the amount of specifically British (or rather, English) history in the final report, already very substantial in the interim report, was placed on the working group by the Secretary of State for Education. Moreover it is British history from a particular perspective, as the following guidelines indicate:

> The programmes of study should have at the core the history of Britain, the record of its past and, in particular its political, constitutional and cultural heritage. They should take account of Britain's evolution and its changing role as a European, Commonwealth and world power influencing and being influenced by ideas, movements and events elsewhere in the world. They should recognize and develop an awareness of the impact of classical civilizations. (National Curriculum History Working Group, Final Report, 1990, p. 189)

The working group sought to reflect the multifaceted nature of school history by incorporating within each unit, sections relating to political, economic, social and cultural historical dimensions of a particular topic or era. This was called the 'PESC' formula (*ibid*, p. 16) and though it aimed to extend historical understanding, the manner in which it appeared in the documentation seemed to encourage conformity rather than diversity in pupil thinking.

In fact, the structure of the National Curriculum is remarkably similar to the prescribed secondary school curriculum for 1904 and the content of the National Curriculum history somewhat resembles that described in 1938 by an ex-Provost of Eton College about his own education at the end of the nineteenth century. He contrasts it with the more 'modern' approaches of the 1930s:

> Moreover since I was a boy, history has broadened. The history I used to learn was political and constitutional with some economics thrown in, and was mainly concerned with Great Britain, with Europe occasionally coming in over foreign policy. But today the histories of science and social life, of literature and culture, are supposed to be within the purview of the history teacher. (Marten, 1938, p. 68)

Thus, even though a large number of historians publically supported the final report against the attacks of those who want to constrain school history yet further (Lodge & Tysome, 1990), conservatism gained some ground in recasting school history in the nineteenth-century public school mould.

Consensus or Prescription

One of the shared goals of all who took part in the history debate was that of assuring a place for history in the school curriculum which seemed to have been lost in the cross-disciplinary (and, it could be argued, more egalitarian) humanities approaches of recent years. There was also little disagreement with the more liberal claims for school history made in the final report, (National Curriculum History Working Group, 1990), such as:

> History is a splendid subject for study at any age but particularly so at school. Children are by nature curious and the past provides a feast for that curiosity. (Para. 1.1, p. 1)

and:

> History raises moral questions: . . . much of the subject matter of history raises implicit or explicit moral questions, notably when human motivation and choice are involved and when the question of the ultimate importance of a great event or episode is discussed: was it 'good', or was it 'bad'? (Para. 11. 17, p. 183)

and:

> Teachers should not hold back from dealing with controversial questions of morality, or of values which unite or divide people. (Para. 11. 18, p. 183)

Yet, these fragmented statements about the educational benefits of school history do not represent or indicate the prescriptive, technocratic and bureaucratic thrust of the documentation. The *prescriptive* nature of the documentation with its 'Ground Rules' (pp. 29–30), 'Programmes of Study' (pp. 31–114), 'Attainment Targets' (pp. 115–45), and 'Statements of Attainment' (pp. 152–65) seems directed towards reducing the status of the documentation to a detailed manual rather than a curriculum document, and lowering the status of the history teacher to an instructor rather than educator. For example, the content of the history syllabus is divided into more or less chronological History Study Units (HSUs), divided into Core (ie compulsory units), Optional and School Designed HSUs. (see Figure 4.1 below) As has already been pointed out, the Core units include principally British (and classical) and a little local history and the optional units segments of European, colonial, world and yet more British history. Each HSU is mapped out in considerable detail as a programme of study and further developed in relation to 'ground rules' and attainment targets. School Designed Units which presumably have been created to provide more flexibility to accommodate local factors, are also firmly circumscribed. For example, for Key Stage 3:[3]

> We have listed a School Designed History Study Unit as an option in each of lists A to D of the optional Study Units for this key stage but stipulated that only two may be selected. In addition there is a further School Designed History Study Unit based on British history. (*ibid*, para. B51, p. 29)

Intentionally, little room has been left for flexible or creative interpretation of syllabus content by teachers or pupils.

The *technocratic* approach of much of the documentation appears even more inappropriate for the history curriculum. Jargon abounds. The full range of terms introduced for the earlier National Curriculum documentation as exemplified in the paragraphs above, for example, key stage, statement of attainment, SATs, programme of study, are further extended to include a subject specific creation — the History Study Unit or HSU. Moreover, much of the terminology used in the history document is unclear: for example the difference between 'knowledge as "information"', 'knowledge as "understanding"' and 'knowledge as "content"' is never adequately explained nor

Figure 4.1 History Study Units by key stage

Key stage 1 (Ages 5 to 7, 2 years, 6 terms)

HSU1 In this first key stage we adopted a straightforward approach designed to introduce pupils to the idea of time, and to people viewed in an historical dimension. The single History Study Unit is made up of the following components:

- i) an element to introduce the past and a sense of time asking the questions 'Who am I?' and 'When and where am I?';
- ii) people (including family) within living memory: life in the 1930s, 40s, 50s, 60s, and so on; and
- iii) an introduction to historical personalities and events through stories from prehistory to the present day; poetry, pictures, TV and radio, local, national and topical festivals.

Key stage 2 (Ages 7 to 11, 4 years, 12 terms)

Core History Study Units:

HSU2 Invaders and settlers: the Romans, Anglo-Saxons and Vikings in Britain;
HSU3 Life in Tudor and Stuart times;

A choice of either:
HSU4 Victorian Britain; or
HSU5 Life in Britain since 1930;
HSU6 Ancient civilizations: Egypt and Greece;
HSU7 Exploration and encounters: c1450 to c1550.

Optional History Study Units:

A choice of two from the following list:
HSU8 Ships and seafarers through history;
HSU9 Food and farming through history;
HSU10 Houses and places of worship through history;
HSU11 The development of writing and printing;
HSU12 Land transport through history;
HSU13 Domestic life, families and childhood in Roman and Victorian times.

School Designed History Study Units:

Three, of which at least one, and not more than two, *must* be based on local history. If the school did not wish to take up the offer of the *remaining* School Designed History Study Unit(s), the remaining option from the core History Study Units ('Victorian Britain' or 'Life in Britain since 1930') could be selected, or selection could be made from the list of Optional History Study Units set out above.

Key stage 3 (Ages 11 to 14, 3 years, 9 terms)

Core History Study Units:

HSU14 Medieval realms: c1066 to c1500;
HSU15 The making of the United Kingdom: c1500 to c1750;
HSU16 Expansion, trade and industry: Britain c1750 to c1900;
HSU17 The Roman Empire.

Optional History Study Units:

A choice of *one from each* of the following lists but not more than two School Designed History Study Units to be selected from Lists A to D:

List A:
HSU18 Castles and cathedrals: c1066 to c1500;
HSU19 Culture and society in Ireland up to early C20th;
HSU20 The British Empire at its zenith: 1877 to 1905;
HSU21 Britain and the Great War: 1914 to 1918;
School Designed History Study Unit which informs and extends the study of the British core History Study Units.

List B:
HSU22 Reformation and religious diversity in Western Europe in C16th;
HSU23 The Italian Renaissance;
HSU24 The French Revolution and the Napoleonic era;
School Designed History Study Unit involving the study of a major European turning point before 1914.

List C:
HSU25 Islamic civilization up to early C16th;
HSU26 Imperial China: 221BC to the Mongol conquest 1279AD;
HSU27 India from the Mughal empire to the coming of the British: 1526 to 1805;
School Designed History Study Unit involving the study of a non-Western culture from its own perspective.

List D:
HSU28 Native peoples of the Americas;
HSU29 Black peoples of the Americas: C16th to early C20th;
HSU30 The American Revolution;
HSU31 The American frontier: c1650 to c1900;
School Designed History Study Unit involving the study of the Americas.

School Designed History Study Unit:
One, long-term in nature, based on British social history.

Key stage 4 (Ages 14 to 16, 2 years, 5 terms [6 terms less 1 for examinations])

Core History Study Units:
HSU32 Britain in the twentieth century;
HSU33 The era of the Second World War: 1933 to 1948.

Optional History Study Units:
A choice of one from List A and one from List B:

List A:
HSU34 East and West: Europe 1948 to the present day;
HSU35 Russia and the USSR: 1905 to the present day;
HSU36 The United States of America: 1917 to the present day.

List B:
HSU37 India and Pakistan 1930 to 1964;
HSU38 Africa south of the Sahara since 1945;
HSU39 Japan: 1868 to the present day;
HSU40 China: 1937 to the present day.

School Designed History Study Unit:
One, based on revisiting British history, studied over a long time-span (starting at least before 1500 and reaching up to the present day).

National Curriculum History Working Group (1990) *Final Report*, DES, April, Annex A to Chapter 5.

how each will fit into the main schemes of work. The matrices which represent the programmes of study for each HSU are even more confusing, especially, one suspects, for primary teachers who will have had to read ten different curriculum documents in all — one for each of the core and foundation subjects.

Finally, the fact that the History Working Group was compelled to use the *bureaucratic* national framework of externally and teacher-determined assessments has meant that much of the content will have to be shaped and squeezed in order to fulfil general assessment requirements. In fact, Commander Michael Saunders-Watson, the chair of the working group, is reported as complaining of being 'lumbered with it. I won't conceal that we found it a difficult framework to fit in' (*Times Educational Supplement*, 13 April 1990). Concern about the application to history of the broad pattern of assessments developed for other curriculum subjects led the working group to identify a number of criteria concerning assessment of school history; that skills, knowledge and understanding should not be assessed separately; that historical learning is not a linear process; and that assessment of history should 'concentrate particularly on that which is peculiar to history' (National Curriculum History Working Group: Final Report, 1990, para. 8.7, p. 168). Yet it is difficult to see, despite the emphasis on different methods of assessment in the final report, how the national framework for assessment based on ten levels of attainment and designed for general use will work for history. It seems likely, however, that it will be more likely to promote conformity and mechanistic learning rather than understanding and the interpretative skills expressly desired by the working group.

Regressive Modernism

How, then, does the history documentation compare with earlier National Curriculum reports? As defined by Stuart Hall, 'regressive modernism' is much in evidence. Hall uses this term to explain the contradictions of Thatcherism and the apparent ability of the Thatcher administration to face two directions simultaneously. Modernism, Hall claims, is evident in the attempts to replace the 'outdated' approach to social welfare of the post-World War II period with free market policies perceived as more in line with the needs of the modern state. Yet at the same time there is a harking back to a golden Victorian Age where subjects were clearly defined and social science was an untried newcomer.

The 'regressive' thrust of the government's project is visible, for example, in the composition of the History Working Group. Its Chair, Commander Michael Saunders-Watson (a former naval officer and owner of a stately home), six male members (director of education, chair of local council, local education advisor, university reader, warden at Oxford, primary teacher), fewer (three) female members (head of department, university lecturer, secretary to Institute of Historical Research) and significant absence of ethnic minority representation, all provide an indication of government intentions. It is no wonder that, despite strong lobbying from history teachers, government expectations for more 'traditional' approaches to history have, in the main, been realized in the final report.

'Modernism', as expressed in attacks on the public sector generally is also evident: in the lack of representation on the working group of professional and subject associations, and in the implied 'instructor' status of teachers of history. The motivation for this form of 'modernism' and particularly its poor regard for the teaching profession can be detected in the words of Henry Hobhouse (1990), one of the members of the History Working Group:

> The damage done to history by slipshod permissiveness disguised as liberalism; the destruction of both history and geography by 'humanities'; the almost complete absence not only of history, but also any possibility of history, in many primary schools; the link between poor literacy and lack of learning; the inevitable limitations of history on TV as a 'turn off'; the profoundly destructive influences of social scientists; the perception that history in general and traditional history in particular were deeply political. These problems could not be addressed (by the working group).

Equality Issues

The final report claims to be concerned about equality issues. Yet the four paragraphs on gender (designated 'equal opportunities') and the two on 'race' (designated 'multicultural education') indicate that they are clearly not a priority. The lack of space given (approximately half a page in a 205 page report) and the fact that they are tucked away towards the end of the final chapter on the 'relationship of history to the rest of the curriculum', indicates the rhetorical nature of the working group's commitment.

'Multiculturalism', in fact, comes off rather worse than gender. The role of history in developing 'the quality of open-mindedness' and the assumption that 'an ethnically diverse population strengthens rather than weakens the argument for introducing a substantial element of British history within the school curriculum' are the principal contributions of the working group to the multicultural/anti-racism debate.[4] In contrast, the advice on gender issues is more specific, concerning the evils of stereotyping and the bias of 'heroic' history. There is also an additional half page on 'pupils with special educational needs' at the end of the assessment chapter. This is principally concerned with appropriate provision for visually and hearing impaired and other disabled pupils. Significantly, a third of this section is devoted to gifted pupils who, it is advised, 'should be given tasks which will fully stretch their ability' (National Curriculum History Working Group Final Report, 1990, paras 8.36–8.40, p. 171).

It is, however, the specified content of the History Study Units which is most revealing. There is no topic devoted entirely to women (even the Suffragettes appear to have lost their usual place) although some of the optional units, e.g., HSU13: Domestic life, families and childhood in Roman and Victorian Times seem designed to focus more on woman's traditional domestic role historically. Attempts have also been made, it seems, to make the history syllabus ethnically diverse. Yet the study of Islam, India or, for example, HSU29: Black peoples of the Americas are set against each other as options at Key Stage 3, as mentioned earlier. So students can choose to specialize in only one of these areas and no student, it seems, can be compelled to have more than a superficial knowledge of Britain's colonial past.

Moreover, as Gill (1990) points out, of the thirty-one named individuals in the core course, only two are women and all are Europeans. Additionally, of the ninety-three named individuals who may be studied in the optional units, only nine are women and a further two (males) originate from outside Europe. Gill concludes, correctly in my view, that 'History in the National Curriculum, it seems, is still to be the history of "great" white men' (p. 2).

Continuity/Fragmentation of Subject Areas

The history documentation may seem less fragmented than other National Curriculum reports because of its emphasis on 'chronology', strengthened as a result of ministerial pressure after the interim report. Undoubtedly adopting a chronological approach can give a sense of coherence to school history. Yet, the fragmentation induced by splitting the syllabus into numerous study units and the widely recognized content overload seem to mitigate against continuity.

Certainly, the emphasis of content over 'understanding' and 'interpretation', despite the working groups stated intentions, denies pupils the possibility of making links between historical topics. For example, although British colonization and imperialism feature in a number of units, few attempts are made to analyse root causes and effects.

Moreover, whilst the working group insists that pupils should be acquainted with 'the writings of historians and (have) a knowledge of typical historical controversies, relating to the content of the course' (National Curriculum History Working Group Final Report, para. 3.28, p. 11), particular perspectives are missing. For example, there is little evidence in various syllabuses of the issues raised by influential Left and feminist historians such as E.P. Thompson (1968), Christopher Hill (1975) or Sheila Rowbotham (1973).

Emphasis on Content

Throughout this chapter there have been allusions to the content-led nature of the documentation. In my view, emphasis has been placed on what teachers should teach and what pupils should know but little on *how* teachers might 'deliver' the syllabus. In a letter to the *The Times Educational Supplement*, Michael Armstrong, a noted primary headteacher, considers this to be the fundamental weakness in the National Curriculum documentation generally:

> It is the fatal weakness of the national curriculum that it isolates these two sorts of questions — what to teach and how to teach. In practice, any curriculum is necessarily an attempt to resolve the interminable conflict between received wisdom, as represented by the established orthodoxies of scholarship, and naive enquiry, as represented by the developing interests and purposes of children. The excitement of teaching is the excitement of of having continually to re-examine and revise one's own understanding of subject matter in response to children's understanding as it emerges from their engagement with that same subject matter.
>
> There is no hint of excitement in the reports of the working parties, no sense of the challenge to knowledge that is inherent in the practice of education. Their's is a comfortable, over-determined world in which the intellectual confusion of the classroom, inseparable from its vitality, is never permitted to disturb the confident and shallow prescriptions. (Armstrong, 1990)

The final report of the History Working Group certainly expresses concern about 'pedagogical problems', such as where slow learners may fall behind and 'mark time' at a lower level topic whilst the rest of the class move on to another topic.

> This situation would run counter to our wish to give all pupils a broad, balanced and coherent historical education, similar in most respects for all pupils, in accordance with the letter and spirit of the National Curriculum. (National Curriculum History Working Group Final Report, 1990, para. A3.3, p. 14)

Yet, no advice is proffered to resolve these 'problems', neither are any examples of good practice included to help teachers achieve 'the letter and spirit of the National Curriculum'. On the contrary, the working group appears to accept the inevitability of 'subgroups' studying different topics at the same time in mixed ability classrooms:

> For example, a secondary school class in Key Stage 3 might contain pupils studying up to five different historical topics simultaneously, since Key Stage 3 assumes a span of levels 3 to 7 in the attainment targets. (*ibid*, p. 14)

Whilst pupils studying different topics according to their interests and motivation are a characteristic of more egalitarian, mixed-ability, pedagogical approaches, pupils consigned to languish at the lower levels of the National Curriculum can only, it seems, indicate the return of ability grouping and streaming and all their accompanying injustices, by yet another route.

Conceptions of School Knowledge

The debates between historians arising from the National Curriculum documentation has led to the emergence of a variety of perspectives on school history. Should it be underpinned with 'facts' and 'dates'? What events might be regarded as significant? Who defines the importance of facts, knowledge, understanding, interpretation, methodology, skills etc.? What has become clear is that differences in perspective on content and approach in relation to school history arise largely as a consequence of the conflicting political and ideological frameworks of historians and policy makers (*TES*, 13 April 1990a). The response of different historians to the National Curriculum History Working Party report is nicely illustrated in Figure 4.2.

Thus, when we come to analyze the National Curriculum syllabuses for history, we can identify the emergence of a specific form of school history. Certainly 'newer' approaches to history are reflected in several of the study units, for example, HSU11: The development of writing and printing; HSU13: Domestic life, families and childhood in Roman and Victorian times; and HSU29: Black peoples of the Americas: C16th to early C20th.

Yet the overwhelming impression of the form of school history emerging from the documentation is one that firmly secures Britain (or England?) at the centre, one that prioritizes ancient civilizations and classical history over colonial history, one that appears to favour political, constitutional and military history over social and cultural history, and one that favours 'the great man' over 'the great woman' or women generally. The perspective adopted by the working

Figure 4.2 Dates that need to be carved in stone (Source: TES, 1990a)

Margaret Thatcher has argued that knowledge itself should be tested in the history attainment targets because 'children should know the great landmarks of British history and should be taught them at school'. The newly-formed History Curriculum Association takes the same line. But how much consensus is there as to what these landmarks are? As a contribution to the debate, *The TES* asked five historians, representing widely differing points of view, to list the events which they think every child should know about. The results were surprising — and illuminating.

RAPHAEL SAMUEL

Tutor in history at Ruskin College, Oxford, and editor of History Workshop Journal

2500BC: Stonehenge.
AD61: Boudicca's rising. 122: Hadrian's Wall and the Roman occupation.
663: Synod of Whitby and the conversion to Christianity.
1086: Domesday Book.
1170: Murder of Thomas à Becket.
1190: Third Crusade and Richard I in the Holy Land.
1192: 'Liberties of London' (abolished 1986); emergence of a self-governing capital city.
1314: Battle of Bannockburn. Scottish wars of independence.
1348–51: Black Death. Depopulation in the countryside and crisis in labour; services and rents.
1397: Dick Whittington, Lord Mayor of London, The first of the historically-authenticated Yuppies.
1477: William Caxton's printing press.
1536–7: Pilgrimage of Grace. North vs South. Catholic defence of the old faith.
1554–5: Fires of Smithfield. 1563 *Foxe's Book of Martyrs.* British Protestantism.
1599: Shakespeare *Henry V.* English nationalism in the age of the Armada.
1620: Sailing of the *Mayflower.* The New England colonies.
1649: Execution of Charles 1. Civil wars in England, Ireland, Scotland.
1649: Siege of Drogheda; 1690: Battle of the Boyne. English conquest of Ireland. 1666: Great Fire of London.
1678: *The Pilgrim's Progress.* English Puritanism.
1707: Act of Union with Scotland. Invention of the idea of 'Great Britain'.
1719: *Robinson Crusoe.* English individualism.
1702–1815: 'The second hundred years war'. France as the national enemy.
1775–1783: American War of Independence. Beginnings of British radicalism.
1789: William Blake's *Songs of Innocence.*
1833: Factory Act.
1834: New Poor Law. 1851: Great Exhibition. 1854: Crimean War—'Victorian Values'.
1870: Education Act.
1882: Married Women's Property Act, Women's rights.
1908: Old Age Pensions. 1920: The Dole. Two faces of 20th-century welfare.
1916: Easter Rising. Irish independence.
1917: Passchendaele. The First World War.
1926: General Strike. British trade unionism and the idea of a working class.
1937: Holidays with Pay Act. 1938: Butlin's. For 20th-century leisure industries.
1940: 'Britain's finest hour'.
1947: End of British rule in India.
1948: Empire Windrush. Start of New Commonwealth immigration.
1968: Enoch Powell. 'Rivers of Blood' speech. Origins of Thatcherism, popular Toryism.
1990: Restoration of history to the school syllabus.
Rationale: 'History for children is a succession of marvellous stories—which has been rather lost sight of recently. So I have tried to stick to the kind of landmarks which appeared in textbooks and "readers" when history was first introduced as a teaching subject in schools. I would find it quite impossible to reduce this list any further.'

SHEILA ROWBOTHAM

Feminist historian and writer

1381: The Peasants' Revolt.
1649: Gerard Winstanley and the Diggers first occupied land, warning; 'If you provide not for the poor, they will provide for themselves.'
1789: Olaudah Equiano, a black member of the radical London Corresponding Society published an attack on slavery.
1792: Publication of Mary Wolstonecraft's *A Vindication of the Rights of Women.*
1838: A woman weaver from Glasgow wrote to the Chartist newspaper *The Northern Star.* 'It is the right of every woman to have a vote in the legislature of her country.'
1848: A Chartist demonstration for universal male suffrage was blocked by cannon and police with cutlasses.
1888: The matchgirl strike.
1906: The Sweated Industries exhibition, which marked a shift in public attitudes to low pay and women's sweated work.
1911: Armed tanks faced dockers and railway workers on strike in Liverpool.
1912: After extensive lobbying from Labour women, the miners' federation supported women's suffrage.
1914: The North London Herald League issued an anti-war leaflet, saying: 'A good soldier is a blind heartless machine; don't be a soldier, be a man.'
1944: Beveridge and the establishment of the post-war Welfare State.
1984–85: The miners' strike mobilized women in mining communities on an unprecedented scale.
Rationale: 'It is important to raise questions about the traditional assumptions which are so often taken for granted. I wanted to use my list to question the usual tramlines — which meant not having room for the tramlines.'

KEITH ROBBINS

Professor of modern history at the University of Glasgow, and President of the Historical Association

1066: Norman Conquest
1215: Magna Carta
1534: Act of Supremacy
1536 and 1543: Acts of Union with Wales
1707: Act of Union with Scotland
1801: Act of Union With Ireland
1832: First Reform
1914: Outbreak of World War I
1918: Representation of the People Act (enfranchising women for the first time)
1922: Establishment of Irish Free State
1926: General Strike
1939: Outbreak of World War II
1940: Battle of Britain
1947: Independence of India and Pakistan
1973: Britain joins the EEC
Rationale: 'The most important landmarks, I think, are to do with the expansion of England and the formation of the United Kingdom, and the major 20th century stress on Britain's international position — the ending of the empire and the opening up of Europe.'

GORDON MARSDEN

Editor of History Today

AD43: Roman invasion of Britain.
597: Christianization of England.
1066: Norman invasion.
1215: Magna Carta.
1338–1453: '100 Years War'. (The exact starting date is a matter for dispute, since war was never officially declared.)
1529: Start of Henry VIII's Reformation.
1588: Spanish Armada.
1642: Outbreak of English Civil War.
1688: Glorious Revolution.
1793: Outbreak of wars with France.
1819: Peterloo massacre.
1846: Repeal of the Corn Laws.
1914: Outbreak of First World War.
1945: End of Second World War; first majority Labour government.
Rationale: 'I have tried to pick out the distinctive forces that have shaped Britain, and particularly its relationship to the outside world, without ignoring the so-called marginalized groups or the human costs and suffering involved.'

LORD BELOFF

Emeritus fellow of All Souls College, Oxford, and supporter of the History Curriculum Association

AD122: The building of Hadrian's Wall.
367: The recall of the legions and the Saxon conquests.
793: The Danish invasions.
1066: The Norman Conquest.
1154: The establishment of the Plantagenets and the acquisition of a continental empire.
Mid-C12th: The conquest and partial settlement of Ireland.
1215: Magna Carta.
1485: The accession of Henry VII and the incorporation of Wales.
1517: Luther begins the Reformation.
1529: Henry VIII and the break with Rome.
1649: The execution of Charles I.
1688: The Glorious Revolution.
1745: Last Jacobite rebellion.
1832: First Reform Act.
1884: Third Reform Act (the real beginning of universal suffrage).
1909: The Lloyd George budget and the foundation of the Welfare State.
Rationale: 'I am keen that children should learn about early history and should have a feeling for the order in which things happened. Dates are very useful as a framework into which you can fit events in other countries — and the discoveries and the buildings too. As a small boy, I was taught through time-charts on great rolls of paper, and I still have the sense of history unrolling.'

group is exemplified, as Gill (1990) points out, by the encouragement students are given in HSU20: The British Empire at its zenith: 1877–1905, to read Rider Haggard and Rudyard Kipling, and to investigate cricket and polo as part of their 'Cultural and Aesthetic' studies. A more balanced understanding of the British Empire might be achieved, one would think, if additional sources from colonial and from others challenging the rampant imperialism of the era were included.

Implications for Feminist Practice

I have attempted, thus far, to show that the various National Curriculum history reports represent a specific view of the purpose and content of school history which cannot be understood outside the political and historical context from which they emerged, i.e., that of Thatcherism. Thatcherism (and its paler sucessor 'Mayorism') may well now be a spent force. Certainly, criticisms are emerging from *within* the Conservative Party about the attacks on education from the New Right. For example, Cox refers to 'right-wing Conservatives . . . particularly . . . the Centre for Policy Studies (whose) attacks (are) based on misunderstandings and prejudice' (Cox, 1991). However, it is likely that the form of school knowledge espoused by the National Curriculum will predominate at least until the end of the decade. In fact, whilst the Labour Party has been fiercely critical of other aspects of the legislation, the creation and content of the National Curriculum has been perceived as relatively uncontroversial.

Moreover, feminist teachers, like their colleagues, have had little influence on the development of the legislation nor on the subsequent documentation — though their views were represented in the Equal Opportunities Commission's submission to the government after the publication of the Education Bill in 1987 (EOC, 1987).

What, then, are the possibilities of recreating feminist practice given this bleak scenario? What forms of action are open to feminist practitioners wishing to mount a challenge to the dominant form of school knowledge as defined by the National Curriculum? It seems to me, that there is still some room for manoeuvre. As Ball (1990) remarks in the last paragraph of his recent book on British education policy, the battle is far from over:

> It is crucial to recognize that the analysis of the noise and heat of reform and the making of national policy still begs questions about the implementation and realisation of reform in schools and classrooms. The struggles over interpretation and accommodation go on. (p. 214)

It seems vital that feminist teachers both maintain their critique of existing school practices and offer new challenges to meet the changing circumstances of schooling. In the latter, they could join the growing number of groups representing 'the new progressivism of educational intellectuals' (*ibid*, p. 221) which, after the onslaught of the New Right, are seeking new understandings, alliances and practices.

In my view, feminist teachers have at least *three* areas of action available: challenging curriculum content, reviewing pedagogy and the hidden curriculum, and in their role as professionals.

Curriculum Content

Feminist teachers have, in the past, collaborated with, and built on the work of, feminist historians to create more girl- or woman-friendly histories. This work could be extended and incorporated into the new history curriculum. For example, it may be possible to put together sections on 'government and social reform' and 'Victorian mothers and fathers' in Core HSU4: Victorian Britain to organize a substantial enquiry into girls' and women's lives in Victorian times. The role that women played in revolutionary France could be incorporated into Optional HSU24: The French Revolution and the Napoleonic era and the lives of women in the colonies into Optional HSU20: The British Empire at its zenith: 1877 to 1905. The influences of the powerful abbesses of the middle ages might be included in the optional HSU18: Castles and Cathedrals: c1066–c1500 and school designed units could utilize feminist oral and documentary history methods to explore the lives of women as well as men in local communities. Extra resources (and energy) will have to be found to ensure the effective teaching of these 'additions' to an already overcrowded syllabus but the possibilities, nonetheless, will be available.

Pedagogy and the Hidden Curriculum

If feminist teachers are to be effective in their challenge to (as well as their 'delivery' of) National Curriculum history, they will need to be able to work with colleagues to develop and exchange a wide range of source materials. Collaborative curriculum development and team teaching (significantly, not encouraged in the documentation) and a commitment from the school staff to tackling educational inequalities will be important. Teachers will also need to develop pedagogical approaches which enable students to derive meaning from the unfolding of historical events. These might include adoption of materials-based or independent learning approaches, collaborative investigative work, small group discussion of 'contentious' issues etc. Emphasis on historical interpretation rather than factual claims, and the introduction to pupils of the work of feminist, as well as mainstream historians, will enable school history to become a more balanced and analytical form of study than it is currently conceived. Students, it is hoped, will then be able to see the importance and relevance of history to their lives, and be encouraged to adopt a more critical view of the historical 'truths' which they find in their school texts. Finally, feminist teachers may wish to collaborate with teachers in higher education to create appropriate teaching materials or extend their own professional skills or personal development, or gain external support for their work.

As Professionals

One of the greatest successes of feminist teachers in the past has been their ability to create lasting networks for communication and support. One such network, Girls and Mathematics Association (GAMMA) for mathematics teachers, has been active for nearly a decade and there have also been similar feminist groups for teachers of history, geography, English etc. However, there are other possibilities for collective as well as individual action. At a political level, feminist teachers are likely to continue to group together, but they need now to lobby for changes in the history curriculum as well as for other areas of education. They may wish to develop critiques of existing forms of school knowledge for discussion within their schools or for publication in the educational press or journals. Collaboration with parents and colleagues may lead to changes in school curricula, if only at local level. The organization of seminars and conferences as means of exchanging information about developments in equality policies and practices in the UK or in other countries is likely to prove mutually supportive. They will, no doubt, continue to work in their trades unions to fight for better career opportunities for women teachers.

As organic intellectuals representing an important political force, feminist teachers, whether they like it or not, are in the cultural front line when it comes to resisting the unacceptable or pushing for the necessary changes that will improve girls' and women's future educational experiences and life-chances. Exhaustion notwithstanding, time alone will tell how effective they can be.

Notes

1 Subsequently, a decision was taken by government to make history (and geography) *optional* from 14 years onwards.

2 Each National Curriculum subject area was developed by a working group, appointed by government, which produced interim and final reports for the Secretary of State. At each stage, the Secretary of State could, and often did, demand changes — and further alterations were also made after the Final Report to ensure that the final published version accorded with government thinking.

3 Key Stages were designated for assessment purposes at the ages of 7, 11, 14 and 16 years of age.
4 There has been a long debate in the UK on the effectiveness of multicultural and anti-racist approaches in eliminating racism from schooling. Multiculturalists adopt a pluralist approach to difference — celebrating within schooling, minority group cultures, traditions and histories. Anti-racists, on the other hand, adopt a more structural perspective in understanding racial inequality not as a system of black disadvantage but as a manifestation of the power relations between black and white people (Arnot, 1986).

References

ARMSTRONG, M. (1990) '"Fatal" weakness in national curriculum', *The Times Educational Supplement*, 29 June.

ARNOT, M. (1986) 'Race, gender, education policy-making', Module 4, Open University Course E333: *Policy Making in Education*, Milton Keynes, Open University Press.

BALL, S. (1990) *Politics and Policy Making in Education*, London, Routledge.

BURTON, L. and WEINER, G. (1990) 'Social justice and the National Curriculum', *Research Papers in Education*, **5**, 3, pp. 203–27.

COX, B. (1991) 'Ignorance behind a right old furore', *Education Guardian*, 19 February.

DEEM, R. (1990) 'The reform of school governing bodies: The power of the consumer over the producer?' in FLUDE, M. and HAMMER, M. (Eds) *The Education Reform Act 1988: Its Origins and Implications*, London, Falmer Press.

EQUAL OPPORTUNITIES COMMISSION (1987) *The Response of the Equal Opportunities Commission to the Consultative Document: The National Curriculum 5–16*, Manchester, EOC.

GILL, D. (1990) *Response on behalf of Hackney teachers to the National Curriculum History Working Group Final Report*, submission to DES.

GOLD, A., BOWE, R. and BALL, S. (1990) 'Special educational needs in a new context: Micropolitics, money and 'Education for All', paper presented to the annual conference of the British Educational Research Association, August, Roehampton.

GRAMSCI, A. (1971) *Selections from Prison Notebooks*, edited/translated by HOARE, Q. and NEWELL-SMITH, G., London, Lawrence & Wishart.

HALL, S. (1988) *The Hard Road to Renewal*, London, Verso.

HARLAND, J. (1987) 'The TVEI experience: Issues of control, response and the professional role of teachers' in GLEASON, D. (Ed.) *TVEI and Secondary Education: A Critical Appraisal*, Milton Keynes, Open University Press.

HILL, C. (1975) *The World Turned Upside Down*, Harmondsworth, Penguin.

HOBHOUSE, H. (1990) 'Time steals a march on history', *The Times Educational Supplement*, 3 August.

KETTLE, M. (1990) 'The great battle of history', *The Guardian*, 4 April.

LITTLE, V. (1990) 'A National Curriculum in history: A very contentious issue', *British Journal of Educational Studies*, **38**, 4, pp. 319–34.

LODGE, B. and TYSOME, T. (1990) 'History dons answer calls to arms', *The Times Educational Supplement*, 1 June.

MACLURE, S. (1990) *Education Re-Formed*, London, Hodder & Stoughton.

MARTEN, C.H.K. (1938) *On the Teaching of History and Other Addresses*, Oxford, Basil Blackwell.

MILLMAN, V. and WEINER, G. (1985) *Sex Differential in School*, York, Longman.
MISCELLANEOUS (1990) 'Letters', *The Times Education Supplement*, 1 June.
NATIONAL CURRICULUM HISTORY WORKING GROUP (1989) *Interim Report*, London, DES, June.
NATIONAL CURRICULUM HISTORY WORKING GROUP (1990) *Final Report*, London, DES, April.
RICHARDS, C. (1978) 'Editorial introduction' in RICHARDS, C. (Ed.) *Power and the Curriculum: Issues in Curriculum Studies*, Driffield, Nafferton.
ROWBOTHAM, S. (1973) *Hidden From History*, London, Pluto Press.
ST. JOHN BROOKS, C. (1990) 'No good reason to turn history into a battlefield', *The Times Educational Supplement*, 13 April.
THOMAS, H. (1979) *History, Capitalism and Freedom*, London, Centre for Policy Studies.
THOMPSON, E.P. (1968) *The Making of the English Working Class*, Harmondsworth, Penguin.
TES (1990a) 'Dates that need to be carved in stone', *The Times Educational Supplement*, 13 April.
TES (1990b) 'MacGregor fails to ruffle history critics', *The Times Educational Supplement*, 3 August.
WEINER, G. and ARNOT, M. (1987) 'Teachers and gender politics' in ARNOT, M. and WEINER, G. (Eds) *Gender and the Politics of Schooling*, London, Hutchinson.

Permissions
The authors wish to thank the Publishers concerned in allowing us to reproduce Abstracts from their publications.

Chapter 5

Othermothers: Exploring the Educational Philosophy of Black American Women Teachers

Michèle Foster

The 1980s will undoubtedly be remembered as the decade of reform reports. In that decade well over thirty reports identifying, analyzing and proposing solutions to the problems in American education were issued. One of the most widely cited, *A Nation at Risk* (NCEE, 1983) issued a battle cry that 'the educational foundations of our society are presently being eroded by a tide of mediocrity that threatens our very future as a nation and a people' (p. 5). According to the National Commission on Educational Excellence (1983), American education was in a crisis. Other reports reached similar conclusions. The reports, however, were marked by important differences, and according to Webb and Sherman (1989), can be classified into four types. Illustrative of reports that take economic and technical approaches to education, *A Nation at Risk* (1983), emphasizes economic development, concentrates on business and competitiveness in a global economy, and recommends closer linkages between business and schools. Other reform documents such as the Paideia Proposal (Adler, 1982) stress intellectual competence. Reports that focus on institutional excellence represent a third type. Unlike reports from the first two categories, these reports address the institutional constraints on the lives of teachers and argue that changing teachers' working conditions will enable them to teach better. The most notable report of this kind is *A Place Called School*, (1983), authored by John Goodlad. Finally, there are a number of reports whose central focus is on excellence and equity. Unlike the reports that comprise the first three categories, these reports contend that appeals to excellence in education are severely compromised unless accompanied by a commitment to serving poor students and students of color,[1] those currently least well served by the existing school arrangements.

Almost without exception, the policy recommendations emanating from the recent reform documents, particularly those that adopt an economic, technical or intellectual approach to education, extol the dominant patriarchal values of competition, power, ambition, money and fame. Recently, in their own report on excellence and equity a group of prominent black scholars indicted most of these reform documents. While not explicitly critical of the patriarchal values undergirding these documents, they charged that such reports are potentially divisive, unresponsive to the needs of the black American community and fail to recognize the centrality of human relationships in the teaching-learning transaction. They contend that African-American children are not likely to excel unless they and their parents can feel a sense of connection and identification with the school and the school personnel assigned to serve them (Committee on Policy for Racial Justice, 1989).

A recent survey suggests that members of the black American community believe that a crisis in education does indeed exist. The majority of those polled expressed dissatisfaction with the current state of education for black children. Sixty-five per cent of those polled reported that the schooling provided for black children had worsened over the past decade.[2] While it can be argued that a similar decline has occurred for all children in the United States, the respondents rated the quality of public schools for white children much higher.[3] Those surveyed were two-and-a-half times more likely to conclude that public schools were more neglectful of the education of black than they were of white students, both at the national level as well as at their respective community level.

Indicators of educational achievement for American blacks are grim. To be sure, black students have made some gains on achievement measures. However, according to national reports even when they attend integrated schools, black students in all parts of the country are more likely than white students to be assigned to classes for the mentally retarded, less likely to be in classes for gifted and talented students and more likely to be enrolled in lower level classes such as vocational and general tracks than in college preparatory classes. On national measures of reading, black students are less likely to perform adequately on complex reading tasks required in college and in a complex post-industrial society.[4]

For teachers of color, including black teachers, the picture is equally bleak. Calls for increasing the number of teachers of color notwithstanding, America's teaching force remains overwhelmingly white and, unaltered, is likely to remain so. The disparity between the number of children and the number of teachers of color for all groups in public schools is seriously imbalanced. In 1987, in the United States, 9.1 per cent of children in public schools were Latino, but Latino teachers made up only 1.9 per cent of the teaching force. Asian/Pacific Islanders comprised 2.5 per cent of the children in public schools, but only 0.9 per cent of the teachers, and Native Americans, and Alaskan Natives represented 0.9 per cent of the children in public schools, but only 0.6 per cent of the teachers. (National Education Association, 1987; Office of Educational Research and Improvement, 1987; Stewart, Meier and England, 1989). Correspondingly, although African-Americans constituted 16.2 per cent of the children in public schools nationwide in 1987, they comprised only 6.9 per cent of the teachers. Nationally, between 1971 and 1986, the percentage of black teachers declined from 8.1 to 6.9 per cent. During the same period, the percentage of white teachers grew from 88.3 to 89.6, an increase of 1.3 per cent.

This imbalance is even more critical when one considers that this decline is occurring at the same time that the number of pupils of color is growing rapidly. It is estimated that by the year 2000, children of color — 'minorities' — will comprise the majority in fifty-three of the nation's largest cities (Goertz and Pitcher, 1985). Merely to keep pace with the growing percentage of pupils of color, at least one-third of the 500,000 new teachers needed by the mid-1990s will have to be from minority communities. Yet, according to some estimates, teachers of color are expected to constitute less than 5 per cent of the entire teaching force by the middle of this decade (National Education Association, 1987; Office of Educational Research and Improvement, 1987; Stewart, Meier and England, 1989). In California, the state where I reside, this imbalance is already apparent. The majority — 54.4 per cent — of the students are children of color but only 18.5 per cent of the teaching force are teachers of color (California Department of Education, 1991).

Even when black teachers are represented in school systems and enrolled in teacher education programs, they often report feeling alienated from the school and its culture, outside collegial and friendship groups, and comment frequently that the teacher education programs and school reform movements do not consider their viewpoints or opinions (Foster, 1992a; Delpit, 1986 and 1988; King, 1991; Murrell, 1991). A recent survey revealed that at all levels of job satisfaction and years of experience, teachers of color are more likely than white teachers to report they were disenchanted with the current conditions (Metropolitan Life Insurance Company, 1988).

It is my contention that life history research can provide a much needed perspective and a different understanding of the current crisis in education, one neglected in most reform documents but one necessary to discovering the appropriate solutions. Rarely are the views of teachers ever considered in discussions about education. And because they are doubly marginalized, the voices of black teachers are even less likely to heard. Drawing on life history interviews, this chapter analyzes the educational philosophies of fourteen black American women teachers all with long tenure in urban and rural school systems across the United States. Selected by 'community nomination' a term and a method of sampling coined for this study, these teachers are part of a larger study of experienced, exemplary African-American teachers.[5] Data were collected using unstructured life history interviews. The fourteen women, whose interviews form the basis of this chapter, are diverse with respect to age, and region of country. Over half grew up in segregated southern or mid-western communities and attended schools that were segregated by law. The others were raised in northern communities and their educational experiences are more complex.

This chapter examines two themes. My analysis of the first theme, 'connectedness', considers how the teachers' relationships in their communities of orientation have shaped their ideas regarding the appropriate relationship between themselves, the students, families and communities they serve. Second this chapter explores how these teachers understand and have dealt with the constraining forces of race, class and gender in their personal lives and careers.

Consistent with the community nomination selection process, my analysis is informed by a black feminist epistemology articulated in the recent scholarship of Collins (1991), a black American feminist, and has been influenced as well by other research that takes the integrity of the black American community as a starting point. Connectedness is a prominent theme among scholars who have examined black family and community life. Several studies have described the strong kinship bonds that exist among extended families in black communities, and the tendency of non-kin to take on social roles. The studies have shown that the extensive kin-networks extant in black communities have contributed significantly both to the material and non-material well-being of children (Hill, 1972; Stack, 1974). Except for Collins, however, rarely have researchers extended the concept to individuals occupying institutional roles, like teachers. In developing a black feminist epistemology, Collins (1991) explores the salutory influence of non-kin women on the social, emotional and intellectual development of black children in greater depth, a phenomenon embodied in her use of the term 'community othermothers'. Moreover, she concludes that black women teachers often shared in this important function (*ibid*, pp. 129–32).

Many black Americans applaud the gains achieved through desegregation, but among intellectuals and lay persons alike, there is a widespread sense of loss for the community cohesiveness, consensus and support that characterized the self-contained, segregated communities, and the realization that desegregation has eroded the supportive community environments that assisted the intellectual, social and emotional development of black children (Committee on Policy for Racial Justice, 1989). Increased economic opportunities for blacks have stripped many black communities of their middle class residents including teachers. In the past, laws or customs consigned blacks to separate communities. In these closed, segregated communities, blacks from all social classes were much more likely than they are today to interact in churches, schools and neighborhoods (Blauner, 1989; Cohen, 1991; Irvine, 1990). Within these constraints and despite these impediments, blacks developed productive strategies for socializing and educating black children within the familiar contexts of families, schools and churches.

This is revealed most clearly in the interviews with teachers who grew up in communities where laws mandated segregation. Women who grew up in these settings spoke of family and community values that reinforced each other, and characterized their communities as places where personal relationships were reinforced in neighborhood, church and school. Pam Owens, a teacher in San Diego, described her childhood and adolescence during the late forties, fifties and early sixties, in Miami, Florida. In the following excerpt she talks about her family of orientation and its relationship to church and community:

> I grew up in a home with a mother, grandmother and great-grandmother. And (I) grew up with a sister who was thirteen months younger. Sometime after that we had a sister, she was ten years younger. Grew up in Miami, of course in a segregated section of Miami, went to segregated schools. Grew up in what is now referred to as a matriarchal home. Course in those days we just thought we grew up with folks who were there to take care of us. And was always surrounded by very, very strong black women and of course we were all close.[6]

Highlighting the interrelationships between family and community, she continues

> You know, growing up in a segregated society, I was born in '44, so I grew up during that time that everything was absolutely separated.

For these women, attendance in segregated public schools, often in buildings housing all grades, staffed entirely by black teachers was the norm. The centrality of schools in the communities and the significance of black teachers feature prominently in the remembrances of the women raised in these communities.[7] These interviews also highlight the constancy and intergenerational continuity that existed in segregated black communities, which were realized and reinforced by the long-term employment and long-term residence patterns of black teachers. The result of these patterns were that teachers were well known members of their communities. Marcia Gray, one of sixteen children, who grew up in a mid-western city and attended school during the thirties and forties describes the linkages between the community, the school and its teachers.

> The teachers knew the parents. Because when you got a job teaching, you just taught forever. They didn't have no what you call retirement or anything. You started and you taught until you died. I think you know, that in my generation, in those times, we didn't have integration. Lincoln was the one high school where all the Negroes went to school. It didn't make any difference whether we were living on Twelfth Street, Twenty-fourth Street or Fiftieth Street. Wherever. That's the way it was. So everybody knew everybody.

In small, rural communities, teachers boarded with families or lived in a teachers' residence during the week and returned home on weekends. Describing the teachers who boarded at her grandmother's house in Haskell, Oklahoma, Lorraine Lincoln notes how non-resident teachers as well as their families were bound to the communities where they worked.

> Except for Mr. Franklin and a couple of others there were no teachers in our community. The others who came to teach at Booker T. Washington were from Tulsa and Muskogee or like Mrs. Brown from Langston. So they had to come and spend a week at a time, sometimes two weeks at a time until their husband or somebody would come and get them and take them back.

By participating in everyday activities these teachers became valued members of family and community, individuals whose well-being mattered. Lorraine continues:

> They walked to the school, a block or two blocks away. We often saw those who stayed with my grandmother because we were frequently there. Well not too frequently, but it was family tradition to go on Sunday evenings and sit with my grandmother and enjoy Lassie and Ed Sullivan. It was interesting to us because we'd see a teacher, one wore braids when she was home. It's kind of interesting to see a teacher in that light. They were part of the family and we cared about them. When it was a special time at school, maybe a baccalaureate then, their family would come.

Though these teachers remember the positive aspects of their communities, they are not entirely uncritical nor totally accepting of all that occurred in them. Despite the interconnections among social classes within the black community and the shared values and aspirations that came from an enforced segregation, several of the women told incidents that revealed the class and color distinctions within their communities. Expressing her anger about an incident that occured during her childhood, Marcia Gray, who grew up in Kansas City, describes how color consciousness affected her

> I'm very serious. They used to say that, meaning the neighbors. I'm the brown skinned one in the family. You know what that means. In those days they used to say that little dark one, you know. I called it brown skinned. You know what they called it. That little dark one she's too serious, we need to watch her. She doesn't laugh when the rest of them laugh. I was too through with that.

Mrs. Gray's comment alludes to the once prevalent view in American and many African-American communities as well that to be black, serious and female was to be evil.[8]

Other women recognized this tendency in their own families. Miss Ruthie attended Avery Institute, a school that offered young blacks 'the best possible opportunities for self-culture, development, training and preparation for life's duties', but also had a reputation for elitism.[9] She recalled her sister's decision not to go to Avery, but to attend the public high school instead:

> She (her sister) wouldn't go to Avery. She said she didn't like the children at Avery. Nun uh. She didn't like them. She wouldn't go. She said they were all too stuck up. Oh yeah, that's right. My mother didn't make her go. She didn't want to go. So, she went to Burke. She finished Burke.

Emma Taylor characterized her parents' attitudes toward some of the children in her Austin neighborhood, and described their inclination toward elitism and snobbishness.

> I think we were poor . . . I look back at what we had you know the material things we had and I've come to the conclusion, we were poor . . . I came from a family that as I grew to be an adult, I made up my mind that there were some things they had done well, some things they hadn't done well and realized that one of them was that I would look back on now and say they were snobs, poor snobs because I was not permitted to play with certain children, not permitted to do a lot of things that other children did. I remember just loving a little girl who lived, I guess we would call it below the tracks. I look back at this now. I didn't understand it then, I simply did what my parents told me to do without any question. And as I look back, I guess it was because of where the child lived. I'm not sure because I dearly loved her and as I look back and try to assess the situation,

she didn't get into trouble. I think she lived with an aunt and maybe it was the wrong part of town. I don't know, but once again I get back to the fact that and perhaps my parents felt this way because, maybe they felt they had to be this way to do what they had to do.

Despite the generally positive characterizations of teachers, some of these women were aware of the tendency of some of their teachers to make class distinctions between themselves and certain children in the community.[10] Remembering her own schooling, Ella Jane assesses some of the negative behaviors she witnessed in her teachers and explains how she refashioned and replaced them with more egalitarian attitudes:

> I think that (treating people with respect) came from elementary school, because I had seen teachers that I thought were mistreated by their peers and I had seen teachers cry. My teachers cried. And I would look at them, decide I will never let someone walk on me that way. You know they cried because someone would hurt their feelings and they would say things in front of the kids to the teacher. You know the principal and his wife and so forth, they'd say harsh things. And I think I had just decided that I didn't want to be like that. And I heard a teacher say one time and this stuck with me and I didn't even have Jackie (her daughter) then. But she said if her son happened to get any girl pregnant, and she thought it was very important that if boys got girls pregnant they wanted them to marry them. But if her son got any girl pregnant well she was not going to make her son marry any of those little natty tailed girls. And that just, that just went all over me. Because I thought at that particular time that she thought that her son was too good to marry some of us who were there. And I just vowed that wasn't kind of person that I would be because I just did think if I ever had a kid *I will not teach her that she's better than anybody else.* And I think that's the thing that stuck with me. (emphasis in the interview)

These women acknowledged the class distinctions within their communities of orientation, as well as the inferior facilities and second-hand books that characterized their schools. Despite these shortcomings they remembered black teachers as significant figures in their personal and academic development. They recalled, moreover, that black teachers imparted more than mere school knowledge. They provided discipline, and guided the young black children entrusted to their care. Looking back at her childhood and schooling, Bobbie Duvon, who grew up in the coal mining town of Dante, West Virginia, remembered one teacher who acted as a surrogate mother.

> The elementary schools were segregated. All the schools were segregated. I loved the teachers in the school. They were just like mothers. You know Miss Waldo was just like our mother and I always remember she would write on my report card, it was always be mischievous, which wasn't bad, but I was always getting into something. We lived in hollows. The school was at other end of the hollow and we were last, at the other end. But everybody knew everyone and if I did something, my mother would know it. I might have gotten a crack on the fanny from Miss Jones down there and then I also got it when I got home too.

Pam Owens describes the means one of her teachers used to enhance each student's development:

> I remember the end of school, almost June, our sixth grade teacher, Miss Pascall. I won't ever forget her name. She called . . . she told us the day before she was gonna call each person up and she was gonna sit you down, we were just sixth graders, and she was gonna actually tell you what she thought about you. And what she thought your good points were and your weak points because we were getting ready to go into seventh grade and she just thought that was something important. She called me up and then she said, 'OK, Pam, what I'm gonna tell you what I think about you, and then ask if you have any questions.' She said, 'You're very bright', well they didn't say bright in those days, they said smart, 'you're smart, but personally I think', because I was only nine then now, 'that you're too young to go to seventh grade'. She said, 'But, don't ever let that be . . . don't ever let that hold you back, but I just want you to know that you are very young.' And now for some reason that's all I remember. She may have told me a lot of other things, but what I remember about it is that at some point, somebody needs to just pull you aside and say, now let me just tell some things that are gonna help you later. Now, I was nine years old, I don't even know how I remember it. But this woman somehow made me understand that you should always look at yourself and know what you're very good at, know what's different about you but don't ever see it as a liability.

More than anything else these early family, community and school experiences, have shaped these women's views of the teachers' role. Immersion in this value system was reinforced by attendance at black colleges and strengthened for two women who returned to their communities of orientation after graduation to work as colleagues alongside former teachers.

Leaving one's neighborhood in order to secure better schooling opportunities is a prominent theme in the narratives of women educated in northern communities. A few of them began their education in racially isolated neighborhood schools, but by the time they reached the upper grades they had left their communities to attend academically advanced or elite exam schools. One consequence of the search for better educational opportunities was that women rarely encountered black teachers. There were some exceptions. But most of these women reported experiences that were similar to those of Linda Morris who grew up in Philadelphia during the fifties:

> In all of my schools, I was basically the only black or it was two or three other blacks in the school. At that particular time, I didn't know there was a color, I just enjoyed being with certain people, whether they were white students or whether they were black friends of mine. I've never had a black teacher, all my teachers from elementary school through high school were white.

Like Linda Morris, Cheryl Thigpen was never taught by a black teacher and often was the lone black student in her classroom. In the following excerpt, she remembers her elementary school years:

> At the Gray, we had one black teacher, a second grade teacher. I didn't have her for second grade, but she was the second grade teachers. And, I knew her because she went to church with some friends of mine, so I used to see her in places other than at the school. At the Everett I don't remember any black teachers. *In the fifth grade is when I really started seeing things a little bit different because we moved and I went to school in my neighborhood which was predominantly Jewish. I don't think there were more than half a dozen black kids in the school at that time. I know I was the only one in my room.* It must have been around '58. Yeah in 58/59 and 59/60 I went to Girls' Latin for two years, 7th and 8th grade. (my emphasis)

Despite their schooling in majority white settings at the pre-college level, the majority of the northern women matriculated at colleges that had been black historically. In these institutions in the company of black students and under the tutelage of black professors, they learned of their responsibilities towards subsequent generations of black children. Mabel Morse recalled her teacher training at Cheney State Teachers College in the 1950s, and though she thought it extreme at the time, remembered Faculty exhorting her duty to serve black children:

> It (the curriculum) did, because one thing they did was to really love the children and to tell you, 'You're their salvation', which I thought was a strong word, but they would say that. But somebody helped all of us black people. Somebody helped us to get where we are and we have to help the the children. Yeah, I believe that. And, they also taught that black people should stick together.

Expressing similar beliefs, Cheryl Thigpen attributed her feelings to the education she received at Hampton:

> *Ms. Thigpen*: One thing, I really feel that all children can learn. No matter what it is, where they are, what the circumstances are. That is my basic philosophy, all children can learn. And I know I picked that up from Hampton. With all the course work that I had, I'm really convinced that all children can learn.
>
> *Interviewer*: And you think that you learned that from Hampton?
>
> *Ms. Thigpen*: I know I did.

Whereas the southern respondents learned of their responsibilities to black children by example, the northern women were taught theirs by precept. Though socialized in different environments, all have established kinlike relationships with their pupils, relating to them as much like family — mothers, aunts, and grandmothers — as teachers. Embedded in these narratives is a conception of the teacher's role, a conception that goes well beyond the narrow institutional goal of promoting cognitive growth specified by the reform reports. Central to these women's conception of teaching is a responsibility to attend to the social and emotional growth of students. Several of the teachers use explicit kin terms to refer to their relationships with students. Commenting on why she likes teaching third grade, a Texas elementary school teacher said, 'Third grade kids you're kinda like Mama to them, and they kind of haven't still weaned themselves away from this mama thing, and you can discipline the kid and the kid still loves you.' Other elementary teachers concurred with this statement. Asked what advice she would give a beginning teacher, 86-year-old Miss Ruthie, who still teaches in a one-room schoolhouse remarked:

> The first thing she's gonna have to do is to get their attention. And then she's gonna have to try and work in there a kind of mother like. She's gonna have to be the mama for all of them, that's the first thing. Then when she gets them to feel that. She's gonna have to let them know I'm your mama until you get back home. That's what I tell them. Long as you're in here with me I'm your mama, until you go

> back. And then when you go back home, you go to your other mother.

A third, this one a high school teacher, noted that during her first encounter with parents she tells them, 'You're the mother at home. I'll be their mother at school.' These comments are not surprising. Involvement with pupils on such an extended and complete basis, as is the case with elementary school teachers, makes it possible to perceive themselves as mother figures. Establishing kinlike relationships is made easier though not certain, in part because, having resided and having taught in the same communities for extended periods, these women occupy permanent roles in the communities and have established powerful reputations. All of these women have worked in their respective schools for at least a decade. Two have taught in the same school for over two decades, and are now teaching their second generation. Miss Ruthie, quoted above, graduated from Avery Institute in 1923 and began her teaching career in what she refers to as the 'rurals', the elementary schools in Charleston County, where she taught for fifteen years, boarded with local families whose children attended her school. In 1938, she moved to Pawley's Island where she has been teaching without interruption in the same one-room school house. After more than fifty years, she is teaching the grandchildren of her original pupils. Of the fourteen women interviewed for this study, ten reside within the geographic boundaries of the school system, and all live within ten miles of the school itself, making intimate knowledge of the surrounding community and its residents likely. Like the teachers they remember from their own childhoods, 'who got a job teaching and just taught forever', patterns of long-term employment and community residence reinforce intergenerational continuity and constancy.

A recurrent theme in the interviews, the constraining forces of race, class, and gender, are considered next. When asked about the constraints on their lives and careers, these women spoke most often about the restrictions of race not gender or class. Attributing oppression to one particular feature over another, to race more than gender or class, is understandable. After all, an individual does not experience oppression based solely on a single aspect of one's identity. What is striking about these narratives is that while the women understand gender and class issues, they are conveyed primarily through individual experiences. In contrast, their analysis of racism is not only mediated through personal experiences, but is also understood structurally. This is not to minimize the influence of gender and class, but to recognize that for these women, at least, the structural issues of race are most prominent. It is therefore, issues of racism that this chapter addresses next.

Whether raised in northern or southern communities, most of these women spent their early years in a segregated society. During their childhoods the majority of them lived in segregated neighborhoods, attended *de jure* or *de facto* separate schools and were aware that their lives, the lives of family and community members were restricted by the color line. While the pattern of racism was clear and unambiguous in southern communities, it was often disguised in northern communities. In southern communities segregation was most visible in segregated schools, which relegated black students and teachers to separate and unequal schools. In northern communities, assigning teachers on the basis of race was a covert but common practice well up into the seventies when desegregation suits forced school boards to change this practice.

Jean Vanderall, who began teaching in the Boston Public Schools in the early fifties recalls how the school board segregated black teachers by race:

> Yeah, right, because at the time I started teaching, black teachers were assigned to just that strip going from the South End into Roxbury, between, let me see Tremont Street and Washington. You didn't get any choice. That's where you were sent and most of the black teachers had a very hard time out of town.

Women who began teaching in the south and later migrated to northern communities found that the kind of opportunities available in the south were unavailable in most northern cities. Though not prescribed by law, the practice of placing teachers in particular schools and restricting them to certain grade levels was a common practice until the sixties when the desegregation suits challenged this practice. Two women grew up in legally segregated communities, began teaching in them and subsequently moved to the north in the forties and fifties seeking teaching positions in Hartford, Connecticut, found there were limited opportunities. A third arrived to teach in Hartford in 1969, a time when some northern school systems were beginning to search for black teachers.

When the older women arrived in Hartford, shortly after World War II, they found that the city concentrated black teachers in specific grade levels and employed unofficial and not so subtle practices to steer black teachers to certain schools. Though certified and having worked as a high school English teacher in Florida, Martha Smith was denied a position in the school system because it was customary not to place black teachers at the high school level and she did not have an elementary credential. Likewise when Bobbie Duvon, who had been a physical education teacher in West Virginia, applied for a teaching position in Hartford, she found it difficult to find suitable employment in the public schools. She explains what happened to her when she tried to secure a teaching position in Hartford:

> Then I came to Hartford. Did not get a job immediately. I applied. This was in '53. I applied each year that I went back to West Virginia,

but they didn't have any openings, or they never called me. So, when I came back to Hartford, I was working at the park department on the playgrounds. I got married, my daughter was born and I subbed at Noah Webster School which was in the North West section of the city which was predominantly white — it was white. There was an African family from the seminary there, and my daughter went to school there after she got old enough, and I was there as a long-term sub for two months because the teacher there was on maternity leave. At the end of June, the principal asked me what was I gonna do next year. I said I didn't know. She said, Well why didn't I put my application in. I told her it had been in. So, she called downtown and she said I want Bobbie here. They say, We don't have an application. Course, I know where the application went. When I applied it went in the waste basket. Because of the color of my skin. This was in '53. I don't know how many black teachers — it might have been maybe six or seven in the city. I'm not sure of how many at that time, but there weren't that many black teachers. And, I was fortunate that my principal liked me.

Occasionally when black teachers decided to challenge discriminatory hiring practices they met with organized community resistance. Evelyn Taylor spent half of her childhood in Austin, Texas, before moving to Boston to finish her elementary and secondary schooling. She spoke of the hostility and resistance encountered, and an unexpected source of support, when she became the first black teacher assigned to a California Bay area community in the late sixties.

All right, so I got the job. But after I got the job, I was assigned to a school on this side of town and it was just horrible. I had been away that summer and when I came back I didn't know that all this stuff had gone on. They had called my house, 'Nigger, nigger, nigger'. They had held a what do you call it, a community meeting in the church and had all the people there. The principal came over to my house . . . It was hard for either of them (her husband or the principal) to tell me. There was even a dispute about the man who led this movement wearing his scouting uniform at that time. There was an article in the paper because you're not supposed to wear your uniform when you do — it was a mess. One of them told the principal that if I were permitted to teach here — and this is a shackey place over here — that I may want to live here. And at that time, there were no Blacks on this side of town. I knew that the whole community didn't want me. But I decided that OK, I'm just going to get through those

> gates that morning. I'm a teacher like everybody else. I'm trained and by golly, that's just the way it's going to be. But it was real good that the teachers at the school supported me.

Because of the dual school systems, there was always greater representation of black teachers in southern school systems. One immediate result of desegregation, however, was that between the 1954 Brown *vs* the Topeka Board of Education decision and the early 1970s, approximately 32,000 black teachers were dismissed in the seventeen southern and border states (Ethridge, 1979, pp. 223–4). Negative evaluations resulted in dismissal for many. In some cases, black teachers were simply relieved of their responsibilities. In other instances, the most competent black teachers were reassigned to white schools. For the most part, the individual stories remain untold. What follows is a close look at one teacher who did not become a statistic of desegregation, but whose experiences in a small East Texas town suggest what life might have been like for black teachers in desegregated schools of the south. Ella Jane grew up in a small town fifty miles east of Dallas, attended the consolidated K-12 school that served black children in the area, matriculated at Prairie View A & M, and in 1955 returned to teach in the consolidated school where she had once been a student. Most compelling is the story she tells about how she was summoned by the superintendent and told that she was to become one of the only black teachers to be sent over to the newly desegregated school.

> I came here in 64. I was teaching at the all-black school, at Brag Morris and I received a telephone call. And the telephone call said, Ella Jane Moore get over here. I want to see you. And I said I can't leave now because my principal isn't here. And the superintendent called and said, 'Come I need you now. The principal will understand.' That's how I got here. And I got in the car and left the school which was about eight miles out and came over to the white school over to the administration building at that time and I was sandwiched between a high school principal, one on one side and one on the other and a secretary to the superintendent. And they carried me through the wringer. That's how I got here.

Recounting the conversation that took place that day she added:

> The questions they asked were ridiculous. They said, 'Did you know,' this is what I remember 'Ella Jane did you know that we have to have some black teachers?' And I said, 'Yes.' And he said, 'Did you know that you are going to be very fortunate because you are going to be one of the black teachers that we're going to hire.' And he said,

> 'You're the best teacher I have in system, black or white I did not have to tell you that, and if you tell anyone I said that I'm gonna tell 'em you lied.' He says, 'Do you get my meaning?' And he said, 'It should make you feel very proud whether you do or not that you're going to be one of the ones who are retained.' That's how that happened.

Though she has managed to survive in the now desegregated schools of Lindale, her experiences — not being assigned students to teach for the first three years of desegregation, being assigned only to remedial reading classes for the next four years, and coping with the hostility of white parents, teachers and school administrators — during the twenty-six years since the schools were first desegregated make it obvious that the constraints imposed on black teachers are not merely idiosyncratic and individual but structural.

Though racial oppression is a central motif theme in the interviews, gender has played a significant role in these teachers' personal development and professional choices. An in-depth analysis that goes beyond what the women are able to express reveals that gender has exerted considerable influence in these women's lives. The obstacles of gender are more easily discerned when the career paths of males and females within the same family of orientation are scrutinized. Eight of the women were raised in families with male siblings. In those families where parents were able to ensure the schooling for all of their children, males had some advantage and tended to achieve higher levels of education and enter more prestigious careers than their female siblings. While in most cases being male assured greater and more varied educational opportunities and career choices, in some instances being male was a clear disadvantage. In three of the families, for instances, males did not receive any post-secondary education even though their female siblings became teachers or entered other female dominated professions. Though such an analysis highlights the relative influence, gender, though powerful, does not always act in favor of males. Further analysis reveals that in larger families where children attended schools staffed primarily by black teachers, males were relatively advantaged. Thus, at least in these interviews, with respect to gender, the influences were uneven.[11]

Though several women became aware retrospectively of the societal constraints imposed on their career choices by gender, only one recalls being aware of this at the time. Born and raised in Boston, Jean Vanderall began teaching in the early 1950s. Asked why she chose teaching, she commented:

> It was either teaching or social work if you were a woman. If you were a man, they didn't even have men teachers. No black men at all. So I don't know what they were gonna do. They didn't go into teaching.

Her narrative reminds us that even though gender acted as a constraining force on the choices of black women, in Boston, at least, gender provided opportunities for black women that were proscribed for black men.

Obstacles to personal and professional development come from many sources. Race, class and gender often combine in ways that are not well understood. In both the black academic and lay communities, there is considerable debate about the relative effects of race, class on determining an individual's life chances (Wilson, 1978; Willie, 1989).[12] Available statistics present conflicting evidence. Figures show that black women frequently depend on government aid and are often located in low-paying female dominated professions. These facts notwithstanding, black women have higher participation and completion rates at all levels of the educational ladder. Recent studies show that except at the higher levels of educational attainment where there has been an increase in the number of black men receiving advanced professional degrees, as a group, black males have lost significant ground at all levels of educational attainment. In California black males are more likely to be murdered or incarcerated than to attend the University of California (Chan and Momparler, 1991). Gender, although not always in the direction generally assumed, has become an increasingly critical factor in determining high school and college participation and completion rates (Wilson and Carter, 1990).

Despite minimal references to the effects of class in their own childhoods, when they talk about the lives of their pupils, it is clear that these teachers understand the changing nature of American society, the widening class cleavages, and devastating consequences of this change on the black community. Asked about the changes in the black community over the course of her career, Jean Vanderall, who has lived in Boston all of her life and taught in its schools continuously since 1953, remarked on the contradictions of the sixties:

> Because I think that, I really believe that the sixties encouraged the use of drugs, too, along with building up of black self-image. I do believe that and I think many of those people are still on drugs. I think that the business of drugs had such a strong hold at the time. I think that it has a strong, a definite strong hold in poor neighborhoods. Because that's the only way of subsisting for some of these people. They are selling the shit. They are selling drugs. And they are selling to whomever will buy. Because they have to live too. And that's getting in the way of progress for us. Yeah, but they (poor blacks) had more stability. There have been poor black people, but they had jobs, and the welfare, it was not like it is now. They're in the projects now. People are doing things outside of the law, so that therefore they do not want any kind of school intervention for fear of legal repercussions. I think that is a major problem. People weren't

> outside the law before. People are more and more outside of the law. People, women are hustling to make money, cause they can't make it with collard greens a dollar a pound. You know what I'm saying. And, don't forget the TV has a great deal to do with it. The level of dressing is changed, these kids want the best jeans, these young kids want the best of everything. You think these kids are going to wear keds sneakers? No, not even in grade one. You can't put no cheap sneakers on this kid and think he's going to walk in school and like it. These kids evaluate the clothes. This little girl came in talking about she should have jherri curls.

The teachers are troubled by recent trends in the way black children have come to view education. Most have witnessed black students become increasingly passive or resistant toward education. Others worry equally about students who have come to view academic excellence in strictly utilitarian purposes. Instead of retreating from these circumstances, these teachers have chosen to remain in their classroom and try to reverse what they believe is an overall decline in education. In order to confront these circumstances, these teachers have fashioned philosophies and pedagogies that draw on their own lived experiences. These women also argue that an appropriate pedagogy for black students can not be limited only to academics, but must deal with the political, social and economic circumstances of children's lives and communities. Pam Owens, the first black California Teacher of the Year, criticizes most of the national reform efforts. While she supports professionalizing teaching, higher salaries for teachers as well the corresponding accountability that will be demanded of them, she questions what the consequences of this movement will be for black students. Based on nineteen years of successfully teaching black students, she foresees little likelihood for change in reforms that merely stress cognitive growth without concomitantly stressing the social, political awareness and the emotional growth of black students. From her perspective not only is cognitive growth linked to other aspects of pupils' development, but cognitive growth without attention to these important elements is neither achievable nor desirable.

These interviews provide substantial evidence that these women have fashioned a 'hidden curriculum' which is designed to reverse the one commonly taught in schools, one that will enable black students to use education to challenge the *status quo*, enrich their own lives and oppose ignorance, poverty and isolation. Though these women do not view their teaching as liberation, feminist or critical pedagogies, it is clear that women not only value their own experiences but those of other oppressed individuals as well. Additionally, they see their experiences an important source of knowledge for themselves and their pupils.

The interviews analyzed in this chapter are not representative of the lives of all black women teachers in the United States. They are presented here specifically to illustrate how these women's experiences and lives diverge from those of white teachers, and how their experiences undergird their educational philosophy. This chapter has illustrated the power and the positive effect of one of these circumstances — connectedness within the African-American community. Connectedness is a central tenet of these black women teachers' philosophy. By recreating a sense of family in their classrooms, one that weaves together race, gender, class and intergenerational continuity, these women have achieved reputations as exemplary teachers in and for their communities.

Reform documents that stress intellectual competence and ignore students' emotional needs, and reports that promote economic and technical excellence and fail to teach social justice will not solve American's educational crisis. Longer school days, extended school years, more courses, and merit pay are solutions that substitute quantity for quality. Until quality and equality can coexist in schools, excellence in education will continue to elude America. Without an acknowledgment that learning requires commitment from students and teachers and this commitment depends on classroom participants' ability to forge productive relationships in classrooms, cycles of educational reforms will continue. Finally, until the voices of those involved in the day-to-day life of classroom, are allowed into the official debate, long-lasting solutions will not be found.

Because they are primarily concerned with relationships, life histories such as those presented in this chapter can provide an alternate view of what schools are and a different vision of what schools could become. Regrettably, the reform documents of the 1980s have avoided or sidestepped most of these critical issues. Hopefully, one day some of these ideas will find their way into mainstream educational discourse. Until that day, America will remain 'a nation at risk'.

Acknowledgment

I acknowledge funding for this work from the University of Pennsylvania Research Foundation, and The Spencer Small Grant Program. A Spencer Post-doctoral Fellowship from the National Academy of Education, a Carolina Minority Post-doctoral Fellowship and a Smithsonian Faculty Fellowship enabled me to work full-time on this study. I am grateful to Jeanne Newman for her careful transcription of the interviews. I also thank Kathleen Weiler for her comments on an earlier draft of this article. In this chapter, the term Black American refers to those individuals who were born and raised in the United States.

Notes

1 In this chapter, the term 'students of color' refers to black Americans, Native American Indians, Latinos and Asian Pacific Islanders.

2 The exact figures are as follows: 63.5 per cent of those polled felt that the quality of public school education for black children had decreased in the past decade. Only 16.6 per cent felt the quality of public school education for blacks had improved and 17.9 per cent felt it had remained the same. The respondents' rating of the quality of public school for white children was significantly different. Asked whether the quality of public school education for white students had improved, worsened or remained the same, the respondents provided the following ratings: 32 per cent felt the quality had increased; 22.4 per cent felt it had decreased and 37 per cent felt it had remained the same. Asked whether the education for black children was better in the thirty-five years since schools were desegregated by court order, 60 per cent felt that the education was the same or worse; 44.5 per cent of the respondents felt the education was worse and 14.3 per cent felt there was no change. For the questionnaire consult *Black Enterprise* (January, 1990a). For the survey results, see *Black Enterprise* (August, 1990b). This finding has also been corroborated by other more scholarly research on attitudes toward school desegregation. See Hochschild (1985).

3 Asked about the quality of schooling for white students, one third reported that the quality was unchanged, just under 40 per cent felt it had increased, and less than 25 per cent felt it had decreased.

4 For a discussion of some of the issues surrounding the school achievement of black American students consult, The College Board (1985); Educational Testing Service, (1985); Oakes (1985); Jaynes and Williams (1989).

5 For a discussion of 'community nomination' see, Foster (1990, 1991a, 1991b, 1992b and 1993).

6 All of the informants' names used in this article are pseudonyms; the names of communities and institutions remain unchanged.

7 The significance of black teachers can be found in Cohen (1991); Blauner (1989); Kluger (1979); Baker (1987); Clark (1962); Fields (1985); Monroe and Goldman (1988); Reed (1990).

8 For additional evidence about color and class distinctions in black communities, see Lightfoot (1988), pp. 34–5, 41–2, 54 and 309–10; Mebane (1981), pp. 70, 182, 208–16 and 219–27.

9 Quoted in Anderson (1988), p. 135; Drago, *Initiative, Paternalism and Race Relations*, pp. 183–95. Also, see Drago and Hunt nd, pp. 183–95.

10 Sociologists employ multiple indicators — income, aspirations and education—to position individuals in the class structure. While these indicators may apply to whites and to a lesser extent to the black community since the 1960s, these indicators do not accurately capture the class structure of blacks prior to the 1960s, the time period when all of these women were born. Landry's work on black class structure is useful for positioning these women's families of orientation into the black community structure of the time. Most of these women were the children of parents who had neither the education or the economic means to be considered middle class. There were five exceptions. One teacher, born at the turn of the century, was the child of a brickmason, an occupation that positioned her family in the black middle class. Two had parents who owned small businesses. Another

was the daughter of the minister, and a fifth had a father who was hampered throughout his life by discrimination and despite his college education spent his lifetime working at a series of menial positions. Often both parents worked although a few of the mothers were homemakers or took in laundry to supplement the family income. Regardless of family constellation, however, all the teachers lived in families that earned regular wages, supplying them with a regular source of income.

11 For a discussion supporting my claim that no evidence exists supporting the tendency of blacks to educate daughters over sons, see Jackson (1973), pp. 229–30. Though I am unaware of any research that documents the fact, it has often been said that black parents have ensured their daughters' education over their sons so that their daughters would not be forced to work as domestics in the homes of white families. The tendency of black families to send their daughters to post-secondary institutions, their reluctance to invest as heavily in their sons and their reasoning for their choices is addressed in Davis (1988), pp. 19, 25 and 71.

12 Scholars have long debated whether race or class is more influential in determining an individual's life chances. Another debate on the race/class issue took place when discussant Niara Sudarkasa (1989) challenged George Frederickson's (1989) claim that class had primacy over race.

References

Adler, M. (1982) *The Paideia Proposal*, New York, Macmillan.

Anderson, J. (1988) *The Education of Blacks in the South, 1860–1935*, Chapel Hill, NC, University of North Carolina.

Baker, H. (1987) 'What Charles knew' in Rubin, L.D. Jr. (Ed.) *An Apple for my Teacher: 12 Authors tell about Teachers who made the Difference*, Chapel Hill, NC, Algonquin Books.

Black Enterprise (1990a) 'Survey, a view of the past, plan for the future', *Black Enterprise*, January, pp. 69–75.

Black Enterprise (1990b) 'Survey Result', *Black Enterprise*, August, pp. 85–94.

Blauner, B. (1989) *Black Lives, White Lives: Three Decades of Race Relations in America*, Berkeley, CA, University of California Press.

California Department of Education (1991) *Fingertip Facts on Education in California*, Sacramento, CA, California Department of Education.

Chan, V. and Momparler, M. (1991) 'George Bush's report card: What's he got against kids?' *Mother Jones*, May/June, pp. 44–45.

Clark, S. (1962) *Echo in my Soul*, New York, E.P. Dutton.

Cohen, M. (1991) 'Growing up segregated', *Emphasis Chapel Hill Sunday Newspaper*, **24** February, C1–2.

The College Board (1985) *Equity and Excellence: The Educational Status of Black Americans*, New York, The College Board.

Collins, P.H. (1991) *Black Feminist Thought: Knowledge, Consciousness, and the Politics of Empowerment*, New York, Routledge.

Committee on Policy for Racial Justice (1989) *Visions of a Better Way: A Black Appraisal of Public Schooling*, Washington, DC, Joint Center for Political Studies Press.

Davis, S. (1988) *The World of Patience Gromes: Making and Unmaking of a Black Community*, Lexington KY, University of Kentucky Press.

Delpit, L. (1986) 'Skills and other dilemmas of a progressive Black educator', *Harvard Educational Review*, **56**, 4, pp. 389–95.

Delpit, L. (1988) 'The silenced dialogue: Power and pedagogy in educating other people's children', *Harvard Educational Review*, **58**, 3, pp. 280–98.

Drago, E. (1990) *Initiative, Paternalism and Race Relations: Charleston's Avery Institute*, Athens, GA, University of Georgia Press.

Drago, E. and Hunt, E. (nd) *A History of Avery Normal Institute from 1865 to 1954*, Charleston, SC, Avery Institute of Afro-American History and Culture, College of Charleston.

Educational Testing Service (1985) *The Reading Report Card*, Princeton, NJ, Educational Testing Service.

Ethridge, S. (1979) 'Impact of the 1954 Brown v. Topeka Board of Education decision on black educators', *Negro Educational Review*, **30**, 3–4. pp, 217–32.

Fields, M. with K. Fields (1985) *Lemon Swamp: A Carolina Memoir*, New York, The Free Press.

Foster, M. (1990) 'The politics of race: Through African-American teachers' eyes', *Journal of Education*, **172**, 3, pp. 123–41.

Foster, M. (1991a) 'Connectedness, constancy and constraints in the lives of African-American women teachers: Some things change, most stay the same', *NWSA Journal* **3**, 2, pp. 233–61.

Foster, M. (1991b) '"Just got to find a way": Case studies of the lives and practice of exemplary Black high school teachers' in Foster, M. (Ed.) *Readings in Equal Education Volume II: Qualitative Investigations into Schools and Schooling*, New York, AMS Press.

Foster, M. (1992a) *Urban African-American Teachers' Views of Organizational Change: Speculations on the Views of Exemplary Teachers*, Madison, WI, Center on School Organization and Restructuring.

Foster, M. (1992b) 'African-American teachers and the politics of race' in Weiler, K. (Ed.) *What Schools Can Do: Critical Pedagogy and Practice*, Buffalo, NY, SUNY Press.

Foster, M. (1993) 'Educating for competence in community and culture: Exploring the views of exemplary African-American teachers' *Urban Education*, **27**, 3, pp. 370–394.

Fredrickson, G. (1989) 'Comparative History of Racism', paper presented at the Symposium on Race in America: The Divided Society Eighty-eighth Annual Meeting of the American Anthropological Association, 17 November.

Goertz, M. and Pitcher, B. (1985) *The Impact of NTE by States on the Teacher Selection Process*, Princeton, NJ, Educational Testing Service.

Goodlad, J. (1983) *A Place Called School: Prospects for the Future*, New York, McGraw Hill.

Hill, R. (1972) *The Strengths of Black Families*, New York, Emerson Hall.

Hochschild, J. (1985) *Thirty Years After Brown*, Washington, DC, Joint Center for Political Studies.

Irvine, J. (1990) *Black Students and School Failure*, Westport, CT, Greenwood Press.

Jackson, J. (1973) 'Black women in a racist society' in Willie, C. (Ed.) *Racism and Mental Health*, Pittsburgh, PA, University of Pittsburgh Press.

Jaynes, G.D. and Williams, R.M. Jr. (1989) *A Common Destiny: Blacks and American Society*, Washington, DC, National Academy Press.

King, J. (1991) 'Unfinished business: Black students' alienation and Black teacher's pedagogy' in FOSTER, M. (Ed.) *Readings on Equal Education: Volume, Qualitative Investigation into Schools and Schooling*, New York, AMS Press.

KLUGER, R. (1979) *Simple Justice*, New York, Vintage.

LANDRY, B. (1987) *The New Black Middle Class*, Berkeley, CA, University of California Press.

LIGHTFOOT, S. (1988) *Balm in Gilead: Journey of a Healer*, Reading, MA, Addison-Wesley.

MEBANE, M. (1981) *Mary: The Autobiography of Mary Mebane*, New York, Viking Press.

METROPOLITAN LIFE INSURANCE COMPANY (1988) *The American Teacher, 1988: Strengthening the Relationship between Teachers and Students*, New York, Metropolitan Life Insurance Company.

MONROE, S. and GOLDMAN, P. (1988) *Brothers: Black and Poor, a True Story of Courage and Survival*, New York, Ballantine Books.

MURRELL, P. (1991) 'Cultural politics in teacher education: What's missing in the preparation of minority teachers?' in FOSTER, M. (Ed.) *Readings on Equal Education*, New York, AMS Press.

NATIONAL COMMISSION ON EDUCATIONAL EXCELLENCE (1983) *A Nation at Risk: The Imperative for Educational Reform*, Washington, DC, US Department of Education.

NATIONAL EDUCATION ASSOCIATION (1987) *Status of the American Public School Teacher 1985–86*, Washington, DC, National Education Association.

OAKES, J. (1985) *Keeping Track: How Schools Structure Inequality*, New Haven, CT, Yale University Press.

OFFICE OF EDUCATIONAL RESEARCH AND IMPROVEMENT (1987) *Digest of Educational Statistics 1987*, Washington, DC, Office of Educational Research and Improvement.

REED, I. (1990) 'Reading, writing and racism', *San Francisco Examiner Image Magazine*, 19 August.

STACK, C. (1974) *All Our Kin: Strategies for Survival in a Black Community*, New York, Harper and Row.

STEWART, J., K. MEIER, T. and ENGLAND, R. (1989) 'In quest of role models: Change in black teacher representation in urban school districts 1968–85', *Journal of Negro Education*, **58**.

SUDARKASA, N. (1989) Paper presented at the Symposium on Race in America: The Divided Society, Eighty-eighth Annual Meeting of the American Anthropological Asssociation, 17 November.

WEBB, R. and SHERMAN, R. (1989) *Schooling and Society*, 2nd edn, New York, MacMillan.

WILLIE, C. (1989) *Caste and Class Controversy on Race and Poverty: Round Two of the Willie/Wilson Debate*, Dix Hills, NY, General Hall.

WILSON, W. (1978) *The Declining Significance of Race: Blacks and Changing American Institutions*, Chicago, IL, University of Chicago Press.

WILSON, R. and CARTER, D. (1990) *Eighth Annual Status Report on Minorities in Higher Education*, Washington, DC, American Council on Education.

Chapter 6

A Post-Modern Pedagogy for the Sociology of Women's Education

Sue Middleton

The term 'sociology of women's education' was coined by Madeleine Arnot (then writing as MacDonald, 1980) to refer to feminist scholarship within the sociology of education. As an academic subject, it has developed since the mid-1970s, when the ideas of the second wave of feminism were increasingly influencing the thinking of many academic women. Since 1981, I have been designing and teaching undergraduate courses in the sociology of women's education in a New Zealand university. In this chapter, I draw on this experience to address some broader pedagogical problems which have emerged as common concerns amongst many of us who 'network' internationally as feminist sociologists and teacher-educators.

We have developed our courses over a period of rapid change. Theoretical shifts in 'contributing' disciplines such as women's studies, the sociology of education, and 'radical'[1] pedagogy have raised new questions about curriculum content and teaching methods. Political events at both national and local levels have altered the professional conditions and the institutional settings in which we work. For example, the various institutions in which we and our students study and teach have been 'restructured'. This restructuring has influenced both the context and the content of our teaching — shaped our material circumstances and become an object of our academic inquiries.

At a more personal level, our experiences of 'aging' are also changing our educational perspectives and methods. As we who teach feminist university courses become older, we notice a widening gap between ourselves and our students. Like many of today's feminist and 'left' educators, I attended university during the 1960s and began my school teaching career in the early 1970s — times of full employment and hope. Today, as a university teacher in the 1990s, I watch my younger students moving into adulthood in times of economic recession and despair. The kinds of feminism and progressive educational theories which offered possibilities to my generation of teachers may seem to today's students irrelevant and quaint anachronisms.

As Maxine Greene (1986, p. 440) has asked, 'what might a critical pedagogy mean for those of us who teach the young at this peculiar and menacing time?' In this chapter I address this question by reflecting upon some of the ways in my own teaching in a New Zealand setting has, over the last decade, been influenced by changing perspectives and power-dynamics in the 'theoretical field' of my discipline; by dynamics between my own, and my students', biographical (and generational) circumstances; and by the political configurations of 'educational restructuring'. I demonstrate specific teaching strategies which are part of my wider project of devising ways in which we, middle-aged and older teacher-educators, can develop feminist courses which are appropriate for the lives and times of today's students.

Theoretical Dilemmas

In 1980 — my first year of employment as an academic — I proposed a new course, 'women and education'. I was the first, and only, woman teaching in my university's education department. Many of my male colleagues expressed grave reservations about this proposal. Some argued that their courses already covered 'women's issues' through lectures on 'stereotyping'. Others were worried that a 'narrow focus on women's issues' would be damaging for me professionally. Their most prevalent concern, however, was that there was too little 'content' upon which to base my curriculum. There was no sound theoretical or disciplinary base.

Accordingly, I set about 'reviewing the literature' — proving that there was, indeed, a discipline, a set of theories, concepts, and debates, into which my students — like those in other disciplines — could be initiated. At the same time as I was developing this curriculum, I was struggling to write a proposal for a doctoral thesis on feminist teachers. To satisfy the relevant committee, I had to position my research questions within an 'acceptable' body of theory. My literature review would serve a dual purpose — I was simultaneously positioned as an academic staff member and as a doctoral student. My teaching, and my research, would begin in a conventionally academic manner. I would draw a 'map of knowledge' which would serve as a navigation guide for my own, and my students' inquiries.

The Sociology of Women's Education — Mapping the Field

Like many of my contemporaries, I approached my task as one of 'marrying' (Hartmann, 1981), or bringing together, two fields of study — sociology of education (and/or curriculum theory) and feminist theory. Similarities were perceived between the theoretical divisions and debates which were commonly described as characteristic of sociology of education and those which feminists had identified within (academic and grassroots) women's studies. With minor variations in categorizations and terminology, those of us who published 'maps' or typologies of the discipline in the early to mid-1980s saw the sociology of women's education as characterized by three or four major sets of theoretical perspectives.

Liberal feminism (for example, Friedan, 1963) is centred on women's individual rights and opportunities. Its political aim is the equitable distribution of the genders across the various divisions of labour and throughout existing social hierarchies. Within liberal feminist educational writing (for example, Byrne, 1975), women are constituted as disadvantaged by our socialization — by 'sex-role stereotyping' — and as in need of measures of compensatory education and affirmative action. As will be illustrated in the final section of this chapter, liberal feminist arguments were readily incorporated into policy-making because they extended to 'women and girls' the kinds of ideas and strategies which were already being applied to the situation of other 'disadvantaged groups'.

More radical theories were based on a rejection of the individualism of liberal approaches which were seen as merely 'adding women in' (Yates, 1987) to hierarchies which were inherently inequitable. The more 'revolutionary' feminist analyses differed according to whether they were grounded in Marxist or in radical feminist assumptions. Marxist feminists researched the ways in which women's education served to reproduce the sexual division of labour and the class differences between women (Deem, 1978). Radical feminists, emphasizing women's oppression by men, studied how schooling reproduced women's sexual subordination and how 'patriarchal curricula' served to alienate us from our own experience (Spender, 1983). They emphasized 'essential differences' between the genders and a distinctive 'women's epistemology' based on 'interpersonal' (rather than abstract) reasoning (Gilligan, 1982). Marxist feminists criticized radical feminists' treatment of women as a homogeneous category and brought into the foreground the class differences between women. Radical feminists accused Marxists of ignoring or underemphasizing patriarchal power.

Socialist feminism emerged as a drawing together of these positions as we struggled to integrate the increasingly dominant neo-Marxist ideas in sociology with our feminist concerns. Students and teachers were studied as simultaneously, and contradictorily, positioned within the relations of class and gender (for example, Kenway, 1990). Socialist feminists developed critiques of the ways many male neo-Marxists had rendered women and girls invisible, marginal, or depicted us only through the eyes of men and boys.

These were the major theoretical tendencies which sociologists of women's education identified in the typologies which were published in key journals and textbooks during the early to mid-1980s. Many such typologies assumed this form, progressed through a similar sequence, and were written from within a socialist feminist problematic. By 'mapping our field' in this way, we conceptualized the sociology of women's education as a conventional academic discipline (for example, Acker, 1981; Arnot, 1981; Arnot and Weiner, 1987; Middleton, 1987b; Yates, 1987). With respect to our teaching in 'women and education' courses, we had produced 'curriculum content' — a 'map' of the sociology of women's education — which could be taught as 'received knowledge'. It was necessary for us to do this in order to gain approval for our courses within the university system.

As a New Zealander, I found myself 'marginal' — positioned both inside and outside the Anglo-American discourses which dominated the discipline. Finding little local writing upon which to base my curriculum, I used overseas texts. As New Zealand children's author, Margaret Mahy has expressed it (in Kedgley, 1989, p. 137), my 'reading imposed a distance between me and my natural environment'.

For example, the 'sex-role stereotype' — a passive, simpering suburban femininity — described by American liberal feminists (Friedan, 1963) was almost unrecognizable to tomboyish New Zealand girls. Liberal feminists' demand for the abolition of 'gender-roles' was antithetical to the traditional gender-differentiation in some Maori rituals. Rather than seeing such differences as oppressive, many Maori women viewed these as a source of strength (Irwin, 1992; Pere, 1988; Smith, 1992). Marxism was criticized as rendering invisible Maori people's experiences of racism and colonialism (Awatere, 1984). British socialist feminism was also 'foreign' — grounded in the experiences of a vast urban industrial proletariat with a culture very different from that of New Zealand working women. Our positioning as New Zealanders made visible the 'conceptual imperialism' (Stanley and Wise, 1983) of Western feminist theories.

Those of us 'on the margins' had long been aware that 'disciplines' are articulated to the ruling apparatus (Smith, 1987). We could not 'see ourselves' clearly in foreign texts which were grounded in the various 'master narratives' of liberalism, Marxism etc. Life-history methods — telling our own and others' stories — offered ways of 'making knowledge' which were grounded in what Sylvia Ashton-Warner (1973) called our own 'native imagery'.

As 'mainstream' northern academics began to hear the voices of those who had been inaudible within their disciplines, the older monolithic or dualistic sets of categories (for example, 'class and gender') were found to be too simplistic to work with. The 'master narratives of the disciplines' (Aronowitz and Giroux, 1991, p. 18) began to collapse. The new 'post-modernist' theories were based on a scepticism about the possibility or desirability of attempting to produce 'totalizing narratives' which 'revealed essential truths about' the world. The 'larger cultural shifts of a post-industrial, post-colonial era' (Lather, 1991, p. 5) required theories which could accommodate people's multiple and simultaneous positionings in complex, changing, and often contradictory, patterns of power-relations — between races or cultures within countries, between the Anglo-American — European nations and those of the 'third world', between indigenous populations and those descended from former colonists, between those of different sexual orientations, those of different religions, the differently abled, etc.

Post-modernists' concerns with multiplicities and differences brought into focus the location of academic and professional 'knowledges' within various multiple relations of power. For example, dominant theories in the social sciences, in educational theory and in pedagogy, are seen as conceptualizing the social world from various vantage-points of 'ruling' (Walkerdine, 1984). While scholars have traditionally been primarily concerned with the scientific 'accuracy', 'objectivity' or 'truthfulness' of their theories or disciplines, post-modernists are more interested in what Nancy Fraser (1989, p. 19) described as 'the processes, procedures, and apparatuses wherein truth, knowledge, and belief are produced'. A post-modernist perspective enables us to study *sociologically* the ways academic disciplines and their associated professional or clinical practices are complicit in the monitoring, surveillance, and regulation of populations (Foucault, 1980; Henriques *et al*, 1984). Disciplines such as sociology (including some versions of feminist sociology) have contributed theories and research data which feed into what Dorothy Smith (1990, p. 14) referred to as 'the governing of our kind of society (which) is done in abstract concepts and symbols'.

The emergence of post-modernism has major implications for our teaching of theories in the sociology of women's education. Those who use the 'flat map' approach to the teaching of theoretical typologies can 'add postmodernism' as a category to existing taxonomies. However, such theories also have major implications for the *ways* we teach theory, for our pedagogy. They raise questions about the experiential grounding, the perspectivity, of the feminist and other social theories we teach. From within a postmodernist perspective, the various feminist theoretical typologies themselves are seen as inscribed in multiple power-relations.

Some Problems with Typologies

While many have disagreed with the ways the various typologies and taxonomies have classified feminist sociological and educational theories, some post-modernists have attacked the very idea of a taxonomy. Here, I shall take up one such criticism. I shall apply to the above typology the post-modernist argument that 'to put into categories is an act of power' (Lather, 1991, p. 125).

In accordance with the conventions of Western academic rationality, I constructed my typology as if I were standing outside it, as if I were looking from an 'eye of God' position. In this, I assumed the standpoint of the scientist, the grounds from which 'sociologists have sought to practice an objectivity constituted in relation to an "Archimedian point" — that is a point external to any particular position in society' (Smith, 1987, p. 71). Such writing, however, is not 'objective'; 'I' am 'in' my text (Jones, 1992). An account such as this can be read as resting upon evolutionary, or 'progressive', assumptions — that our analyses have been getting us nearer to 'the truth'. By concluding with socialist and post-modernist feminisms, I implied that these positions are the evolutionary apex of feminist theory and thereby position myself within them. As Donna Haraway (1990) has expressed it such typologies tend 'to make one's own political tendencies appear to be the telos of the whole' (p. 198). The 'overview' I have sketched, then, is not a view 'from the skies' but is a landscape drawn from my own perspective.

When such a typology is used as a framework for curriculum design, the students are positioned 'outside' the theories. They are like spectators, looking in. Theory is presented as a map, a chart drawn by those with the expertise to depict objectively 'what is there' in the theoretical terrain. The international debates in the sociology of women's education appear to students as 'abstracted from particular participants located in particular spatio-temporal settings' (Smith, 1987, p. 61). Theories appear as disembodied and decontextualized abstractions.

We can use the kinds of insights post-modernist theories can provide without teaching the theory in a formal sense — for a premature confrontation with the vocabularies of post-modernism can terrify some undergraduate students right out of social theory. Rather than presenting theories as a flat or two-dimensional, map, we can assume a post-modernist stance as teacher-educators by demonstrating ways in which — as teachers, as students, as social researchers — we are positioned 'inside' the social and educational phenomena which are the object of our inquiries. The personal, political, and theoretical dimensions of educational experience are studied holistically. In the remainder of this chapter, I shall demonstrate ways in which I have approached my own teaching from such a perspective. However, before doing so, I shall contextualize my approach in previous discussions about the place of 'the personal' in feminist pedagogy.

Feminism, Pedagogy and the Place of 'the Personal'

Many have argued that a feminist pedagogy is a 'student-centred' pedagogy, which emphasizes the educational worthwhileness of using students' (and sometimes teachers') personal experiences as a basis for learning. Discussions of such questions can usefully be grouped into three major sets of arguments — empirical, psychological and political.

There is empirical research which supports the claim that women teachers, to a greater degree than men teachers, prefer the pedagogies which are based on students' 'personal knowledge'. For example, in a study of academic women in Massachusetts, Nadya Aisenberg and Mona Harrington (1988) noted a tendency for women's scholarship in their various disciplines to focus 'on the relation of actual daily experience to larger social or moral patterns' (p. 94). Similarly, all of the feminist school teachers in Kathleen Weiler's study 'mentioned the value of nurturance and caring in themselves and their work — values that are emphasized as positive aspects of women's experience . . .' (Weiler, 1988, p. 78). The Catholic religious and Jewish women in Kathleen Casey's thesis on feminist teachers spoke of 'a genuine care of children' as their major motivation for becoming teachers; a 'kind of attachment', argues Casey (1988, p. 225) which 'has enormous potential for progressive action'. The New Zealand feminist teachers in my own study (Middleton, 1987a and 1989) expressed similar concerns.

A second set of writers have based their arguments on psychological or psychoanalytic theories. Drawing on 'object relations' theory (for example, Gilligan, 1982), some radical feminist curriculum theorists see feminists' espousal of student-centred pedagogies as expressions of women's 'essential femininity'. For example, Madeleine Grumet (1988) has argued that, as teachers, women draw their 'experiences of reproduction and nurturance into the epistemological systems and curricular forms that constitute the discourse and practice of public education' (p. 3). Concerns with what Nel Noddings (1991) calls 'caring and interpersonal reasoning' structure such feminist, or women-centred, curricula. Such radical feminist positions have been criticized as essentialist (Grosz, 1990).

The political rationales derive from various versions of the 'consciousness-raising model', which developed in the early phases of the second wave of feminism. Consciousness-raising originated in 'grassroots' settings, and has been adapted for more academic situations. It was a technique of finding words for what Betty Friedan (1963) described as 'problems with no names', as women met in informal groups to share their 'sense of something wrong' (Mitchell, 1973) with their experiences as women in particular (usually middle-class, white, Western, urban) settings. It was a way of 'making knowledge' where no prior written records remained.

Critics argued that, within this framework, 'experience' was conceptualized as unproblematic — it was assumed that 'pure experience' could be described and was of itself valid knowledge. A politics grounded in consciousness-raising rested on 'women's experiences' to provide a basis for an oppositional 'women's knowledge' and 'feminist culture'. Such assumptions, said socialist feminists, rendered invisible the material conditions and power-relations of the wider (capitalist/patriarchal) society which 'structured' such experiences (for example, Rowbotham, 1973). What was needed, they argued, were historical and materialist analyses which would contextualize 'women's experiences' within the wider power-dynamics in which they had come to form. Socialist feminism (a combination of Marxism and feminism) could help us locate our biographies within the wider, oppressive, power-relations of gender and class. The 'teaching of theory' was an aid to liberation.

Some such feminist arguments were influenced by theoretical shifts within the wider, and 'overlapping', disciplines of the sociology of education and curriculum theory. During the early to mid-1980s — the years when the sociology of women's education was in its formative stages as a discipline — the increasingly dominant neo-Marxist perspectives in the sociology of education had constituted educational institutions primarily as sites of social and cultural reproduction. Rejecting the liberal view that schools and tertiary institutions were agents of social mobility and human emancipation, many sociologists had studied how such institutions constructed and reproduced the oppressive power-relations of class, racism and gender in the wider society. As intending, preservice, or practising teachers, many students found the reproduction theories profoundly depressing. If the educational institutions in which they studied and taught merely reproduced existing social and cultural inequalities, they as teachers were mere agents of oppression and preservers of privilege.

Perhaps partly as a response to the pessimism of 'reproduction theories', many 'left' and feminist educators paid increasing attention in their writing to 'radical' (or 'critical') pedagogy. They argued that radical teachers could make visible to students the patterns of power-relations which constrained their own and others' lives and could help make audible the voices of students from oppressed and marginalized groups. Writers such as Giroux (1982) suggested that teacher-educators could teach their students life-history techniques to enable them, as prospective teachers, to develop 'the concepts and methods to delve into their own biographies, to look at the sedimented history they carry around, and to learn how one's cultural capital represents a dialectical interplay between experience and history' (p. 24).

Recently, some feminists have expressed reservations about the usefulness of critical pedagogy. Although they recommended teaching techniques which required students to analyze their lives, many 'critical pedagogues' rendered invisible their own biographies (for example, Giroux, 1986). Similarly, 'reproduction theorists', who may themselves have been of 'educationally marginalized' backgrounds and yet have been empowered and politicized by means of their own education, usually bracketed out in their writing the conditions of their own intellectual production. Feminists noted a kind of evangelical tendency in 'critical' pedagogies which positioned radical (including feminist) teachers as conduits to revealed truths about students' and others' oppressions (Ellsworth, 1989; Lather, 1991; Miller, 1990).

Somewhat ironically, this was also true of some feminist post-structuralist writers — authors such as Chris Weedon (1987) positioned themselves as 'masters of truth and justice' (Lather, 1991), as knowers or revealers of the truth about others' oppression, through addressing such questions at a purely rationalist level — omitting to mention the problem of what made their own ideas possible. As Linda Nicholson (1990) has argued, academic feminism has shared the

> failure, common to many forms of academic scholarship, to recognize the embeddedness of its own assumptions within a specific historical context. Like many other modern western scholars, feminists were not used to acknowledging that the premises from which they were working possessed a specific location. (p. 1)

A Life-history Approach to Feminist Pedagogy

If we are to take seriously such post-modern insights about relationships between our 'feminist educational knowledge' and power, we must 'problematize' our own perspectives — make visible to, and explore with, our students those aspects of our own life-histories which impact upon our teaching. We must analyze relationships between our individual biographies, historical events and the broader power relations which have shaped and constrained our possibilities and perspectives as educators. As Elizabeth Ellsworth (1989) has argued, 'a relation between teachers/students becomes voyeuristic when the voice of the pedagogue . . . goes unexamined' (p. 312). Our academic perspectives are viewed as historically, socially, and biographically constructed. The everyday world is viewed as 'problematic' (Smith, 1987) and is studied as that in which our research and pedagogical questions originate.

A Teacher's Voice

To give you an example, I should like to invite you into my undergraduate 'women and education' classroom. It is the first class in the twelve-week course. There are about forty undergraduate students. The majority are teacher-trainees, taking this course as part of their education major.[2] A few are taking it as part of the women's studies programme. While some of the 'education' students (and all of the women's studies students) identify themselves as feminists, some are suspicious of, or hostile to, feminism. For example, one student described her image of feminism as 'some strange type of religion which only women belong to. Some of their (feminists') characteristics are hairy bodies, wearing lots of purple and necklaces with "the symbol". They enjoy hating men and do body building.'[3] The majority of the students are Pakeha (New Zealand-born white); some are Maori or of Pacific Islands descent. The majority are in their early twenties.

I begin this first session of the course with slides — images from my own school exercise books and childhood paintings produced in the late 1950s and early 1960s in New Zealand — in a rural primary school and a state girls' secondary school in a provincial town. These give access to my 'native imagery' — to my interpretations of the world in which I grew up and to my dreams, wishes and fantasies. They are of interest in this course not as personal memorabilia, but as examples of ways in which the 'grand narratives' and historical events of my childhood and adolescence contributed to the development of my adult perspective as a feminist educator. More broadly, they identify several of the generative themes of the academic women's studies created by my (post-World War Two) generation of Pakeha academic feminists. They depict an experiential basis for the feminist theories we came to adopt and develop as adults. I shall share with you three of these slides.[4]

The first illustrates my positioning in the 'grand narrative' of colonialism as reproduced in my childhood reading of the social studies curriculum in the late 1950s (McGeorge, 1981). This was the title page of an 11-year-old rural schoolgirls' social studies exercise book in 1959. The 'good ship social studies' bears — in descending order — the signs of the Christian cross, the British crown, the Union Jack. God, King, Country. On the beach stand 'hostile natives' — black men in grass skirts brandishing spears. What counted as 'school knowledge' (the social studies curriculum) rendered legitimate this 'way of knowing' colonization. Indigenous peoples were constituted as 'other'. We learned about the history of exploration — how Europe 'discovered' and 'took possession' of much of the rest of the world. The poems we studied reinforced the ideology of 'our glorious empire' and male battles. We learned that New Zealand had been part of this process. However, during the years of my schooling — the 1950s and early 1960s — it was believed that modern New Zealand was a truly egalitarian society. We were taught that equal rights and opportunities for Maori and Pakeha had been guaranteed in 1840 with the signing of the Treaty of Waitangi by Maori chiefs and the colonial government.

At primary school colonial power-relations were taken for granted. We never questioned them. However, during our secondary schooling, 'our

glorious empire' was to collapse. These momentous changes led many of my generation to question taken-for-granted ideas about the 'nature' of 'races' and the legitimacy of Pakeha domination.

It has proved very useful to discuss in classes these 1950s images of a child's interpretation of colonial relations. This was particularly true in 1990, for this marked the sesquicentenary of the signing of the Treaty. Unlike Australia, which had marked its bicentenary with a huge celebration, New Zealand 'commemorated' rather than 'celebrated' its anniversary. For many Maori, as for Australian Aborigines, the birth of the colonial state was not cause for celebration. The 1980s had seen strong protests by Maori that the Treaty had not been honoured, that they had been dispossessed of their lands, forests, and fisheries. The Treaty became one of New Zealand's most contested political issues. Today it is used as a basis for arguing for Maori people's rights to be educated in the Maori language and to cultural autonomy.

In New Zealand university education and women's studies courses, as in other educational and feminist settings, the Treaty has been a central issue of debate. Issues of Maori–Pakeha relations and biculturalism have become

increasingly prominent in New Zealand Pakeha feminist theory, and in women's studies courses (Smith, chapter 3 in this volume). New Zealand students are helped through this exercise to position themselves (variously, and multiply — for example, as middle-class and Maori and female) within the power-relations of colonialism.

The next group of slides (one of which is reproduced here) are indicative of the 'possibilities and constraints' experienced by Pakeha rural girls of the time and place. In these childhood impressions of everyday life in a rural town in the 1950s clear gender relations are apparent in the work force. Access to certain kinds of technical knowledge and occupations was not at that time seen as suitable for girls. For example, this painting of a shearing shed suggests a great fascination with machines and technology. As the daughter of a stock agent (a person who buys and sells livestock on behalf of farmers), I was around farms and machinery a great deal. In this painting, the men are doing the shearing — handling the machines — while the women clean up. To be able to take the 'academic' subjects which had at the time high status (Latin and French), I had to leave home and board at a state girls' school in a nearby provincial city. During this time in our adolescence, 'sexuality' became an important concern. 'Sexuality' and 'intellectuality' were often constituted as being in conflict or contradiction, as is evident from this painting done when I was a junior at the boarding hostel. 'Seniors swotting' shows girls reading

'love comics', setting one another's hair in rollers and perfecting their suntans. ('Swotting' was our term for 'cramming' for exams). Such pictures are helpful in exploring the ways in which young girls of my age-group and class were constituted as 'gendered subjects' (Henriques *et al*, 1984) within the 'regulatory apparatus' of the time. Drawing on a feminist reading of key education policy texts, as well as other women's life-histories and empirical research (Middleton, 1987a), I show how, as children of the post-World War II baby boom, we were members of the first generation to be *promised* equality of opportunity in education. Children of both sexes, all races and classes were promised 'equal opportunities' to what the policy-makers had described as 'a free education of the kind for which he is best fitted and to the fullest extent of his powers' (cited in Beeby, 1986, p. xxxii). The promise was one of 'meritocracy'.

However, at the same time, it was believed that the morality, stability and cohesion of society rested on women's domesticity. Girls' experiences, then, were contradictory. On the one hand, within the discourse of liberal individualism, we were educable, potentially rational and autonomous, individuals who were to be accorded equal opportunities with men. On the other hand, within the 'pre-feminist'[5] assumptions of patriarchy, our domesticity within the patriarchal nuclear family (with the husband/father as 'breadwinner') was essential to the maintenance of social cohesion and stability. Our education, and our socialization, would prepare us for our 'natural functions' as wives and mothers. Our intellectuality and our feminine heterosexuality were constituted as contradictory.

In this early stage of the course, I use my own constructed account of my own educational life-history, previous research, other women's stories, and key 'official' policy documents of the time to suggest ways we can connect 'the personal, the theoretical, and the political'. Such combinations of materials can show clearly how certain gendered sociological assumptions have been productive of specific professional practices or 'technologies of the social' (Henriques *et al*, 1984) which have served to classify, regulate, and rank students. The use of personal texts can help us to avoid the deterministic assumptions which can be made when, for example, theoretical and policy texts alone are used as curriculum content. For example, my own generation of feminist teachers did not become mere passive victims of our socialization. We were creative strategists who resisted and resolved the contradictions we experienced. For some of us, such contradictions — together with the alternative possibilities our historical circumstances made visible to us — were generative of our feminism (Middleton, 1987a, 1989 and 1993).

Students' Assignments

Students keep a diary during the first half of the course. In their 'responses' to my slide presentation, and in their written reactions to various set readings, many choose to write about their own experiences. I do not require them to write autobiographies because I respect their right to privacy. I do not wish to 'pry', to engage in the monitoring and surveillance of their private lives (Foucault, 1980). I do not wish to be what Ellsworth (1989) termed a pedagogical 'voyeur'.

However, after the session on my own schooling, I run one class based on the students' 'official personal' texts — photographs, school reports, exercise books — an 'archaeology of our schooling'. As 'official records' these 'depersonalize', objectify, make public aspects of personal biographies. Because I have used such artifacts as part of my own biographical narrative — made aspects of my schooling visible to them — the students do not seem shy about doing this. They choose whether, or what, to provide. We discuss these documents in small groups whose membership is determined by the age of the student. This enables the younger students (aged 19 or 20) to speak freely — many in previous years had felt intimidated by what they saw as the greater experience of the mature students.

As a woman in her early forties I found that my own life-history and my writing about the radicalization of post-war feminist teachers spoke to the mature students, but alienated, constituted as 'other', some of the younger students. I try to provide for them a space in which my generation's analysis and experience does not silence or distort theirs. Within the groups the students discuss how their educations were similar to, and different from, one another. We then 'report back' and bring together the experiences and documents from the different generations. This becomes a basis, a grounding for our theorizing during the course.

The students then undertake a research assignment on women's educational life-histories. They are required to interview two women with at least a twenty-year age gap between them. They are to compare and contrast the two women's experiences of education, taking into account not only their individual biographies, but the historical events, educational policies and provisions, and the relevant power-relations (for example, race, class, gender, town/country) characteristic of the time and place. In C. Wright Mills' (1959) terms, the focus of the assignment is simultaneously on 'biography, history, and social structure'.

The use of life-history methods as pedagogical techniques can help teachers and students understand the circumstances of one another's possibilities. In our feminist pedagogies, as Dorothy Smith (1987) has argued with respect to sociology, 'Opening an inquiry from the standpoint of women means accepting our ineluctable embeddedness in the same world as is the object of our inquiry' (p. 127).

Teaching About Educational Policies 'From the Inside'

Many of our students, especially younger women without teaching experience, feel alienated, not only by theory, but also by talk about policy, which they see as dull conversations and texts produced by grey-suited men in remote offices. Life-history techniques can make policy 'three-dimensional' as students study the educational 'choices' of individual women of their own and other generations as contextualized in the constraints and possibilities of their circumstances and come to see the part played by policy-makers in these. As 'discourses', educational 'theories' and policies are constitutive of our subjectivities. As sociologists of women's education, we are positioned within, produced by, and productive of, that which is the object of our inquiries.

While my own schooling was shaped by 'pre-feminist' education policies, that of many of my younger students took place during the 1970s, a time when the second wave of feminism was influencing the kinds of 'choices' offered to girls and boys in schools. However, issues of racism, sexism and contradictions between 'the intellectual and the sexual' come through strongly in many of the younger students' oral and written comments. For example, one young woman wrote of her experiences in a woodwork class: 'I remember purposefully getting things wrong so that the boys would come to my aid and help me. I got the attention I wanted, but I also reinforced the notion that girls were clumsy, needed help and aid when attempting male subjects.' Unlike the women of my generation, this younger student had the 'insider's knowledge' of a former pupil whose educational experiences were shaped within a feminist-inspired 'equal opportunities' policy in a school in the early 1970s. Such students position themselves 'inside' feminist-inspired education policy.

To teach about more recent policy changes (the educational restructuring of the late 1980s and 1990s), I rely on the discourse analysis of key policy documents. Rather than approach the teaching of the various feminist theoretical perspectives as a 'flat map', I focus on the ways various feminist theories have become 'articulated to the ruling apparatus' in the New Zealand setting — become tools of the policy-makers. The various feminisms (liberal, radical, Marxist, etc) are studied sociologically. 'Feminisms' are conceptualized as historically, and variously, located within the broader political configurations and institutional apparatus of New Zealand education.

Many previous feminist writers have discussed the ways in which various versions of 'liberal feminism' have been incorporated into educational, and other social, policy. The more radical versions of feminism are seen as having had less influence on, as being incompatible with, the central projects and perspectives of, policy-makers. The various 'feminisms', then, are seen as being of 'unequal weight and power' within the political configurations of the wider society (Haraway, 1990; Weedon, 1987). New Zealand provides a particularly dramatic example of the ways different forms of feminism have been articulated to, and marginalized by, various apparatus of state policy-making during rapid changes of government. Our experiences provide particularly useful 'content' for the teaching of post-modern insights about relationships between feminist theories and power. For the benefit of overseas readers, I shall briefly outline these political and theoretical shifts.

New Zealand's Fourth Labour Government (1984–1990) undertook a radical restructuring of school administration. Following recommendations in a document which has become popularly known as the 'Picot Report' (Taskforce to Review Educational Administration, 1988), policy-makers devolved responsibility for many major educational decisions from central government authorities to elected school boards of trustees. The powers of the boards were listed in school charters, which contained detailed statements of broad objectives and specific goals. School successes and failures in achieving these were to be monitored regularly by state Educational Review Officers.

New Zealand's 'left-wing' critics identified similarities between these reforms and those in Britain, North America, and Australia (Lauder and Wylie, 1990). They claimed that 'new right' economic discourses were having an undue influence — that the language of competitiveness, efficiency, effectiveness, and accountability dominated the new educational policies. Education was being increasingly conceptualized as primarily an economic (not a social, political or moral) activity. An extreme form of liberal individualism in which the role of the state was minimal was being put forward.

However, alongside its libertarian economic policy, the Labour government had also made a strong commitment to 'equity'. In contrast to the individualistic free-market ideas which have been so frequently described as characterizing the educational reforms, Labour's view of 'equity' involved conceptualizing the population as groups. Certain groups (rather than individuals) were seen as having been disadvantaged educationally — through no fault of their own — in the past. Compensation was owed. Schooling became a site for the bringing about of 'compensatory justice' (O'Neill, 1977). 'Equity objectives' were to 'underpin all school activities' (Ministry of Education, 1989, p. 8).

During 1989 and 1990, the boards of trustees of all educational institutions were required to write their charters. In this, they were — in the words of the school charter guidelines — to ensure that their

> policies and practices seek to achieve equitable educational outcomes for students of both sexes, for rural and urban students; for students from all religions, ethnic, cultural, social, family and class backgrounds, and for all students irrespective of their ability or disability. (*ibid*)

With respect to gender, school boards of trustees were required to develop specific targets for bringing about equal opportunities, to provide role-models along non-sexist lines, to develop a non-sexist and non-racist curriculum, and to provide freedom from sexual harassment. Boards were also required to develop policies on biculturalism: 'The board of trustees accepts an obligation to develop policies and practices which reflect New Zealand's dual cultural heritage' (*ibid*, p. 6).

The belief that state 'intervention' is necessary to achieve equal opportunities between individuals is characteristic of liberal feminism. Measures of 'affirmative action' are seen as 'compensation' for disadvantage. The requirements to develop 'non-sexist and non-racist curricula' are somewhat more radical as they raise questions about the nature of knowledge and the possibility of 'feminine' and 'culturally pluralist' epistemologies. The requirement to address issues of sexual harassment challenges the taken-for-granted behaviours of many men and raises radical questions about relations between the genders. Labour's policies, then, embodied strong liberal feminist and radical feminist assumptions. Both liberal and radical feminisms had become inscribed within an apparatus for the surveillance, monitoring and regulation of the population.

However, in October 1990, New Zealand had a general election and Labour was defeated by a landslide majority. During the election campaign, Lockwood Smith (now Minister of Education) announced that 'Under National schools will be free to renegotiate their charters if they wish to do so. They will no longer be compelled to adhere to Labour's "Orwellian" social agenda' (NZ National Party, 1990b, p. 8). During the first weeks of its administration, the National Party announced that 'equity provisions' in educational institutions were to be optional.

In contrast to the National Party's view of society as consisting of autonomous competitive individuals, Labour's 'collectivist' requirements to bring about social equity for disadvantaged groups were constituted as 'social engineering'. In describing their paramount educational aim as being the creation of an 'enterprise culture', the National Party constituted education as an economic, not a social, activity (Middleton, 1992a). During the early months of 1991, the National government attacked other women-oriented social policies: pay equity legislation (based on the radical feminist notion of 'equal pay for work of equal value') was repealed and social welfare benefits cut.

Within New Zealand's ruling apparatus, liberal and radical feminist discourses are power-differentiated and unequal (Haraway, 1990; Weedon, 1987). A 'non-interventionist' liberal 'equal opportunities' position — one of allowing both sexes 'freedom of choice' of available options — is compatible with the free market model espoused by conservative or libertarian right governments. A more interventionist (liberal and feminist) model of affirmative action and compensation may become — and has been in the New Zealand setting — a site of struggle between sexual conservatives and those espousing more interventionist positions (for example, Labour Party politicians). A radical feminist approach — which challenges both the sexual power and the epistemological authority of men — is less likely to enter the discursive practices of governing and, if it does, as in New Zealand, is particularly vulnerable in a new-right or conservative backlash.

As teachers, my students are likely to find themselves involved in struggles over their schools' charters. They will need a knowledge and understanding, as well as an opinion on, the theoretical assumptions and the political dynamics which are shaping the institutional settings within which they work. They are 'positioned inside' the feminist debates which, in a course on the 'sociology of women's education', are their topic of study. It is important, then, that we continue to teach the various 'feminist theories.' However, such teaching need not take the traditional form of the 'flat map' which position students as spectators, but can be approached as 'three-dimensional', from our various points of view as 'insiders'.

Conclusion

Like other feminist methodologies, a post-modern feminist pedagogy is subversive to traditional social science approaches which, following the dictates of 'natural science', have required what Dorothy Smith (1987, p. 146) referred to as 'the suppression of the personal'. Because such a 'scientific' world-view is said to be detached from the social world and to provide an objective, bird's-eye view of reality, researchers and teachers are required within such a tradition to 'begin outside ourselves'. Women's studies' reliance on 'the personal' is antithetical to such approaches and its apparent 'subjectivity' has frequently been used in the past by academic gatekeepers as a basis for its exclusion from, or devaluation within, what counts as high-status or 'proper' academic knowledge. For example, making visible to students aspects of one's own biography lays the feminist academic open to accusations (from students as well as colleagues) of being unscholarly. Developing a feminist pedagogy can involve taking professional, as well as personal, risks.

We can reduce such risks by giving our practices a strong theoretical base. In this chapter, I have used post-modernist theory to help develop such a position. However, to my New Zealand undergraduate students, most post-modernist theoretical texts appear as abstracted conversations between overseas intellectuals — feminism receding into terrifying reifications. For post-modernism — the perspective which seeks to deconstruct relations between knowledge and power — is itself 'articulated to the ruling apparatuses' and can become an instrument for the perpetuation of academic conceptual imperialism.

I have argued that, at undergraduate level, we can use post-modernist insights without directly teaching the theory. To develop pedagogies which are authentic to our personal and collective histories, we must explore the ideas and imagery which are indigenous to our circumstances — geographical, cultural, historical and material, generational. This provides teachers and students with ways of understanding how our own subjectivities have been constituted and with means of making visible the alienations which can result from interpretations of our personal and collective histories purely through the eyes of theorists whose perspectives have arisen elsewhere.

Notes

1 By 'radical' I include both 'critical pedagogy' (for example, Giroux, 1982) and feminist pedagogy.

2 The BEd degree has been jointly taught by university and teachers' college staff. As part of the 'education major' my course is 'academic'. I am not involved with the teaching practice side of the students' professional training.
3 The students' comments used in this paper are excerpts from Middleton (1993).
4 The full text of this lecture — including additional pictures — is in Middleton (1992b). The complete text is also contained, and a detailed theoretical rationale developed, in Middleton (1993).
5 By 'pre-feminist' sociological theories, I mean those 'master narratives' in the sociology of women's education, such as the various forms of functionalism which dominated the field in the 1950s and 1960s (Friedan, 1963), which constituted women according to patriarchal or sexist assumptions (see Middleton, 1993).

References

ACKER, S. (1981) 'No-woman's land: British sociology of education 1960–1979', *Sociological Review*, **29**, 1, pp. 77–104.

AISENBERG, N. and HARRINGTON, M. (1988) *Women of Academe: Outsiders in the Sacred Grove*, Amherst, MA, University of Massachusetts Press.

ARNOT, M. (1981) 'Culture and political economy: Dual perspectives in the sociology of women's education', *Educational Analysis*, **3**, 1, pp. 97–116.

ARNOT, M. and WEINER, G. (Eds) (1987) *Gender and the Politics of Schooling*, London, Hutchinson.

ARONOWITZ, S. and GIROUX, H. (1991) *Postmodern Education*, Minneapolis, MN, University of Minnesota Press.

ASHTON-WARNER, S. (1973) *Teacher*, New York, Simon and Shuster.

AWATERE, D. (1984) *Maori Sovereignty*, Auckland, Broadsheet Books.

BEEBY, C.E. (1986) 'Introduction to W.L. Renwick', *Moving Targets*, Wellington, NZ Council for Educational Research.

BYRNE, E. (1975) *Women and Education*, London, Tavistock.

CASEY, K. (1988) 'Teacher as author: Life-history narratives for contemporary women teachers working for social change', DPhil dissertation, Department of Curriculum and Instruction, University of Wisconsin, Madison.

DEEM, R. (1978) *Women and Schooling*, London, Routledge and Kegan Paul.

ELLSWORTH, E. (1989) 'Why doesn't this feel empowering? Working through the repressive myths of critical pedagogy', *Harvard Educational Review*, **59**, 3, pp. 297–324.

FOUCAULT, M. (1980) *A History of Sexuality, Volume One*, New York, Vintage.

FRASER, N. (1989) *Unruly Practices: Power, Discourse and Gender in Contemporary Social Theory*, Minneapolis, MN, University of Minnesota Press.

FRIEDAN, B. (1963) *The Feminine Mystique*, Harmondsworth, Penguin.

GILLIGAN, C. (1982) *In a Different Voice*, Cambridge, MA, Harvard University Press.

GIROUX, H. (1982) *Ideology, Culture, and the Practice of Schooling*, Philadelphia, PA, Temple.

GIROUX, H. (1986) 'Radical pedagogy and the politics of student voice', *Interchange*, **17**, pp. 48–69.

GREENE, M. (1986) 'In search of a critical pedagogy', *Harvard Educational Review*, **56**, 4, pp. 427–41.

GROSZ, E. (1990) 'Conclusion: A note on essentialism and difference' in GUNEW, S. (Ed.) *Feminist Knowledge*, London, Routledge.

GRUMET, M. (1988) *Bitter Milk: Women and Teaching*, Amherst, MA, University of Massachusetts Press.

HARAWAY, D. (1990) 'A manifesto for cyborgs: Science, technology, and socialist feminism in the 1980s' in NICHOLSON, L. (Ed.) *Feminism/Post-modernism*, New York, Routledge.

HARTMANN, H. (1981) 'The unhappy marriage between Marxism and feminism: Towards a more progressive union' in SERGENT, L. (Ed.) *Women and Revolution*, Boston, MA, South End.

HENRIQUES, J., HOLLWAY, W., URWIN, C., VENN, C. and WALKERDINE, V. (1984) *Changing the Subject*, London, Methuen.

IRWIN, K. (1992) 'Towards theories of Maori feminisms' in DU PLESSIS, R. *et al* (Eds) *Feminist Voices: Women's Studies Texts For Aotearoa/New Zealand*, Auckland, Oxford University Press.

JONES, A. (1992) 'Writing feminist educational research: Am 'I' in the text?' in MIDDLETON, S. and JONES, A. (Eds) *Women and Education in Aotearoa 2*, Wellington, Bridget Williams Books.

KEDGLEY, S. (Ed.) (1989) *Her Own Country*, Auckland, Penguin.

KENWAY, J. (1990) 'Privileged girls, private schools and the culture of "success"' in KENWAY, J. and WILLIS, S. (Eds) *Hearts and Minds: Self-esteem and the Schooling of Girls*, Lewes, Falmer Press.

LATHER, P. (1991) *Getting Smart*, New York, Routledge.

LAUDER, H. and WYLIE, C. (Eds) (1990) *Towards Successful Schooling*, Lewes, Falmer Press.

MACDONALD, M. (1980) 'Sociocultural reproduction and women's education' in DEEM, R. (Ed.) *Schooling For Women's Work*, London, Routledge and Kegan Paul.

MCGEORGE, C. (1981) 'Race and the Maori in the New Zealand school curriculum since 1877', *Australia and NZ Journal of History*, **10**, 1, pp. 13–23.

MIDDLETON, S. (1987a) 'Schooling and radicalisation: Life histories of New Zealand feminist teachers', *British Journal of Sociology of Education*, **8**, 2, pp. 169–89.

MIDDLETON, S. (1987b) 'The sociology of women's education as a field of academic study' in ARNOT, M. and WEINER, G. (Eds) *Gender and the Politics of Schooling*, London, Hutchinson.

MIDDLETON, S. (1989) 'Educating feminists: A life-history study' in ACKER, S. (Ed.) *Teachers, Gender, and Careers*, Lewes, Falmer Press.

MIDDLETON, S. (1992a) 'Gender equity and school charters — Some theoretical and political questions for the 1990s' in MIDDLETON, S. and JONES, A. (Eds) *Women and Education in Aotearoa 2*, Wellington, Bridget Williams Books.

MIDDLETON, S. (1992b) 'Towards an indigenous women's studies for Aotearoa' in DU PLESSIS, R. *et al* (Eds) *Feminist Voices: Women's Studies Texts for Aotearoa/New Zealand*, Auckland, Oxford University Press.

MIDDLETON, S. (1993) *Educating Feminists: Life Histories and Pedagogy*, New York, Teachers College Press.

MILLER, J. (1990) *Creating Spaces and Finding Voices: Teachers Collaborating for Empowerment*, Albany, NY, SUNY Press.

MILLS, C. WRIGHT (1959) *The Sociological Imagination*, Harmondsworth, Penguin.

MINISTRY OF EDUCATION (1989) *Charter Guidelines for Schools*, Wellington, Government Printer.

MITCHELL, J. (1973) *Woman's Estate*, Harmondsworth, Penguin.

NEW ZEALAND NATIONAL PARTY (1990a) *National: Investing in Achievement*, abridged version of National's Education Policy, released by Lockwood Smith, 5 May.

NEW ZEALAND NATIONAL PARTY (1990b) *National Party Policies For the 1990s: Creating a Decent Society*, (election manifesto), Wellington.

NICHOLSON, L. (1990) 'Introduction' to NICHOLSON, L. (Ed.) *Feminism/Post-mcdernism*, New York, Routledge.

NODDINGS, N. (1991) 'Stories in dialogue: Caring and interpersonal reasoning' in WITHERELL, C. and NODDINGS, N. (Eds) *Stories Lives Tell: Narrative and Dialogue in Education*, New York, Teachers College Press.

O'NEILL, O. (1977) 'How do we know when opportunities are equal?' in VETTERLING-BRAGGIN, M. *et al* (Eds) *Feminism and Philosophy*, Totowa, NJ, Littlefield Adams.

PERE, R.R. (1988) 'Te wheke: whaia te maramatanga me te aroha' in MIDDLETON, S. (Ed.) *Women and Education in Aotearoa*, Wellington, Allen and Unwin/Port Nicholson.

ROWBOTHAM, S. (1973) *Woman's Consciousness, Man's World*, London, Penguin.

SMITH, D. (1987) *The Everyday World As Problematic*, Boston, MA, Northeastern University Press.

SMITH, D. (1990) *The Conceptual Practices of Power: A Feminist Sociology of Knowledge*, Toronto, University of Toronto Press.

SMITH, L. (1992) 'Maori women: Discourses, projects, and mana wahine' in DU PLESSIS, R. *et al* (Eds) *Feminist Voices*, Auckland, Oxford University Press.

SPENDER, D. (1983) *Invisible Women: The Schooling Scandal*, London, Writers and Readers Cooperative.

STANLEY, L. and WISE, S. (1983) *Breaking Out: Feminist Consciousness and Feminist Research*, London, Routledge and Kegan Paul.

TASKFORCE TO REVIEW EDUCATIONAL ADMINISTRATION (1988) *Education For Excellence* ('Picot Report'), Wellington, Government Printer.

WALKERDINE, V. (1984) 'Developmental psychology and the child-centred pedagogy: The insertion of Piaget into early childhood education' in HENRIQUES, J. *et al* (Eds) *Changing the Subject*, London, Methuen.

WEEDON, C. (1987) *Feminist Practice and Post-Structuralist Theory*, New York, Basil Blackwell.

WEILER, K. (1988) *Women Teaching For Change: Gender, Class, and Power*, New York, Bergin and Garvey.

YATES, L. (1987) 'Theorizing inequality today', *British Journal of Sociology of Education*, **7**, 2, pp. 119–34.

Chapter 7

Contradictions in Terms: Women Academics in British Universities

Sandra Acker

This chapter asks two deceptively simple questions: How can we best conceptualize the situation of women academics in British universities? How can we change it? Having spent my working life as a woman academic and sociologist of education and gender, I have strong personal and intellectual interests in these questions. For nineteen years I taught in a British university. My move to Canada was in part a search for a more nourishing environment for women, for feminists and for women's studies scholars.

There is, of course, the view that there is no real problem. Otherwise, the 'problem' can be variously located: in sex-typed socialization; family-career conflicts; under-investment in women's education; sex discrimination and career structures; the workings of capitalism and patriarchy. I shall discuss these perspectives in the context of feminist theory — that is, ways of understanding gender relations and the structural subordination of women — as theory helps to group the 'explanations' and to extend our thinking. I shall use the familiar divisions of liberal, socialist and radical feminism, recognizing that they are much-criticized for making artificial distinctions which divide the women's movement (Delmar, 1986); for failing to include the full range of women's experiences, especially the experiences of black women (Carby, 1982); for making overstated claims to be essential truths (Fraser and Nicholson, 1990). For me, these theoretical approaches are heuristically useful, both in describing the dominant discourse about women academics (which, if feminist at all, is liberal feminist) and in pointing to ways in which our conceptualizations, arguments and strategies might be extended by drawing upon socialist feminist and radical feminist perspectives.

In recent years, feminist writers have furiously debated how differences among women can be simultaneously accorded the respect and analytical importance they deserve without destroying the integrity of the concept of 'woman' upon which much of feminism as a political practice rests (Hirsch and Keller, 1990). Yet ways in which 'differences' among women academics are typically construed can be rather limited, as, for example, when confined to comparisons of those who are more or less successful in achieving publications or promotions (Davis and Astin, 1990). Feminist work can become more sensitive to diversity when it crosses national borders, as in this collection. Certainly women's position within higher education responds to particular social, cultural and economic forces (Moore, 1987). Feminism itself takes different forms in different countries (Gelb, 1989; Eisenstein, 1991).

I begin my discussion by summarizing some of the statistics on academics which demonstrate the differential positions typically occupied by women and men in the hierarchical structures of British universities.[1] The statistics confirm that a problem, indeed, exists. In the main body of the chapter, I examine the three major forms of feminist theory in terms of their contribution to an adequate conceptualization of the situation of women academics. I also look at some 'missing links', areas where scholarship is underdeveloped yet required for further progress on this topic. I argue that while the typical rhetoric about women's place in the university derives from liberal feminism, other theoretical approaches are necessary if we are to grasp why resistance to change is so deep-seated. Designation of some theoretical approaches as providing better explanatory frameworks than others does not, however, preclude the use of political strategies derived from less-satisfactory frameworks.

Documenting the Differences

Among academics in Britain, women are not only a minority but disproportionately in lower ranks and in less secure posts. In 1988/89, women were about 19 per cent of all full-time academics in universities (UFC, 1990). The figures can be broken into two subsets, as shown in table 7.1: those faculty who teach and are expected to do research as part of their normal work (termed 'traditional academics' in the table) and those who do 'research only'. Women are much more likely than men to be in the second category, so much so that the 19 per cent figure becomes misleading: women are 31.1 per cent of the research-only group but only 13.4 per cent of those following traditional university careers. Even this figure of 13.4 per cent obscures subject variations. Women are 26.6 per cent of the 'traditional academics' in language, literature and area studies and 22.9 per cent of those in education. At the other extreme they are 6.1 per cent of academics in biology, mathematics and physical science and an even smaller 3.3 per cent of those in engineering and technology (*ibid*, p. 77).

Table 7.1 Distribution of academic staff across ranks by sex, Great Britain 1988–89

	Percentages			
	Traditional academics		Research only	
Rank	Men	Women	Men	Women
Professor	15.2	3.2	0.8	0.1
Reader/Senior Lecturer	29.3	16.4	3.3	1.6
Lecturer	54.9	76.2	67.0	55.8
Other	0.6	4.2	29.0	42.6
TOTAL (%)	100.0	100.0	100.0	100.0
TOTAL N	(27,371)	(4,231)	(10,119)	(4,561)

Source: Universities Funding Council, 1990. (All figures are rounded up).

Most of the people in the research-only group are on contracts, which means their salaries come from bodies outside the universities, such as research councils. Their job security only extends for the duration of their contract, which might be as short as six months. For some, a succession of contracts constitutes a career. Contract researchers are often excluded from other academic employee benefits such as maternity leave and are not always well-integrated into departmental life. The contract research sector, which now contains about a third of full-time academics, is the growth area in British universities, up from around 5,000 in 1972 to 14,000 in the late 1980s (Rees, 1989; UFC, 1990).

Do women in the traditional career lines fare any better? In British universities, the lectureship is the so-called career grade. Above it in rank are readerships and senior lectureships, different from one another on promotion criteria but equivalent on salary scale. Readerships and senior lectureships are usually internal promotions, with a restricted number available each year in each institution. Only a small proportion of British academics achieves the rank of professor. There are rarely more than one or two in a department and apart from a small number of 'personal chairs', more can be hired only when a position is vacant. The system does not favour women. Among men, 15.2 per cent are professors and 29.3 per cent readers or senior lecturers; among women, 3.2 per cent are professors and 16.4 per cent readers or senior lecturers.

Figures such as those in table 7.1 tell us what proportion of each sex reaches a given academic rank. They give us an indication of career chances for each sex. Our other option is to show the relative proportions of each rank that are held by women and men. The two options give us different information. If women are severely under-represented in the academic population as a whole, then even if most were to rise to the top level, they would remain a small proportion of that grade.

Table 7.2 Representation of women and men in each rank, Great Britain, 1988–89

	Percentages			
	Professor	Reader/ senior lecturer	Lecturer	Other
Men	96.9	92.1	82.3	46.9
Women	3.1	7.9	17.7	53.1
TOTAL (%)	100.0	100.0	100.0	100.0
TOTAL N	(4,307)	(8,720)	(18,233)	(337)

Source: Universities Funding Council, 1990. 'Research only' staff are not included in this table.

Table 7.2 shows the figures arranged accordingly. It gives us an idea of what the outside world sees. Nearly all professors in Britain are men; men also hold the vast majority of other senior positions. The impact of the imbalance on British academic life is extreme, especially when combined with tendencies towards hierarchy and elitism still found within many of the universities. Professors in British universities are the people who head departments, represent the university to the government, serve on working parties, act as external examiners, make hiring and promotion decisions. In many universities the numbers of women professors can literally be counted on the fingers of one hand, while the men number in the hundreds. When I left my British university post in December 1990, only two women there were professors. The number has since increased to four.

Explanations and Strategies

What needs to be explained is why we find women academics so relatively disadvantaged and men so firmly in control — why we have a man-centred university (Rich, 1979) with some women in it. The literature on academic women in Britain is rather sparse, probably reflecting a tendency to consider them members of an elite rather than a disadvantaged group worthy of feminist concern (Acker, 1984b). Their numbers are small, as table 7.1 demonstrates. Interested readers tend to rely on articles in *The Higher* (formerly the *Times Higher Education Supplement*) and the very useful *AUT Women*, a newsletter supplement published by the Association of University Teachers.

To answer the question posed here, we have to go beyond works specifically on women academics and extrapolate from feminist theory. The next sections review the three main strands of feminist theory in terms of their potential for explaining the unequal position of women academics in British universities.

Liberal Feminism

Most accounts of women in higher education draw at least loosely on liberal feminist perspectives. The aim of liberal feminism is to alter women's status and opportunities within the existing economic and political frameworks. It concentrates on removing barriers that prevent girls and women from attaining their full potential; that is, on the creation of equal opportunities for the sexes. Key concepts include equal opportunities, sex stereotyping, socialization, role conflict and sex discrimination (Acker, 1987).

In Britain, the liberal feminist discourse of 'equal opportunities' is the most widely acceptable analysis (Acker, 1986; Weiner, 1986), despite a number of limitations. With respect to higher education, there are several strands. Liberal feminists consider the impact of socialization; conflicting roles; inadequate social investment in women's education; and sex discrimination. Strategies which follow from these arguments tend to depend on individuals changing their practices, in response to better information or appeals to fairness. The extent to which observed patterns are rooted in structures resistant to change is de-emphasized.

Socialization

A common explanation for women's 'failure' to achieve high status places responsibility on parents, schools and other socialization agencies which have encouraged women from early childhood to develop a constellation of characteristics not easily compatible with achievement, especially in certain fields. Women are said to display lack of confidence, low aspirations and ambition, concern with people and nurturance, need for approval, desires for dependency, motives to avoid success. Feminist researchers have moved away from simplistic versions of such conceptualizations, recognizing their potential for 'blaming the victim' and taking the 'male-as-norm'.

Conflicting Roles

A similar argument adduces that women put family first ('domestic responsibilities') and thus are unable to compete effectively. In this view they are held back by overload and time problems; by guilt; by the demands of a husband's career; by anticipation of the demands of a husband's career; by their consequent inability to plan a career for themselves which is compatible with the age norms of high status occupations. It is necessary to look carefully at these arguments. Many studies report that women academics are less likely than male colleagues to be married or have children, although the gap may be culturally and historically variable (Sutherland, 1985). Researchers in various countries have tried to calculate the effects of marriage or parenthood on publishing productivity, with contradictory results (Lie, 1990).

It seems there are so many variables interacting here — age, experience, subject, ages of children, rank and others — that it is difficult to come to any firm conclusions. Accounts which invoke family-career role conflict as explanation too often simply blame the victim for not achieving a successful resolution of competing commitments or suggest that women are powerless in the face of social expectations. These are inadequate conceptualizations. Yet marriage and parenthood are facts of women's (and men's) lives.

A more convincing approach considers the role of marriage and parenthood in conjunction with institutional factors which make these statuses more or less compatible with academic life. For example, a report from Cambridge University (Spurling, 1990) finds that women academics experience strains caused by conflicts between family and work. These are analyzed, however, in an institutional context specific to Cambridge University and King's College, a formerly all-male constituent college within it. The university offers no part-time posts and no assistance with childcare, holds meetings in late afternoon or evening, and operates age restrictions affecting access to jobs or funding for those whose careers have been interrupted.

Investment in 'Womanpower'

Another view of the problem is that society fails to invest sufficiently in 'womanpower'. This approach can be pursued with or without feminist input. In the 1950s and 1960s a frequently encountered argument was that individuals benefit from investment in education and so does the country. With women there was too much 'wastage' (movement out of the labour force; failure to practice after training; failure to train up to capacity). Writings, especially about graduate women, claimed 'the country needs them' (Arregger, 1966). These arguments are often elitist as it is 'talented' or 'able' women who are needed, not the others (except perhaps to look after the children of the talented?).

Discrimination

Can we explain the position of women in higher education in terms of sex discrimination? This is a common argument, made both by feminists and others concerned with equality and justice.

What is sex discrimination? Legally speaking, discrimination consists of less favourable treatment of a member of one sex than would be accorded to a person of the other sex whose relevant circumstances are the same or not materially different. There is parallel legislation for race relations. Built into the UK legislation is a greater concern for the fate of individuals than for the welfare of groups. In most cases discrimination has to be established by means of comparisons between individuals rather than by demonstrating statistical patterns. Discrimination may be *direct* (unequal treatment because of one's sex) or *indirect* (unequal treatment using some other criterion that puts one sex at a disadvantage and is not otherwise justified).

Figures collated by the Association of University Teachers (AUT) demonstrate women's poor chances for promotion (Aziz, 1990). For example, in 1986, 536 people were promoted from lecturer to senior lecturer or reader. Only fifty-three of these were women. From 1984 to 1986 the figures hardly varied: 'the proportion of women promoted is consistently smaller than the proportion of women in the pool of lecturers from which the promotions are made' (*ibid*, p. 36).

But are these figures proof of discrimination? Not according to the law, which requires direct comparisons between named individuals. In a recent example, four women lecturers from Newcastle Polytechnic (now the University of Northumberland) took their case under the Sex Discrimination Act to an industrial tribunal, with support from the Equal Opportunities Commission (Buswell vs. Newcastle City Council, 1989). They claimed they had been directly discriminated against for promotion. A principal lectureship (a senior position) had been advertised within the department and four women and two men applied. One of the men was appointed. The women felt he was junior to them in seniority and experience, and less qualified than some of them in other respects. Various witnesses appeared for each side before a tribunal made up of two men and one woman. The women *lost*.

The official report shows, first, the enormous difficulty of proving discrimination in cases where 'academic judgments' are involved. It is clear the tribunal was unable to understand in-depth the politics of academic institutions; 'this was a foreign world' the chairman admitted (p. 10). Second, it shows how a tribunal is itself likely to rely on stereotypes about the sexes. The tribunal was impressed by the coolness and rationality of the Polytechnic management; it declared itself unimpressed by the 'obsessive, emotional involvement' of the women (p. 12).

What about indirect discrimination? Several interesting legal cases have concerned part-time work in universities. The figures in tables 7.1 and 7.2 were for full-time academics only. Part-time workers are more likely to be female. In one successful case involving a woman scientific researcher at the University of Dundee, a tribunal ruled that making part-time workers as a group redundant would affect women more heavily than men, thus constituting indirect discrimination. Also successful in establishing indirect discrimination have been several cases challenging age requirements, using the argument that women are more likely to be older when they reach certain points of their occupational careers, especially if they have taken time out of work to look after children.

Indirect discrimination may take more subtle forms. Simply working in a mostly-male environment imposes different pressures on women. The career structure is designed on a 'male norm' — career breaks or part-time work do damage to promotion chances. Time out from full-time work may be more damaging still in areas where knowledge is proceeding rapidly and where there is little provision for catching up (Jackson, 1989). Women may also be at a disadvantage in the informal socializing that aids promotion chances.

Strategies

What strategies follow from the liberal feminist perspectives reviewed above? If the problem lies in women's attitudes or personalities, as formed through socialization, the solution appears simply for the individual to make the best of a bad situation. One can simply try harder. I have a post-it note pad from the United States which sums it up as the 'career woman's checklist for success: look like a lady, act like a man, work like a dog'. Women are to 'dress for success', learn career-planning strategies from mentors and develop assertiveness through training.

This path is full of pitfalls, for double standards make such strategies difficult. Women academics who are highly successful at publishing or obtaining research funding, or who try to be 'one of the boys', risk disapproval for breaking norms for feminine women. Meanwhile feminist women criticize them for their lack of concern about other women's progress. Those who do take a feminist stance are regarded as eccentric if not actually strident and uncongenial. Whatever one does seems only to reinforce the male-as-norm definitions.

For family-career conflicts, a helpful partner, clever manoeuvring, luck and money might provide a nanny or other solution. But again, these are *individual* solutions, and not open to all. One woman finds a way, but the same problem is there for the next.

The womanpower and discrimination arguments shift the analysis somewhat, still staying within the liberal framework, but examining structures rather than individuals. We become more sociological, understanding women's actions within the frameworks that constrain them. But there are still difficulties. The demand for womanpower is bound to fluctuate over time and some groups are not perceived as being in shortage. For example, there has not yet been a call for women to come into university teaching comparable to the one for school teaching, although a 'womanpower' argument has been made in a project which recruited highly-qualified women returners to university fellowships in science and engineering (Jackson, 1988). There have also been rumours that contract researchers in universities are becoming more difficult to recruit, perhaps because of their poor remuneration and prospects. The university academic population in Britain is aging, a result of expansion in the 1960s and early 1970s followed by contraction since the 1980s. At some point, mass retirements from the 'bulge' will require replacement. But recent government policies have squeezed the universities and starved them of funds, hardly auspicious circumstances for extending equal opportunities to women or minorities. Arts and humanities, and certain social sciences, have experienced particularly severe cutbacks. It is difficult to defend a 'womanpower' argument that supplies talent only to fields designated by the government of the day as in the national interest.

If discrimination is seen to be the problem, use may be made of the law, the Equal Opportunities Commission and union procedures. Steady pressure can be put on colleagues. The situation can be brought to the notice of the wider public. Generally strategies rely on persuasion, rational argument, the assumption of goodwill and distaste for injustice. Using the law and publicizing successful outcomes, as the Equal Opportunities Commission does, may raise the level of consciousness but there is little evidence of fundamental change. The number of successful cases is small and there are few effective sanctions to stop the same discriminatory treatment occurring again elsewhere.

Extending the Analysis: Socialist and Radical Feminisms

The approaches discussed thus far give us an idea how social arrangements operate to the detriment of women but not why they have developed this way. We can deepen our understanding of women in higher education if we go beyond the various varieties of liberal feminist thought outlined above. Both socialist feminist and radical feminist theories are concerned with underlying causes.

Socialist Feminism

The long-term aim here is to end oppression under capitalism but the immediate task is to elucidate the processes involved. Most socialist feminist theoreticians have focussed on women's position within the economy and the family. For those concerned with education, the key question is 'how is education related to the reproduction of gender divisions within capitalism?' (Arnot and Weiner, 1987).

For example, women and men occupy different typical spheres in the labour market as well as in the home; details of such divisions change but the broad outlines are perpetuated over time, or 'reproduced'. Questions arise. Why is it that women are concentrated in certain manual occupations with little job security and few fringe benefits; or in lower white collar (secretarial) work; or in the caring professions? Why is it that within professional occupations, women are found in lower grades and lower status specialities? If education is about increasing social mobility, why does the same amount of education bring a lower rate of return for women and minorities than for white men?

The internal labour markets in institutions of higher education contain gender and other social divisions. Universities now even have their own 'academic proletariat' (Aziz, 1990): temporary contract research staff, disproportionately female, who act as a kind of reserve labour force. The abolition of academic tenure in universities (for all who join, move or are promoted) through the Education Reform Act of 1988 would seem to suggest 'traditional' academics are vulnerable, too.

Higher education can be seen to reinforce divisions in other ways. It is a scarce prize which sections off an elite, dividing the credentialed from the remainder. Williams *et al.* (1989, p. 8) point out that in 1984 only 8.6 per cent of male school-leavers and 6.3 per cent of female school-leavers entered degree courses. The overall participation rates are somewhat higher because some students go first to further education or tertiary colleges to get the requisite qualifications for entry to university or polytechnic; nevertheless higher education is still only available to a small minority.

This minority is disproportionately white and middle class. The latter monopoly is scarcely news, as British sociology of education has a long history of interest in 'political arithmetic', charting the probabilities of children from different social class backgrounds achieving educational outcomes such as examination passes or access to higher education (Gray, 1981). Gray comments that the universities are still 'comparatively inaccessible to the working class' (p. 82). Reid (1989, p. 320) shows that in 1988, 68 per cent of the candidates accepted to universities came from the top two categories of the six-part Registrar General's social class scale (based on father's occupation). These categories contain only 27 per cent of the population at large.

Such figures point to a role for the university as the imprimatur of class privilege. One difficulty with such statistics is that they rarely record more than one social division at a time. What are the interconnections of class, sex and 'race' in determining access to university? While 'women' as a category are approaching parity among undergraduates (UFC, 1990), ethnic minorities are scarce indeed. New procedures for ethnic monitoring suggest that only about 1 per cent of university students and 4 per cent of polytechnic students are black (Utley, 1991). We also lack figures on the class background and ethnic composition of the academic profession (and other workers in higher education); we have no easy way to assess the combined effects of class, sex, 'race' and other attributes such as sexual orientation (Kitzinger, 1990) on subject specialities, promotion prospects, or any other aspect of being an academic.

Radical Feminism

In radical feminism, the operation of patriarchy is the fundamental reason for observed social patterns. Although there are different definitions of patriarchy, most depict a system whereby men as a group (not necessarily every individual man) are dominant. Figures shown earlier amply support the argument that men dominate universities numerically. Radical feminists want to eliminate patriarchal structures and put girls and women at the centre of concern. In higher education, male dominance is expressed through curriculum, pedagogy and the sexual politics of everyday life.

Feminists have produced extensive critiques of scholarship in many fields. A classic of this genre is Dale Spender's (1981) collection, *Men's Studies Modified*. Jeri Wine (1989) identifies stages feminist criticism goes through, starting with correcting the record and finally attempting to construct woman-centred alternatives. Writers like Stanley and Wise (1983) try to develop a specifically feminist research methodology.

Feminist scholarship is exciting, 'producing a critical and analytical literature of an intellectual liveliness and practical relevance unmatched in any other field of social science' (Connell, 1985, p. 260). Nevertheless, there are numerous examples of important ways in which feminist work is outside the mainstream. For example, Sara Delamont (1989) shows that the Winfield Report on submission rates for social science higher degree theses ignored all the research on *women* graduate students. Specializing in feminist scholarship may harm one's promotion chances (Gumport, 1990; MA pioneer . . . 1991).

How much scope is there for finding a feminist way to organize pedagogy, curriculum and management? Women's studies are gaining ground quietly in Britain (Brookman, 1991), but the field is subdued in comparison with developments in the United States, where a different organization of higher education permits new courses and programmes to flourish provided they attract students. Attempts to create new ways of working within the relatively rigid world of British higher education can be painful, as high expectations held by the students clash with university conventions. Women who do become heads of department or professors find themselves allowed in as individuals to a culture which is shaped by men. They are always highly visible. Simply being a woman academic in a male dominated institution brings forms of 'sexual politics' — dilemmas of power, visibility, relationships — into everyday life (Acker, 1980; David, 1989).

Power men hold over women can, at an extreme, become sexual harassment. This means unwanted sexual attentions or advances, which may be looks, gestures, pictures, physical advances, threats, etc. In the United States many institutions have developed policies on harassment and there have been widely publicized court cases. Consciousness was further raised by the issue surfacing during the confirmation hearings of Supreme Court Justice Clarence Thomas. American surveys suggest widespread sexual harassment in universities (Simeone, 1987) but little is known about its incidence in British universities.

Strategies

The goals of socialist and radical feminism are unrealizable in the immediate future; one cannot devise strategies for ending capitalism and patriarchy in the same way as, for example, introducing an equal opportunities policy or encouraging women to apply for promotion. Consistent with socialist feminist analysis would be efforts to develop further a class-gender-race analysis of the university's social role; to encourage alliances of university workers, especially women, across occupational segments and social divisions; to raise consciousness of oppression among these groups; to increase awareness of, and commitment to, gender issues in the more left-leaning political parties and trade unions; to increase access to universities for groups traditionally deprived of it.

Radical feminist strategies focus on putting women at the centre of concern: developing woman-centred knowledge, making institutions safe for women, finding space for women within (or outside) the academy. Putting women first may mean encouraging women-only courses and groups. The difficulty is that the territory is still controlled by men, as the figures show. Women's studies courses in Britain — as, indeed, is any input on 'gender' to any course — are frequently marginal, poorly resourced, dependent on the energies of a few committed individuals doing the work 'on top' of their responsibilities in traditional departments.

Missing Links, Alternative Models

It seems to me that there are at least three underdeveloped areas within British feminist work on women in higher education. These are socialist feminist writing on the topic; considerations of 'race'; and imaginative projections towards a woman-centred university.

First, in the literature on universities, there are few examples of a socialist feminist (or even a socialist) perspective. Earlier I referred to questions of access and the lack of simultaneous consideration of class, sex and 'race' divisions among the student body, academics and other staff. Other questions could be raised concerning the extent to which the university operates in tandem with the interests of industry and in support of capitalist development (Esland and Cathcart, 1981). Under the Conservatives, central government has intervened extensively in higher education in recent years, for example by modifying the curriculum in initial teacher education; abolishing academic tenure; taking polytechnics out of local government control; differentially distributing funds so as to increase institutions' accountability and dependence on market forces.

What implications have these developments had for women? How do the subject divisions and hierarchies of the university contribute to the reproduction of gendered divisions of labour in society at large? How do particular forms of knowledge become enshrined in academic discourses; do they then become differentially accessible to different groups; do their curricula transmit messages which aid in the cultural reproduction of beliefs about gender? We need more scholarship and research from a socialist feminist perspective on higher education; that there is so little, especially when British socialist feminist work is so strong in other areas, is itself a 'problem'.

Second, there is a near-silence about 'race' and ethnicity in terms of their impact on British academic women. This is perhaps surprising in view of the incisive critiques of ethnocentrism which have been levelled against some British feminist work (for example, Carby, 1982; Murphy and Livingstone, 1985) and the reconceptualizations which followed. Although there is a body of literature on experiences of black and Asian schoolgirls in Britain (for example, Amos and Parmar, 1981; Brah and Minhas, 1985), there are only a few references to black women students in higher education (Tomlinson, 1983; Bryan *et al*, 1985) and an almost total absence of information about the ethnic composition of the academic profession.

An exception is McKellar (1989), who gives an account of her own experiences as a teacher educator. McKellar cites a study which found only twenty-seven black teacher educators in England, Scotland and Wales, only eight of whom were in universities (p. 69). There does not seem to be much serious effort to increase the representation of minority ethnic groups among academics, despite institutional claims to be equal opportunities employers (Williams *et al*, 1989), nor are there commentaries which explore the consequences for the curriculum, role modelling or other aspects of university life of the absence of academics from minority ethnic communities.

In North America, where representation is somewhat better, one regularly finds discussion of ethnic diversity among academic women (for example, Pearson *et al*, 1989). A recent Canadian volume (Bannerji *et al*, 1991) provides a model of a collection by women working in universities as students and academics which engages seriously with class, gender, race and sexuality issues in academic life and their impact on the construction of knowledge and the shaping of subjectivities. The authors 'recognize that this is a racist, classist and heterosexist society and that the university is structured to perpetuate those relations' (p. 8). In their individual chapters they examine their own 'different — and sometimes contradictory — location in these relations' (*ibid*).

Third, a leap of the imagination might allow us to go beyond the structures and inequities of universities as we know them. In reviewing research on women graduate students for another paper, I noticed that a typical concern of the 70s and early 80s — the extent to which women were taken seriously and sponsored by male faculty members — had in more recent North American literature nearly disappeared. The themes of feminist pedagogy and radical revision of the curriculum, which I earlier associated with radical feminist scholarship, had developed further into an exploration of women's preferred ways of learning and working, thought to involve valuing community over competition, attachment and caring over justice and objectivity (Desjardins, 1989). Gray (1989), for example, speculates what education would look like if 'the culture of separated desks' gave way. In a woman-centred university (Rich, 1979) the figures on women's underrepresentation in the upper reaches of the hierarchy I gave earlier would no longer provide the linchpin of an argument; they would be beside the point, as the hierarchy itself would dissolve. Meanwhile, we can at least think creatively and innovate wherever possible.

Moving Towards Equity, Slowly

The feminist theories discussed in this chapter advance reasons for the structural subordination of women. Those considered under the liberal feminist umbrella tend to answer the question of *how* women become disadvantaged, for example, through processes of socialization and discrimination. The socialist and radical feminist approaches aim for a deeper, more fundamental understanding, addressing the question of *why* such disadvantage occurs (Acker, 1984a). As it is impossible to ascertain 'why' with any certainty, we are left with competing but untestable hypotheses. Moreover, behind every 'how' question, a 'why' is lurking, untestable as it may be; for example if we believe socialization to be the cause of women's subordination, we still must question why socialization operates in this particular fashion.

While feminist theory gives broad reasons for inequalities of gender, focussed studies in specific countries and educational systems are necessary to fill in the detail. Britain appears to lag behind other, similar, countries in its commitment to improving the status of women in general and women academics in particular (Johnson, 1990). Reasons might be sought in its particular historical and political traditions (Gelb, 1989). Gelb argues that in comparison with the United States and Sweden, British feminist groups are more radical, ideological and decentralized. Like other grassroots groups, they lack input into the policy-making process. Britain has no active and effective liberal feminist network of committees and pressure groups pushing for implementation of feminist priorities. There has been no extensive feminist infiltration into bureaucracies such as observed in Eisenstein's (1991) account of 'femocrats' in Australia. Feminism in Britain remains a fringe pursuit, outside the dominant discourse. The years of Conservative government have enshrined this principle; a few women, like Mrs Thatcher, could 'make it', but only by their own efforts, not by virtue of socially progressive policies.

Canada provides an interesting contrast. In neither Britain nor Canada is there a network of privately financed universities, as in the United States. Women make up 17.9 per cent of Canadian academics, a figure similar to the British one (Statistics Canada, 1991). There is also a tendency for women to be disproportionately located in contractually-limited appointments and part-time positions (Drakich *et al*, 1990). But once in the 'tenure track', women's chances of advancing to middle levels are greater than those of their counterparts in Britain. Slightly over a third of each sex holds the middle rank of associate professor. The difference comes at the full professor rank which is held by about 13 per cent of the women and 40 per cent of the men (Statistics Canada, 1991).

In Canada there are policies at both federal and provincial level which have as their aim the reduction of gender (and other) inequality (Breslauer and Gordon, 1990; Canadian Association of University Teachers, 1991). The Federal Contractors Program requires employees of more than 100 people who wish to receive federal contracts for $200,000 or over to put into place plans to increase equity for women, visible minorities, aboriginal people and the disabled. Many universities have joined this programme. Some provinces have introduced additional equity measures. Canadian universities also benefit from a higher level of feminist activism than British ones, reflecting the greater prominence of the women's movement generally, and there is evidence that such efforts have been influential (Drakich *et al*, 1991).

Education in Canada is a provincial responsibility. In contrast, central government is particularly influential in the British case; local and county levels of government have no control over universities. Although the central government in Britain has pursued a number of aggressive higher education policies in recent years, none are concerned with gender equality.

The use of a competitive promotion procedure in British universities, together with minimal commitment from the government to redressing gender inequities, may produce the contrast with the Canadian situation. Unlike the American practice of allowing individuals to compete against a standard to attain higher ranks, judged by one's peers, the typical British university makes its candidates for internal promotion (senior lectureships and readerships) compete against one another for a restricted number of promotions, usually judged by senior personnel (professors and deans). The academic profession is aging and there are large numbers at the top of the 'lecturer scale' (reached at about age 40) competing for promotion. The system discourages geographical mobility (why start over again in a lectureship somewhere else?) except at the professorial level and is open to micropolitical manoeuvring as professors struggle to get 'their' candidate promoted.

The individuals making these judgments, as we have seen, are almost all men. Few will be familiar with research on gender, thus placing women doing research and scholarship in that area at a possible disadvantage (MA pioneer . . ., 1991). Because women are concentrated in relatively few subject fields, they also in effect compete against one another to the extent promotions are 'shared out' among departments. It is also possible that when promotions are restricted, and many candidates are of equal merit, that male preference will operate, however unconsciously.

A further, ironic, consequence of the small numbers of women in the system is that opportunities for organizing to improve matters are thereby limited. Women academics are too scattered to provide a critical mass, nor do they hold many positions of influence. Johnson (1990) makes this clear using the example of music, a subject with a majority female undergraduate enrolment. As of 1988, two-thirds of university music departments had no women academic staff. There were no readers or professors. Wales had no women lecturers. One of the limitations of women's studies is that it will make few inroads where there are few women already present.

Finally, the economic situation has been perilous for some time in Britain. Universities have been experiencing cuts and retrenchment since the early 1980s (Reynolds, 1990). It would not seem the best of times to push for feminist reform. But there are always contradictions and points of intervention. For example, the increasing impact of market forces means that student preferences should be a factor in shaping provision. Women have been steadily increasing their share of student places. During the 1990s mature women are expected to be in demand to make up some of the shortfall left by an unusually small cohort of individuals of traditional university-going age. The massive rise in temporary teaching and research staff has unsettled old certainties about the meaning of the university as a workplace and undermines the image of the academic as an autonomous professional. The very business of education carries contradictions in its simultaneous reproductive and liberating potential. The institution is reproducing the divisions of the labour market while at the same time providing the means for challenge and critique.

So feminists need not give up just yet. As I have suggested, liberal feminist analysis is inadequate to explain the persistence of deep gender divisions in academic life. Socialist and radical feminisms go further to explain why the barriers to women are so strong. Yet when considering strategies, we confront something of a paradox. Either strategies are long term (working towards the end of capitalist or patriarchal oppression) or provocative and likely to arouse opposition or even ridicule (challenging the disciplines with women's studies; constructing feminist methodology). Liberal feminist strategies, on the other hand, tend either to put too much responsibility on the individual to make changes, often in herself, or to rely on arts of persuasion and assumptions of goodwill. Nevertheless, it may be that even those with radical or socialist sympathies need to pursue liberal strategies in the short run, given that the liberal ones — as in the Canadian case — may be as, or more, constructive than the others. The difference is that for liberal feminism they are an end; for other feminisms, a means to an end. Liberal strategies have not failed in Britain; they have not sufficiently been tried.

The strategies will need to be adapted to their context: institutions complacent towards certain issues but in flux and crisis. Working through academic unions may provide a relatively 'respectable' base. Feminist academics need to use their skills as scholars to look at their own institutions. The pioneering work by Thomas (1990) and Greed (1991) draws our attention to ways in which institutional, disciplinary, and departmental cultures in higher education may be transmitting a hidden curriculum of gender and thereby creating or reinforcing gendered subjectivities: a phenomenon which demands further study.

Feminists are not as happy about our theories as we once were. The post-modern critique has forced us to deal with the puzzle that in arguing 'women's' case, we downplay disparities of class, race and other divisions which fragment the category 'women'. The theories I have worked with here are not convincing as total truth (did we ever think they were?) yet played off against each other, they give us different angles of vision on an elusive 'problem'. As Linda Alcoff (1988) argues, we cannot afford to abandon our politics because our theories lack perfection. We need to recognize the historical and cultural specificity of our case, and within it actively take up the position and the identity which feels most compelling as a political point of departure (Alcoff, 1988; Nicholson, 1990). Feminist theories help us understand how serious the situation is, and why change is so frustratingly slow. Accepting this, we can work at deepening the cracks, crevices and contradictions of the patriarchal university.

Acknowledgments

This chapter has been evolving for some time. Earlier versions were presented at a conference on women in higher education at King's College, University of Cambridge, April 1989, and as part of the symposium on Feminism and the Struggle for Social Justice: Comparative Perspectives, at the American Educational Research Association annual meeting, Chicago, April 1991. Some passages in the present chapter also appear in another article of mine entitled 'New perspectives on an old problem: The position of women academics in British higher education', *Higher Education*, **24**, 3, 1992, copyright Kluwer Academic Publishers, The Netherlands, and are reproduced here by kind permission of Kluwer Academic Publishers. I would also like to thank Kari Dehli, Maureen Dyer, Madeleine Arnot and Kathleen Weiler for their comments on drafts of the conference paper or the chapter; Carol Buswell for providing transcripts and other materials from her tribunal proceedings; Linda Fitzsimmons for updating me on Association of University Teachers activities concerning women; Helen Breslauer and Dorothy Smith for pointing me towards materials on Canadian women academics. Over the years I have had many discussions with friends and colleagues which contributed to the ideas in this paper, among them Elizabeth Bird, Patricia Broadfoot, Miriam David, Clara Greed, Sara Meadows and Andrea Spurling.

Note

1 I have concentrated on universities rather than polytechnics, given limitations of space and my own experience in the university sector. As most polytechnics have now become universities, certain statements may need alteration. However, women's representation in polytechnics is similar to the pattern in universities, i.e. they are a minority overall and are scarce in top positions (DES, 1987). Similarly, I have considered women academic staff rather than other university workers, many of whom are women in support positions, such as secretarial or library staff. Little is written about women in universities who are neither students nor academics.

References

ACKER, S. (1980) 'Women, the other academics', *British Journal of Sociology of Education*, **1**, pp. 81–91.

ACKER, S. (1984a) 'Sociology, gender and education' in ACKER, S., MEGARRY, J., NISBET, S. and HOYLE, E. (Eds) *World Yearbook of Education 1984: Women and Education*, London, Kogan Page.

ACKER, S. (1984b) 'Women in higher education: What is the problem?' in ACKER, S. and WARREN PIPER, D. (Eds) *Is Higher Education Fair to Women?* Guildford, Society for Research into Higher Education.

ACKER, S. (1986) 'What feminists want from education' in HARTNETT, A. and NAISH, M. (Eds) *Education and Society Today*, Lewes, Falmer Press.

ACKER, S. (1987) 'Feminist theory and the study of gender and education', *International Review of Education*, **33**, pp. 419–35.

ALCOFF, L. (1988) 'Cultural feminism vs post-structuralism' in MINNICH, E., O'BARR, J. and ROSENFELD, R. (Eds) *Reconstructing the Academy*, Chicago, IL, University of Chicago Press.

AMOS, V. and PARMAR, P. (1981) 'Resistances and responses: The experiences of black girls in Britain' in MCROBBIE, A. and MCCABE, T. (Eds) *Feminism for Girls*, London, Routledge & Kegan Paul.

ARNOT, M. and WEINER, G. (1987) *Gender and Education Study Guide*, Milton Keynes, Open University Press.

ARREGGER, C. (1966) *Graduate Women at Work*, Newcastle upon Tyne, Oriel.

AZIZ, A. (1990) 'Women in UK universities: The road to casualization?' in LIE, S. and O'LEARY, V. (Eds) *Storming the Tower: Women in the Academic World*, London, Kogan Page.

BANNERJI, H., CARTY, L., DEHLI, K., HEALD, S. and MCKENNA, K. (1991) *Unsettling Relations: The University as a Site of Feminist Struggle*, Toronto, Women's Press.

BRAH, A. and MINHAS, R. (1985) 'Structural racism or cultural difference: schooling for Asian girls' in WEINER, G. (Ed.) *Just a Bunch of Girls*, Milton Keynes, Open University Press.

BRESLAUER, H. and GORDON, J. (1990) 'Redressing the imbalance: The public policy agenda and academic women', paper presented at the annual meeting of the Canadian Society for the Study of Higher Education, Victoria, British Columbia.

BROOKMAN, J. (1991) 'Graceful coming of age for women', *Times Higher Education Supplement*, 2 February, p. 4.

BRYAN, B., DADZIE, S. and SCAFE, S. (1985) *The Heart of the Race: Black Women's Lives in Britain*, London, Virago.

BUSWELL, C. vs. NEWCASTLE CITY COUNCIL (1989) *Decision Document Folio Ref: 9/213/179. 6 Feb. 1989* (available from Regional Office of Industrial Tribunals, Newcastle Upon Tyne NE1 6NT, England).

CANADIAN ASSOCIATION OF UNIVERSITY TEACHERS (1991) *Status of Women Supplement*, Ottawa, CAUT.

CARBY, H. (1982) 'White woman listen! Black feminism and the boundaries of sisterhood' in CENTRE FOR CONTEMPORARY CULTURAL STUDIES *The Empire Strikes Back*, London, Hutchinson.

CONNELL, R. (1985) 'Theorizing gender', *Sociology*, **19**, pp. 250–72.

DAVID, M. (1989) 'Prima donna inter pares? Women in academic management' in ACKER, S. (Ed.) *Teachers, Gender and Careers*, Lewes, Falmer Press.

DAVIS, D. and ASTIN, H. (1990) 'Life cycle, career patterns and gender stratification in academe: Breaking myths and exposing truths' in LIE, S. and O'LEARY, V. (Eds) *Storming the Tower: Women in the Academic World*. London, Kogan Page.

DELAMONT, S. (1989) 'Gender and British postgraduate funding policy: A critique of the Winfield Report', *Gender and Education*, **1**, pp. 51–7.

DELMAR, R. (1986) 'What is feminism?' in MITCHELL, J. and OAKLEY, A. (Eds) *What is Feminism?* Oxford, Basil Blackwell.

DEPARTMENT OF EDUCATION AND SCIENCE (1987) *Statistics of Education: Teachers in Service, England and Wales 1985*, London, HMSO.

DESJARDINS, C. (1989) 'The meaning of Gilligan's concept of "different voice" for the learning environment' in PEARSON, C., SHAVLIK, D. and TOUCHTON, J. (Eds) *Educating the Majority: Women Challenge Tradition in Higher Education*, New York, Macmillan.

DRAKICH, J., SMITH, D.E., STEWART, P., FOX, B. and GRIFFITH, A. (1991) *Status of Women in Ontario Universities: Final Report.* September Government of Toronto, Canada.

EISENSTEIN, H. (1991) *Gender Shock: Practicing Feminism on Two Continents*, Boston, MA, Beacon Press.

ESLAND, G. and CATHCART, H. (1981) *Education and the Corporate Economy* Unit 2 of Course E353, Society, Education and the State, Milton Keynes, Open University Press.

FRASER, N. and NICHOLSON, L. (1990) 'Social criticism without philosophy: an encounter between feminism and post-modernism' in NICHOLSON, L. (Ed.) *Feminism/Postmodernism*, London, Routledge & Kegan Paul.

GELB, J. (1989) *Feminism and Politics*, Berkeley, CA, University of California Press.

GRAY, E. (1989) 'The culture of separated desks' in PEARSON, C., SHAVLIK, D. and TOUCHTON, J. (Eds) *Educating the Majority: Women Challenge Tradition in Higher Education*, New York, Macmillan.

GRAY, J. (1981) 'From policy to practice — some problems and paradoxes' in SIMON, B. and TAYLOR, W. (Eds) *Education in the Eighties: The Central Issues*, London, Batsford.

GREED, C. (1991) *Surveying Sisters: Women in a Traditional Male Profession*, London, Routledge.

GUMPORT, P. (1990) 'Feminist scholarship as a vocation', *Higher Education*, **20**, pp. 231–43.

HIRSCH, M. and KELLER, E.F. (Eds) (1990) *Conflicts in Feminism*, New York, Routledge.

JACKSON, D. (1988) *Fellowship Scheme for Women Returners to Science and Engineering: Personal Experiences of the Returners*, Guildford, University of Surrey.

JACKSON, D. (1989) 'Women returners', paper presented at the Conference on Women and Higher Education, King's College, Cambridge, 29 April.

JOHNSON, J. (1990) 'Behind the bastion', *Times Higher Education Supplement*, 20 April, p. 14.

KITZINGER, C. (1990) 'Beyond the boundaries: Lesbians in academe' in LIE, S. and O'LEARY, V. (Eds) *Storming the Tower: Women in the Academic World*, London, Kogan Page.

LIE, S. (1990) 'The juggling act: Work and family in Norway' in LIE, S. and O'LEARY, V. (Eds) *Storming the Tower: Women in the Academic World*, London, Kogan Page.

MCKELLAR, B. (1989) 'Only the fittest of the fittest will survive: Black women and education' in ACKER, S. (Ed.) *Teachers, Gender and Careers*, Lewes, Falmer Press.

'MA PIONEER CHARGES KENT WITH SEXISM' (1991) *The Higher*, 29 November, p. 6.

MOORE, K.M. (1987) 'Women's access and opportunity in higher education: towards the twenty-first century', *Comparative Education*, **23**, 1, pp. 23–34.

MURPHY, L. and LIVINGSTONE, J. (1985) 'Racism and the limits of radical feminism', *Race and Class*, **26**, pp. 61–70.

NICHOLSON, L. (1990) 'Introduction' in NICHOLSON, L. (Ed.) *Feminism/Post modernism*, London, Routledge.

PEARSON, C., SHAVLIK, D. and TOUCHTON, J. (Eds) (1989) *Educating the Majority: Women Challenge Tradition in Higher Education*, New York, Macmillan.

REES, T. (1989) 'Contract research: A new career structure?' *AUT Woman*, **16**, 1, p. 4.

REID, I. (1989) *Social Class Differences in Britain* (3rd edn) London, Fontana.

REYNOLDS, P.A. (1990) 'How long is a piece of string: Reflections on British higher education since 1945', *Higher Education*, **20**, pp. 211–21.

RICH, A. (1979) *On Lies, Secrets, and Silence*, New York, Norton.

SIMEONE, A. (1987) *Academic Women: Working Towards Equality*, South Hadley, MA, Bergin & Garvey.

SPENDER, D. (1981) *Men's Studies Modified: The Impact of Feminism on the Academic Disciplines*, Oxford, Pergamon.

SPURLING, A. (1990) *Report of the Women in Higher Education Research Project*, Cambridge, King's College.

STANLEY, L. and WISE, S. (1983) *Breaking Out*, London, Routledge & Kegan Paul.

STATISTICS CANADA (1991) *Teachers in Universities 1987/88*, Ottawa, Minister of Supplies and Services.

SUTHERLAND, M. (1985) *Women Who Teach in Universities*, Stoke-on-Trent, Trentham.

THOMAS, K. (1990) *Gender and Subject in Higher Education*, Milton Keynes, Open University Press.

TOMLINSON, S. (1983) 'Black women in higher education: Case studies of university women in Britain' in BARTON, L. and WALKER, S. (Eds) *Race, Class and Education*, London, Croom Helm.

UNIVERSITIES FUNDING COUNCIL (1990) *University Statistics 1988–89, Vol. 1*, Cheltenham, Universities' Statistical Record.

UTLEY, A. (1991) 'Blacks fare badly in entry stakes', *Times Higher Education Supplement*, 21 June, p. 1.

WEINER, G. (1986) 'Feminist education and equal opportunities: Unity or discord?', *British Journal of Sociology of Education*, **7**, pp. 265–74.

WILLIAMS, J., COCKING, J. and DAVIES, L. (1989) *Words or Deeds: A Review of Equal Opportunities Policies in Higher Education*, London, Commission for Racial Equality.

WINE, J. (1989) 'Gynocentric values and feminist psychology' in MILES, A. and FINN, G. (Eds) *Feminism: From Pressure to Politics*, Montreal, Black Rose Books.

Chapter 8

Feminism and Australian State Policy: Some Questions for the 1990s

Lyn Yates

Introduction

What happens when feminist issues get taken up as an agenda of the State? This chapter offers a consideration of almost two decades of Australian government commitments to girls and education. In doing this, the chapter will raise some issues about the nature of the state's activity in educational reform in this area, and also about the feminist theories which have provided frameworks for reform. In particular, I will discuss some changes in the ways gender has been framed as an issue for education in the 1980s compared with the 1970s.

My discussion is located in Australia. Here, in contrast to many other Western, post-industrial countries, Labor governments, formally committed to programs of social reform, held power throughout the 1980s. It is true that these Labor governments shared many elements of 'new right' economic rationalism with Conservative governments in other countries. Nevertheless, the formal progressive commitments and associations of the Australian governments provided a distinctive context for reform related to girls and schooling. Questions for feminism take different forms in countries which overtly sanction feminist agendas, as compared with those where gaining a hearing for a critique of sexism is still a major issue. Parallels for many of the issues raised in this chapter can be found in Swedish reflections on the history of feminist reform in that country (Andrae-Thelin and Elgqvist-Salzman, 1989).

For one thing, the relationship between 'radical' intellectual production and public policy is framed differently in this setting:

> In Australia, a Left largely given to the pursuit of socialist science in the 1970s has now itself become deeply involved in the production and advocacy of policy. (Beilharz, 1987, p. 388)

And particularly is this the case in relation to education policy (cf. Yates, 1986) and in relation to feminism.

Commentators exploring Australian feminism's concern with state policy and with achieving power in the state bureaucracies, have drawn attention to the 'state-centric' nature of Australia (Yeatman, 1988), as well as to the very large public sector in the composition of the Australian workforce (Porter, 1983; Franzway, Court and Connell, 1989). Yeatman (1988) makes the following point, one that might well be applied to most feminists working in education in the Australian context:

> A relatively centralized state structure is conducive to the rationalized social reform orientations of the new class, i.e., the class which makes its political, cultural and economic claims on the basis of its cultural capital, its knowledge claims. The new class, wherever it is, tends to view the state as the vehicle of its claims to power as social planners and national policy makers. (p. 143)

While the concern to shape, work within, and influence government policy is strong within Australian feminism, there has been a considerable debate about the effects and the desirability of such a relationship to the state. Critics of those working within state bureaucracies argue that 'femocrats' are shaped and contained by the conditions of their work. Others argue that some involvement with state institutional structures is inescapable for feminist politics. These theorists argue that what is important is to examine reflexively the sources and reformations of power within the institutions of the state, and to assess the strengths of different strategies of reform. (Baldock and Cass, 1983; Eisenstein, 1988; Yeatman, 1988 and 1990; Franzway, Court and Connell, 1989; Yates, 1990 and Kenway, 1990 are some examples of this discussion.)

The discussion which follows is part of this ongoing attempt to reflect on state action and feminist theory, in a context where theory, and indeed the services of the theorists themselves, may well be called on in the development of policy. My assumption is that schooling as a system (and as a compulsory form of acculturation) will continue to be important, and that the theories and debates of academics can have some impact on the policies that are developed.

A second context of the discussion which follows is the emergence of post-structuralism as a dominant wave of contemporary social theory, and as a strong but contested framework feminism.

Post-structuralist writings in feminism and in education, especially those associated with the widespread taking up of the work of Foucault, have been interested in the unmasking of power inherent in claims to knowledge and truth (see, for example, Diamond and Quinby, 1988; Ball, 1990; Giroux, 1991; Nicholson, 1990). The interest in knowledge and power is not a new development for theorists concerned with gender and education. What is new is the extension of the critique to liberatory movements themselves, and to a suspicion of any search for general answers by theorists and activists.

Any 'universalizing' theory, it is suggested, is a form of domination in silencing differences and voices from the margins. This issue has been particularly developed in relation to racism within feminism, extending to a challenge to those speak of 'women' as a category to note the 'violence' to minority women that their concept entails.

Moreover, power is no longer seen as having a structured relation to an identifiable set of material and institutional conditions but as something to be identified within particular cultural ways of being, seeing and, above all, speaking. An interest in ideology has been replaced by an interest in discourse. Discourses (of educational practice, for example) are historically constituted frameworks of material and conceptual organization (as Walkerdine discusses in relation to the progressive primary school classroom (1984); and in relation to what counts as mathematical ability (1987)). For the theorist and activist, what is possible is not a general theory of the state (of ideology, of ideological state apparatuses), but an unpicking of particular discursive formations in particular contexts ('deconstruction', 'local knowledges').

The interest of this line of contemporary analysis then, is in showing the power relations inherent in the framing of policy, institutional arrangements, cultural concepts ('femininity', but also 'feminism' and 'non-sexist education'). This is approached not by pointing to some ongoing interests (capitalism, patriarchy) that lie outside the discourse (though whether it should do so remains an issue for feminism), but by revealing the oppositions and silences set up by the discourses (cf. Walkerdine, 1985; Davies, 1989a and 1989b). Among feminist theorists, there has been much debate about the viability of post-structuralism as a political framework (see Pateman and Gross, 1986; Alcoff, 1987; Nicholson, 1990; Hirsch and Fox Keller, 1990; Lather, 1991). There is wide recognition that concerns about difference are important, and that theories which speak in general terms yet make some groups 'other' to the voice that is speaking, are inadequate. Yet there are ongoing worries about where this form of theory is leading: that the continuing interest only in unpicking the silences and deconstructing the categories, disowning even the term 'woman', is a dangerous one for feminist practice. What association, what movement for change, it is said, can persist on such a basis? As well, there is the question of whether current theories produce abstractions satisfying to intellectuals, while losing touch with palpable discriminations and inequalities which continue to affect most women.

The discussion of policy on gender and education in Australia which follows takes up (not necessarily in their own terms) some of these themes of recent feminist theory. In terms of policy as discourse, it asks, what is being constructed as the terms of the framework concerning gender and education, and what is being silenced? What 'regulation' is embodied in this sphere of government action? In terms of the debate *about* post-structuralism, the question is what happens to the project of curriculum reform in a schooling *system*? Can there be lines of action which work with cultural difference and avoid positioning some groups as other? Is the feminist attempt to work on developing policy (as compared with maintaining a critique of policy) a mistaken one?

The discussion which follows pays particular attention to the *National Policy for the Education of Girls in Australian Schools*, (Schools Commission, 1987) and contrasts this with an earlier Commonwealth Report on the issue of gender and education, *Girls, School and Society*, (Schools Commission, 1975.) In discussing the text of two national policy documents here, it is not assumed that they translate straightforwardly into practices, either of the government or of schools. The changing emphases discussed here, I would argue, *are* reflected in a wide range of curriculum projects, policy statements, and writings by feminist academics over the same period. But to analyze them as I do here for the purpose of interpreting some developments within theory, policy and practice, is certainly to oversimplify the positions individuals take and also to exaggerate certain aspects of the policies themselves.

Girls, School and Society, the 1975 Australian report, signalled the beginning of a period of major government involvement in school reform concerned with gender. The 1987 *National Policy* represented an attempt to draw together, systematize and bring a new accountability in relation to the strands of reform that had developed. The movement between the two reports also, I will suggest, reflect some movements within feminism between these two dates, which now need to be examined.

Sexual Inequality and Education: The Changing Shape of Policy

Girls, School and Society, the 1975 Report by a Study Group to the Commonwealth Schools Commission, had many of the hallmarks which feminists dismiss as a 'liberal' (meaning individualist and non-radical) approach (cf. Middleton, 1984 and 1990; Arnot, 1986; Weiner and Arnot, 1987). The problem of sexism, the report suggested, was apparent in the invisibility and biased treatment of women in the curriculum, but this effectively was an oversight, a contingent matter at odds with the principles for which education was designed, which themselves were sound:

> Sexism is a process through which females and males not only progressively learn that different things are required and expected of them

> because of their sex, but learn these things in an unexamined way. Good education is incompatible with such a process; central to it is the examination of assumptions and the rational consideration of alternatives. Hence 'sexist education' is a contradiction in terms; good education is non-sexist, it makes no assumptions about sex differences. (Schools Commission, 1975, p. 17)

This policy was framed in a discourse of liberal education. Its terms were that education could give access to real knowledge about the world (as opposed to distortions and stereotypes) and that the mode of building knowledge was by critical reasoning.

Girls, School and Society would also be categorized as inadequate by many feminist theories of the 1980s and 1990s for its treatment of girls and women. There is no acknowledgment — indeed there is an implied rejection — that women have different 'ways of knowing'. (This is hardly surprising given that, in 1975, such theories of difference were largely represented by psychological rationales for women's inferiority, rather than by the exploration of difference as a suppressed term and condition of language and culture, as seen in later writings of French feminists and American object-relations theorists.)

Even more strikingly, from the perspective of the 1990s, differences among women are not seen as central to an analysis. Instead, the report discusses 'woman's' (in the singular) changing role and outlines a 'universalizing' case about sexual inequality and sexism. That is, this report is not afraid to treat 'woman' (or 'girls') as a category from which a meaningful analysis of inequality in schooling can be made. A late chapter, entitled 'groups with special needs', treats these as an addendum to the main argument. The groups are defined as 'migrant girls and women', 'Aboriginal girls and women' and 'country girls and women'. (The point here is discussed further in Tsolidis, 1990; Yates, 1989 and 1990; Kenway, 1990.)

Nevertheless, the position taken in this early report is not exactly a weak 'equal opportunities' approach, one which looks to change as a matter of very minor adjustments within the political *status quo* (cf. Weiner and Arnot, 1987). In *Girls, School and Society*, the issue of gender and schooling, or girls and schooling, is named explicitly as an issue relating to the *broad sexual inequality of women in society*:

> An observer not raised with our cultural assumptions would be struck by the fact that one half of the population was assigned by birth to activities which, whatever their private gratifications and social importance, carried no economic reward, little public status, and very limited access to public power. Such an observer would note that the terms on which the female population was admitted to public,

> economically rewarded activities were such as to ensure that they retained inferior positions in them. (School Commission, 1975, p. 8)

Notwithstanding the ethnocentric assumption that all cultures would be equally interested in 'economic reward', 'public status' and 'public power' as the measures of what was important about a society, there is a strong point being made here. The analysis is not being confined to measured inequalities in some moments of schooling; rather its starting point, its point of reference, is women's subordination in the general social form. It is from that concern that the question of schooling is addressed.

As well, this 1975 report had a clear proposition about how schooling, a compulsory institution in which young people are inducted into the culture, might be expected to contribute to change. Schooling should teach students (girls and boys) a different history, a different account of the world, one which attends to women as much as to men. And it should interrupt the taken-for-grantedness of students' enculturation into gender by asking them to 'examine' this. To learn gender roles 'in an unexamined way' is 'sexism'; central to 'good education' is 'examination of assumptions and the rational consideration of alternatives'.

By 1987, the influence of a further twelve years of feminist research and action could be seen in the framework of the new *National Policy for the Education of Girls in Australian Schools*. The framework offers an approach that appears more comprehensive, more systematic, more challenging of traditional assumptions about liberal education, more attuned to the claims of minority groups. No 'universalizing' here. Being a girl in an Australian school means being different sorts of girls in different sorts of locations:

> Strategies to improve the quality of education for girls should be based on an understanding that girls are not a homogeneous group. (Schools Commission, 1987, policy framework)

What is heard strongly in this document is the need to listen to different girls, the need to make them feel comfortable. What is there in only the most indirect way, is the reference to the social inequality of women within which schooling is located:

> This report is about education for a society where women and men relate to each other as equals, unconstrained by factors relating to gender. In this context the Report is concerned with addressing the educational experiences of girls in Australian schools.
>
> A comprehensive and realistic understanding of those experiences can only be gained at school level. (*ibid*)

Linked to the changed emphasis on the voices of the girls in the definition of the problem, was a changing assumption about the nature of the knowledge they might acquire. In 1987, there is no longer such a clear assumption that 'liberal education', with adjustments, is all that is required for progressive action. This policy places much more emphasis on the 'educational needs of girls'. One of its four objectives is named as the development of a 'supportive school environment'. Another refers to 'equal access to and participation in appropriate curriculum'. (The other aims are 'raising awareness' and 'equitable resource allocation'.)

By the late 1980s then, issues such as sexual harassment, racism, and the physical environment of the school, are seen as matters which are part of the conditions of learning of girls. And what is to be learnt is not one 'non-sexist' picture of the world, or an ongoing 'critical examination' of sexism, but rather is a curriculum which should be differentiated according to the 'needs' of learners. In the terms of this policy, curriculum should be 'appropriate' and 'inclusive'.

In one sense these shifts in the discourse of policy mirror some shifts in the discourse of feminist educational writing over the same period. In the 1970s and for much of the 1980s, the approach that was being taken assumed either a liberal concept of knowledge (whose basic lines were sound, but whose biases and omissions needed remedy), or a neo-Marxist line of ideology critique (students were to be taught to understand the nature of power and inequality in their own society, including in their own school) (cf. Byrne, 1978; Branson and Miller, 1978; Whyld, 1983, etc.). The more pluralistic position of the *National Policy* reflects the growing significance of two other lines of feminist work (which, at the level of theory, would be seen as different paradigms, and not easily combined). The first stream of work, largely deriving from psychologically-trained intellectuals, takes up an interest in 'women's ways of knowing', and the challenges this poses to 'rationality' (for example, Gilligan, 1977 and 1982; Gilligan, Lyons and Hanmer, 1990; Martin, 1982 and 1984; Harding and Sutoris, 1987). The second stream of debate and research gives priority to the issue of differences amongst women, and particularly to the issue of race and ethnicity as a challenge to general frameworks for understanding sexism or movements against sexism (see, for example, in the UK, the exchanges in *Feminist Review* 17 (July 1984), 25 (March 1987) and 26 (July 1987); in the USA, Hooks, 1984; and in Australia, Tsolidis, 1984 and 1986; Bottomley and De Lepervanche, 1984).

But the approach suggested by the *National Policy* builds the emphasis on difference and cultural identity into a framework far removed from any of the political challenges and deconstructive strategies outlined in the latter literature. The concerns of different groups (women's ways of knowing; culturally specific frameworks and priorities) might be added (curriculum, after all, should be 'appropriate' and 'inclusive') but little is to be brought into question. The illustrative strategies for curriculum reform are full of the language of embracement and not of critique: 'to *broaden* students' perspectives', 'to *include*', 'to *enhance* girls' participation and achievement', 'developing *confidence* and *self-esteem*', 'to meet the *needs* of girls', 'to ensure *inclusive* content, practices, processes and environment', 'increasing girls' *confidence* in mathematics through the *involvement* of parents', '*collaborative* work' (Schools Commission, 1987, pp. 49–51).

Some Issues

Difference, Girl-Centredness and Women's Inequality

In an earlier typology, Weiner and Arnot (1987) contrasted an 'equal opportunities/girl friendly' approach to school reform with a more powerful 'anti-sexist/girl-centred' list of strategies. The Australian developments raise questions about the conflation of 'anti-sexist' and 'girl-centred'. As a policy discourse, a 'girl-centred' strategy, though it may be highly attentive to differences among girls, can operate to contain challenges from feminism.

Not surprisingly, given that they are policy documents, both of the reports discussed above construct schooling as an institution that can act fairly in relation to the different students that enter it (in this case, girls and boys). But the documents present different cases as to the strategies for reform in this area, and different frameworks for the measure of this area as a problem.

Girls, School and Society in 1975 'universalizes' woman as a category, but the *National Policy* in 1987 universalizes difference. The huge body of feminist writing since the 1970s has been heard. The issue of gender and education is complex and broad: sexuality (sexual harassment), race and class differences, different 'ways of knowing' must all be attended to. But, as policy, the attention to difference must be held together within some general framework, and it does so in the form of a needs-based pluralism. The voice through which the issue of difference was raised (the challenge that feminist agendas were racist, or Australian agendas of multiculturalism sexist) and the question of how issues of race and class may be brought together as a movement for change (cf. Hooks, 1989) are both suppressed in this discourse. The emphasis shifts from the discussion of social inequality and how schooling may contribute to change, to a discussion of listening to girls, being nice to girls, attending to the comfort of girls.

The point is particularly apparent if we consider how policies (and funded reform projects) construct the claims of Aboriginal girls, girls of non-English speaking background, and working-class girls. The statements of the 1980s eschew the deficit perspectives of earlier formulations; formally, the research and policy proclaims that any problem is not in the girls, it is in what schooling is doing. But the strategies of action are heavily oriented to the 'needs' of particular groups, rather than to any acknowledgment of ongoing power of the dominant groups, or of structural elements maintaining the *status quo*.

At conferences, Aboriginal women respond to feminist discussions by expressing sympathy for the sexism experienced by Western women, but an insistence that for themselves self-determination, land-rights and anti-racism are the key issues, and that, within their own traditional culture, the division of labour is sex-based, but not patriarchal. Australian education policies concerned with girls and schooling have commonly treated Aborigines and Torres Strait Islanders as a special case, in which those communities will have the right to direct how and to what extent general policy initiatives in relation to girls are taken up. This aspect of formal policy is in line with that proposed by the National Aboriginal Education Council (the formal body through which the Aboriginal community is heard in education discussions), though Aboriginal women writing about schooling in urban settings have also discussed how these city schools are both culturally insensitive and also quick to use 'cultural difference' as an excuse for inferior education (Daylight, 1987; Burnley, 1987; Holland, 1987). However, while the calls of the *Report of the Aboriginal Education Policy Task Force* (Department of Employment, Education and Training, 1988) have been accepted in so far as they relate to a considerable degree of self-determination and some funding support for Aboriginal children, little has been heard about recommendations related to Aboriginal studies in the mainstream curriculum and the problem of racism in the schooling of non-Aboriginal children.

The danger then in moving via policy to listen to the voices of 'the other' is in confining reform to focus on the schooling of those groups. Inequality and subordination in society do not simply arise from the subordinate groups, and schooling's contribution to inequality comes not simply from what it does to those groups.

Beyond the Liberal Curriculum?

In terms of a policy for curriculum, the movement between the mid-70s and the late-80s was from a clear but narrow view of the action to be taken to one which was much broader but much less clear. Moving with the intellectual currents of the times, the policy frameworks had discarded a vision of non-sexist knowledge, for one of multiple meanings, deconstruction, and knowledge as ongoing construction. (White, 1987–88; and Luke and Luke, 1990 provide some further discussion of these developing directions in Australian school curricula.)

For theorists concerned with critical pedagogy, it has been difficult to illustrate a practice sensitive to race, class and gender, even in terms of what one teacher might do with one group of students. In practice, teachers concerned with one issue continue to cut across others (Weiler, 1988); to find that strategies of deconstruction and collage, so popular with the theorist, find a less than enthusiastic response from the captive students (Taylor, 1989); or to posit such an abstract and extreme move beyond existing categories that it is hard to conceive them as practice (as in Davies, 1989a; Giroux, 1991; and discussed further in Yates, 1992). The liberal curriculum of truths and critical rationality may be naive in terms of these contemporary lines of theory, but the move beyond it, in terms of those policy frameworks discussed above, may blunt, rather than extend the challenge of feminism within the mainstream curriculum.

The questions raised here continue some problems raised by Mica Nava over a decade ago, in assessing two of the early British books to address gender and education, Eileen Byrne's *Women and Education* (1978) and Rosemary Deem's (1978) *Women and Schooling* (Nava, 1980). Byrne's work, Nava wrote, was marked by a naivety of theoretical framework, by contradictions, and by a 'quaint' and rambling style ('We need a simple national declaration that it is no longer British to discriminate'). Yet, Nava argues, Byrne's case nevertheless captures a 'positive political engagement', an uncompromising attack on male blindness which perpetuates the invisibility of girls in official documents, and a workable program of (admittedly partial) reforms. Deem's work, Nava argued, was set in a more sophisticated Althusserian framework yet in fact offered a less clear intervention in relation to schooling and sexism. More significantly, Deem in fact, at a level of strategy, supported 'reformist' action, which implicitly brought into question the theoretical framework she had used, by recognizing 'the heterogeneous nature of the structures of oppression' (*ibid*, p. 74).

In terms of curriculum and student learning, theoretical critiques have become very sophisticated. The question of what pedagogical practice engages student learners differently is much less worked out. (I have discussed this further in Yates, 1992.)

Feminism Within State Policy

To date, my discussion has focussed on some changing emphases in policy and their connection to changing emphases in feminist theoretical work. The shape of policy is not simply a translation of work within feminism concerning difference and the nature of knowledge, but it does raise the question of what these lines of feminist discussion can propose as a framework for schooling as a system. When deconstruction and difference are themselves universalized as curriculum policy, is it enough to go on calling for more deconstruction and critique?

In this section, I want to consider more directly what the Australian government is doing when it takes up issues concerning gender and education reform: how does the discourse of policy shape issues from feminism?

In relation to gender and schooling, a number of writers (McHoul, 1984; Arnot, 1986; Lingard, Henry and Taylor, 1987; Kenway, 1990; Middleton, 1990) have shown how the language of feminist politics is taken up but transformed and contained when it is made policy. One theme is that state policy in liberal-democratic societies will continue to assert and 'naturalize' the rule of law, the rights of individuals, the absence of structured conflict and inequalities of power, and will modify challenges of groups given political legitimacy (here, the women's movement) where they propose any fundamental challenge to these principles. As Yeatman (1990) puts this in her discussion of a large range of Labor government policies in Australia:

> The feature which all these have in common as instances of the policy genre concerns the way in which the interest of the state in the management of issues means that the policy text is written in such a way as to deny the politics of discourse (a politics of contested meaning). (p. 160)

The point being made in Yeatman's analysis is that the transformation and containment takes place not simply because policy-makers represent a 'ruling class', and not because there is a deliberate effort to continue to silence subordinate groups, but because contested meaning, contested lines of exclusion and inclusion, contested vision, are excluded in the terms of its own discourse.

This is seen very clearly in the treatment of 'difference' in the policies I have discussed. 'Difference' was a marginalized addendum in the first policy framework, and in the second was pervasive, but as mere variety which could be unproblematically held together in a common schooling. It is not acknowledged as a challenge which concerns the fundamental shape of that schooling (of rationality, of language, of what knowledge is important). Within feminism there is vigorous debate about centre and margins, about post-colonialism, about feminisms. Within policy discourse the taking up of claims about women's ways of knowing or about Aboriginal self-determination is treated as part of incremental reform, not as contesting what is to count as the problem.

Secondly, there is the issue of the substantive terms within which feminism is constituted in the policy discourse. Formally the Labor government in Australia is committed both to affirmative action for women and to economic rationalism. Formally too these are constructed as two separate discourses. Yet, if we consider which projects have actually been emphasized under both of the policy frameworks discussed earlier, we can see that the discourses of gender and those of economics are mutually constituting.

In schools as in higher education, government money committed to women and education has been overwhelmingly reserved for increasing their numbers in mathematics and science (cf. *Girls in Schools*, 1988; Yates, 1990; Yeatman, 1990). The discourse constructs the problem of gender and education as the problem of women and non-traditional careers. The problem of boys and men for women's equality is suppressed. As well, the discourse shapes the overall curriculum question for policy as that of its relation to paid work and public life, in a period when many feminist writers on education have been mounting critiques of women's exclusion by definition through such an emphasis (cf. Martin, 1982; Harding and Sutoris, 1987).

More broadly, the identification of the gender and schooling problem as that of their failure to continue with mathematics, or to take on scientific and technical jobs, 'naturalizes' (that is, makes appear as common-sense) that women's position in society is a result of their individual choices and achievements. And it materially contributes to women's continuing inequality by using the discourse of women's rights to increase funding to engineering, science and technology, and to construct these rather than the service sector (which is in fact the major area of employment) as the important part of the workforce.

Enforcing Feminism Via the State

Since International Women's Year in 1975, Australian governments have been providing funding specifically tagged for issues of girls and schooling. Initially, funding was primarily available to be taken up by states and schools who wished to develop projects in the area. It was decentralized and intended to support school-based initiatives and a 'grass-roots' development of reform (see Yates, 1987). When reassessments of the effectiveness of these initial developments took place in the early 1980s, what was largely heard from feminists working in education was the need to make these reforms more systematic and mandatory rather than optional on the part of schools and teachers. On the surface at least, much of this has now occurred.

Recently, for example, there has been a major restructuring of teacher career paths, in particular through the introduction of a new promotion classification, 'advanced skills teacher'. This position is officially described as one designed to recognize the classroom skills of the teacher, and to begin to overturn a career structure which rewarded only qualifications and administration.

At the time of writing, teachers are being assessed for these positions. The guidelines for these applications emphasize above all else that teachers are to be judged on their knowledge of and commitment to, current government policy. In Victoria, they are expected to know the Labor government's 'social justice' policy for education and the more specific policies related to 'equal opportunity' for girls and 'inclusive curriculum'. They are asked to show what actions and initiatives they have taken in terms of such policies.

Or consider this. Most states in Australia have now developed affirmative action employment policies for teachers which regulate the gender composition of appointment committees, the texts of advertisements, appointment procedures. These strategies to date have produced little change in the shape of the hierarchies of teaching (a majority of women in the lowest positions; a minority in the senior positions, particularly as principals of schools), as well as many complaints from female principals, that such approaches constitute 'gender charity', that they construct as token the women who are successful, and undermine their credibility.

Or again, consider the apparatus surrounding the *National Policy for the Education of Girls in Australian Schools* discussed earlier. This has spawned an ongoing avalanche of paper, as it requires annual reports by states on what they are doing (and the states in turn have produced their own 'action plans' with their own reporting requirements), and the information produced is circulated and recirculated in the form of formal annual reports (the *Girls in Schools* series); a computerized National Data Base; a monthly newsletter for interested teachers (*The Gen*); and other publications and curriculum resources for schools.

In sum, two things have happened in the course of the taking up by the Commonwealth government of the concern about gender and schooling. First, it has used these issues to considerably extend its formal involvement in, and control of, schooling. Second, the regulation of schooling and of the activities of teachers has been greatly increased through the new policies.

The *National Policy for the Education of Girls* was in fact the first 'national policy' of any kind for schooling in Australia. Previously, schooling was a matter for state governments and Education Departments. The Labor government which introduced the National Policy was engaged in developing a 'unified national system' of education, and had largely completed this in relation to the tertiary sector. By using a reform agenda for its first national policy on schooling, the government has avoided criticisms that might be expected from intellectuals on the left regarding the extension of its powers.

As a parallel to this current move, one might consider that a major increase in the government funding of 'independent' schools was introduced by a Labor government in 1973, as part of its attention to 'disadvantage' (many of the schools in the Catholic sector in particular rated high on its various criteria of disadvantage). This funding has steadily been increased, and the idea that non-state schools are entitled to have a large part of their recurrent costs funded by the government is now 'naturalized' in the current discourse. Here an institutionalized funding mechanism, initiated as part of a strategy to 'compensate disadvantaged students', has been transformed into one of 'individual rights', where all individuals and schools are assumed to be entitled to an individual share of taxes allocated to schools. A policy to compensate disadvantage has been turned into a central source of disadvantage, by strengthening the viability and size of the private sector, and making the state sector a more residual one (cf. Anderson, 1990; Connell, White and Johnston, 1990).

The new involvement in the control of schooling by the Commonwealth Government, of which the *National Policy for the Education of Girls* is a part, was a response to calls from feminists for broader and more effective enforcement of reform. But it is also part of a general development in the past decade towards more direct control of schooling and curriculum by politicians (cf. Sherington, 1990).

Secondly, as a result of the new policies and systems of management, teachers, schools, selection committees, curriculum consultants and principals are all now required to spend a good deal of time documenting, checking, accounting for their activities in relation to girls and schooling.

The greater the incursion into schools of the forms of bureaucratic management, the less is likely to be the space for the pedagogic conditions of any lively critical pedagogy (cf. Ferguson, 1984; Kenway and Blackmore, 1988). As well, the institution of new forms of control, designed for progressive ends, remain to be used for other purposes as the political climate changes (and the example of the funding of independent schools is one example of this). And, as the examples at the beginning of this section were designed to illustrate, the developments are building a considerable resentment and evasion by teachers.

Yet across all this we need to remember that one source of these developments was a call for greater regulation and enforcement of 'non-sexist' principles by a wide range of feminist groups concerned with education, and disenchanted with the effectiveness of the decentralized and piecemeal activity of the first wave of reform.

Conclusion

This discussion of Australian government policy on gender and schooling leads to questions rather than conclusions. They are questions from a particular context and for a particular context, but also questions that touch on feminist theory more broadly.

In relation to the form of the state's involvement in gender reform, this chapter identified some continuities as well as some changes in the framing of policy. Throughout the period, feminist issues, when they are taken as policy, are not located as part of a 'politics of contested discourse' (to refer back to Yeatman's argument), but as reforms achievable within the existing frameworks. Throughout it too, despite the rhetorical taking up of feminist challenges to treat schooling rather than girls as the source of the problems, the initiatives supported, and indeed the very policy documents themselves, continue the focus on girls as the problem, on women and girls as other. What could begin to turn this around?

In terms of changes in the policies, we saw some shifts from an 'equality' agenda to a 'difference' agenda. Joan Scott (1990) has discussed how versions of both agendas failed to support women in the Sears court case regarding affirmative action in the USA. Scott argues that the appropriate response is to reveal the excluded voices within particular versions of equality, but also to recognize that equality rests on differences rather than identity (that is, it is a needed term only in so far as there is not absolute identity, but rather an agreement to treat as equal a group who have some other qualities of diversity). In the case of the policies discussed in this chapter, the problem is not at the level of formal frameworks. Both reports endorse equality for girls and boys within schooling, and neither argues that girls are identical either to boys or with each other. The problem is at the level of substantive choices in curriculum strategy: the degree of emphasis given to a common knowledge and expectation of students, as compared with that given to the 'needs' of students. This is why the conflation of 'girl-centred' and 'anti-sexist' begs some questions.

In Australia, we saw too that experience with local action and piecemeal reforms led most people working for change in relation to gender and schooling to call for a general and mandatory approach. But this approach brings increasing government incursion in all teachers' lives (and in their non-teaching duties) and provokes some backlash. Is the answer to continue with this direction and work to improve these policies of management, or to withdraw, criticize and deconstruct, leaving policy to develop untainted by feminist involvement, with all that that might imply?

And what of post-modernism and its uses in the context I have been discussing? We have seen that some directions of this contemporary theory (the concern with difference, and with local knowledges) are in fact being drawn into the shaping of policy. However, as curriculum policy, these frameworks are not necessarily a stronger force for change than the discourse of liberal education which they replaced.

The insights of post-structuralist theory have been useful in pointing to silences in both the 'inequality of woman' form of policy and the 'inclusive curriculum' form of policy. They have also been useful for attending to the form of state discourse and regulation of this recent period. This next step, presumably, would be to move beyond the terms of the oppositions in the 'equality versus difference' formulation, and beyond my own 'either/or' question above, regarding reform from within versus an oppositional stance. But the answers cannot come simply from theory.

References

ALCOFF, L. (1987) 'Cultural feminism versus post-structuralism: The identity crisis in feminist theory', *Signs*, **13**, 3, pp. 405–36.

ANDERSON, D.S. (1990) 'The public/private division in Australian schooling: Social and educational effects' in SAHA, L.J. and KEEVES, J.P. (Eds) *Schooling and Society in Australia: Sociological Perspectives*, Sydney, Pergamon.

ANDRAE-THELIN, A. and ELGQVIST-SALZMAN, I. (1989) 'Sweden' in KELLY, G. (Ed.) *International Handbook of Women's Education*, New York, Greenwood Press.

ARNOT, M. (Ed.) (1985) *Race and Gender: Equal Opportunities Policies in Education*, Oxford, Pergamon Press.

ARNOT, M. (1986) 'State education policy and girls' educational experiences' in WHITELEGG, L. (Ed.) *Women in Britain*, Milton Keynes, Open University.

BALDOCK, C. and CASS, B. (Eds) (1983) *Women, Social Welfare and the State*, Sydney, Allen & Unwin.

BALL, S. (Ed.) (1990) *Foucault and Education*, London, Routledge.

BEILHARZ, P. (1987) 'Reading politics: Social theory and social policy', *Australian and New Zealand Journal of Sociology*, **23**, pp. 388–407.

BOTTOMLEY, G. and DE LEPERVANCHE, M. (Eds) (1984) *Ethnicity, Class and Gender in Australia*, Sydney, Allen & Unwin.

BRANSON, J. and MILLER, D. (1978) *Class, Sex and Education in Capitalist Society*, Melbourne, Sorrett.

BURNLEY, L. (1987) 'Meeting the educational needs of young Aboriginal women' in FOSTER, V. (Ed.) *Including Girls: Curriculum Perspectives on the Education of Girls*, Canberra Curriculum Development Centre, Canberra.

BYRNE, E. (1978) *Women and Education*, London, Tavistock.

CONNELL, R.W., WHITE, V. and JOHNSTON, K. (1990) 'Poverty and education: Changing conceptions', *Discourse*, **11**, 1, pp. 5–20.

DAVIES, B. (1989a) 'Education for sexism: A theoretical analysis of the sex/gender bias in education', *Educational Philosophy and Theory*, **21**, 1, pp. 1–19.

DAVIES, B. (1989b) *Frogs and Snails and Feminist Tales: Pre-School Children and Gender*, Sydney, Allen & Unwin.

DAYLIGHT, P. (1987) 'Overview' in FOSTER, V. (Ed.), *Including Girls: Curriculum Perspectives on the Education of Girls*, Canberra, Curriculum Development Centre.

DEEM, R. (1978) *Women and Schooling*, London, Routledge.

DEPARTMENT OF EMPLOYMENT, EDUCATION AND TRAINING (1988) *Report of the Aboriginal Education Policy Task Force*, Canberra.

DIAMOND, I. and QUINBY, L. (1988) *Feminism and Foucault*, Boston, MA, Northeastern University Press.

EISENSTEIN, H. (1988) 'Dilemmas in theory and practice: Theorizing gender difference' in BLACKMORE, J. and KENWAY, J. (Eds) *Gender Issues in the Theory and Practice of Educational Administration and Policy*, Waurn Ponds, Deakin University.

FERGUSON, K. (1984) *The Feminist Case Against Bureaucracy*, Philadelphia, PA, Temple Press.

FRANZWAY, S., COURT, D. and CONNELL, R.W. (1989) *Staking a Claim: Feminism, Bureaucracy and the State*, Sydney, Allen & Unwin.

GILLIGAN, C. (1977) 'In a different voice: Women's conception of the self and morality', *Harvard Education Review*, **47**, 4, pp. 481–571.

GILLIGAN, C. (1982) *In a Different Voice: Psychological Theory and Women's Development*, Cambridge, MA, Harvard University Press.

GILLIGAN, C., LYONS, N. and HANMER, T.J. (1990) *Making Connections: The Relational Worlds of Adolescent Girls at Emma Willard School*, Cambridge, MA, Harvard University Press.

GIRLS IN SCHOOLS (1988) Report on the National Policy for the Education of Girls in Australian Schools, AGPS, Canberra.

GIROUX, H. (Ed.) (1991) *Post-modernism, Feminism, and Cultural Politics: Redrawing Educational Boundaries*, New York, SUNY Press.

HARDING, J. and SUTORIS, M. (1987) 'An object-relations account of the differential involvement of boys and girls in science and technology' in KELLY, A. (Ed.) *Science for Girls?*, Milton Keynes, Open University Press.

HIRSCH, M. and FOX KELLER, E. (Eds) (1990) *Conflicts in Feminism*, New York, Routledge.

HOLLAND, W. (1987) 'Aboriginal women in education: A community initiative' in FOSTER, V. (Ed.) *Including Girls: Curriculum Perspectives on the Education of Girls*, Canberra, Curriculum Development Centre.

HOOKS, B. (1984) *Feminist Theory: From Margin to Centre*, Boston, MA, South End Press.

HOOKS, B. (1989) *Talking Back: Thinking Feminist/Thinking Black*, Boston, MA, South End Press.

KENWAY, J. (1990) *Gender and Education Policy: A Call for New Directions*, Waurn Ponds, Deakin University.

KENWAY, J. and BLACKMORE, J. (1988) 'Gender and the green paper — privatization and equity', *Australian Universities Review*, **31**, 1, pp. 49–56.

LATHER, P. (1991) *Feminist Research in Education: Within/Against*, Waurn Ponds, Deakin University.

LINGARD, B., HENRY, M. and TAYLOR, S. (1987) 'A girl in a militant pose: A chronology of struggle in girls' education in Queensland', *British Journal of Sociology of Education*, **8**, 2, pp. 135–52.

LUKE, A. and LUKE, C. (1990) 'Schooling knowledge as simulation: Curriculum in post-modern conditions', *Discourse*, **10**, 2, pp. 75–91.

MCHOUL, A. (1984) 'Writing, sexism and schooling: A discourse-analytic investigation of some recent documents on sexism and education in Queensland', *Discourse*, **4**, 2, pp. 133–48.

MARTIN, J.R. (1982) 'Excluding women from the educational realm', *Harvard Education Review*, **52**, 2, pp. 133–48.

MARTIN, J.R. (1984) 'Bringing women into educational thought', *Educational Theory*, **34**, 4, pp. 341–53.

MIDDLETON, S. (1984) 'The sociology of women's education as a field of academic study', *Discourse*, **15**, 1, pp. 42–62.

MIDDLETON, S. (1990) 'Women, equality and equity in liberal educational policies 1945–1988' in MIDDLETON, S., CODD, J. and JONES, A. (Eds) *New Zealand Education Policy Today; Critical Perspectives*, Wellington, Allen & Unwin.

NAVA, M. (1980) 'Gender and education', *Feminist Review*, **5**, pp. 69–78.

NICHOLSON, L. (1990) *Feminist/Postmodernism*, New York, Routledge.

PATEMAN, C. and GROSS, E. (Eds) (1986) *Feminist Challenges*, Sydney, Allen and Unwin.

PORTER, P. (1983) 'Social policy, education and women in Australia' in BALDOCK, C. and CASS, B. (Eds) *Women, Social Welfare and the State*, Sydney, Allen & Unwin.

SCHOOLS COMMISSION (1975) *Girls, School and Society*, Report of a Study Group to the Schools Commission, Canberra.

SCHOOLS COMMISSION (1987) *National Policy for the Education of Girls in Australian Schools*, Canberra.

SCOTT, J.W. (1990) 'Deconstructing equality-versus-difference: Or, the uses of poststructuralist theory for feminism' in HIRSCH, M. and FOX KELLER, E. (Eds) *Conflicts in Feminism*, New York, Routledge.

SHERINGTON, G. (1990) 'Organization and control in Australian schools', paper presented to the National Conference of NBEET, Coffs Harbour.

TAYLOR, S. (1989) 'Empowering girls and young women: The challenge of the gender-inclusive curriculum', *Journal of Curriculum Studies*, **21**, 5, pp. 441–56.

TSOLIDIS, G. (1984) 'Girls of non-English speaking background: Implications for an Australian feminism' in BURNS, R. and SHEEHAN, B. (Eds) *Women and Education*, Papers of the ANZCIES Annual Conference, Melbourne, La Trobe University.

TSOLIDIS, G. (1986) *Educating Voula: A Report on Non-English Speaking Background Girls and Education*, Melbourne, Ministry of Education.

TSOLIDIS, G. (1990) 'Ethnic minority girls and self-esteem' in KENWAY, J. and WILLIS, S. (Eds) *Hearts and Minds: Self-Esteem and the Schooling of Girls*, Lewes, Falmer Press.

WALKERDINE, V. (1984) 'Developmental psychology and the child-centred pedagogy' in HENRIQUES, J., HOLLOWAY, W., URWIN, C., VENN, C. and WALKERDINE, V. (Eds) *Changing the Subject: Psychology, Social Regulation and Subjectivity*, London, Methuen.

WALKERDINE, V. (1985) 'On the regulation of speaking and silence: Subjectivity, class and gender in contemporary schooling' in STEEDMAN, C., URWIN, C. and WALKERDINE, V. (Eds), *Language, Gender and Childhood*, London, Routledge.

WALKERDINE, V. (1987) 'Some issues in the historical construction of the scientific truth about girls' in KELLY, A. (Ed.) *Science for Girls?*, Milton Keynes, Open University Press.

WEILER, K. (1988) *Women Teaching for Change: Gender, Class and Power*, Massachusetts, Bergin & Garvey.

WEINER, G. and ARNOT, M. (1987) 'Teachers and gender politics' in ARNOT, M. and WEINER, G. (Eds) *Gender and the Politics of Schooling*, London, Hutchinson.

WHITE, D. (1987–88), 'Individual, curriculum and society: The post-modern curriculum?', *Melbourne Studies in Education*.

WHYLD, J. (Ed.) (1983) *Sexism in the Secondary Curriculum*, London, Harper & Row.

YATES, L. (1986) 'Theorizing inequality today', *British Journal of Sociology of Education*, **7**, 2, pp. 119–34.

YATES, L. (1987) 'Australian research on girls and schooling 1975–1985' in KEEVES, J.P. (Ed.) *Australian Education: Review of Recent Research*, Sydney, Allen & Unwin.

YATES, L. (1989) 'Gender, ethnicity and the "inclusive" curriculum', paper presented to the annual conference of the American Educational Research Association, San Francisco.

YATES, L. (1990) *Theory/Practice Dilemmas: Gender, Knowledge and Education*, Waurn Ponds, Deakin University.

YATES, L. (1992) 'Post-modernism, feminism and cultural politics — or, if master narratives have been discredited, what does Giroux think he is doing?, *Discourse*, **13**, 1, (forthcoming).

YEATMAN, A. (1988) 'Contemporary issues for feminism and the politics of the state' in BLACKMORE, J. and KENWAY, J. (Eds) *Gender Issues in the Theory and Practice of Educational Administration and Policy*, Waurn Ponds, Deakin University.

YEATMAN, A. (1990) *Bureaucrats, Technocrats, Femocrats: Essays on the Contemporary Australian State*, Sydney, Allen & Unwin.

Chapter 9

A Crisis in Patriarchy? British Feminist Educational Politics and State Regulation of Gender

Madeleine Arnot

Few recent sociological analyses of the New Right in the United Kingdom have addressed the interconnections between the rise of the radical right and critical feminist traditions in education. A surprising fact perhaps, given the evident hostility of Conservative politicians to feminist and anti-racist politics and their explicit references to the ending of the 'age of egalitarianism'.[1] Sophisticated analyses, such as those by Whitty (1989), Dale (1989) and Ball (1990), offer us insights into the various discourses and ideological tendencies of the Conservative government and its party advisors. From their perspective, we are encouraged to see education policy as 'infused with economic, political and ideological contradictions' (Ball, 1990, p. 211); a site of struggle between different groups for domination, prestige or economic advantage where the most significant context is the restructuring of capitalism. As Stephen Ball argues:

> The (National) curriculum . . . is a particular focus for contradiction and struggle. The economic provides a context and a 'vocabulary of motives' for reform. The overall repositioning and restructuring of education in relation to production is evident. (p. 211, my addition)

No reference here to patriarchal ideologies, nor indeed to the logic of patriarchy. The New Right is represented instead as a set of political responses to the necessity of 'restoring authority' and 'responding to the contemporary logic of capitalist development' (*ibid*, p. 213). As Dale (1989) earlier explained, this logic implies that educational systems are structured around three problems:

> direct support for the capital accumulation process; the provision of a wider social context not inimical to the continuing capital accumulation

> and the legitimation of the work of the state and the education system. (p. 95)

Yet, given such emphasis on the effects of economic formations on educational discourses, it seems extraordinary that feminist and 'race' politics are so absent from such sociological accounts. It is surely hard to deny the impact of the women's movement and black community politics on the post-war economy and the considerable increase in married women's economic activity on economic, familial and cultural spheres. Yet again, it seems male radical sociologists in the United Kingdom have failed to address gender relations and, as a result, have avoided explanations of the rise of the New Right based upon 'moral/traditional/familial ideologies and policies' (ten Tusscher, 1986). According to Kenway (1990), mainstream policy analysts

> . . . have rather arrogantly failed to notice that they (most often men) write largely for and about men. Insensitive to matters of gender, they have little or no apparent consciousness of how gender inflected are their theories, concerns and interests. (Further) many mainstream/malestream policy analysts seem unaware of an increasing body of feminist scholarship which both exposes many of the limitations of the presuppositions of the policy field and brings matters of gender into the foreground. (p. 7)

For Jane Kenway, the solution is to develop 'gender and educational policy analysis' as a new field of study. This field, she argues, already exists insofar as one can find a diversity of research literature which focusses upon state policy-making. Such literature includes, for example, analyses of the gendered assumptions behind government policies and studies of the impact of the women's movement and feminist struggles on state policy-making processes. Contained within this new field are studies of the success and the limitations of legislation which attempts to promote equal opportunities for women. Particularly in Australia, state administrative apparatuses through which such equality policies are implemented, are being analyzed by feminists. In this context, reports on the ways in which feminists have been incorporated within the state bureaucracy as 'femocrats' are especially instructive.[2]

This chapter contributes to Kenway's new field of study. It offers a preliminary analysis of the ways in which gender issues were part of the political context behind the recent radical reorganization of education in the United Kingdom. I intend to reconsider the circumstances which allowed for the promotion of those aspects of New Right ideology which we tend to associate with the doctrines of Margaret Thatcher's government (1979–1991) — doctrines which many have described as a mixture of neo-liberal influences emphasizing a free market approach and an absence of state controls, and neo-conservative influences which reassert 'an orientation to the past, traditional values, and collective loyalties' (Ball, 1990, p. 214).

The impact of 'Thatcherism' as a constellation of different discourses on the educational system has been far reaching. However, it is my belief that the full significance of the last two decades of policy-making cannot fully be understood without more questions being asked about the gendered assumptions which underpin these educational reforms. Such questions will need to deal, for example, with the tensions between New Right approaches to patriarchal relations in the public and private spheres and to women's position within both spheres. As I, along with others have argued (for example, David, 1983a and 1983b; Arnot, 1991 and 1992b), the New Right educational discourses are significant precisely because of the contradictions between, on the one hand, encouraging a 'moral crusade' in support of the patriarchal family and, on the other, promoting the principles of a 'free market' society in which individuals are to find their full potential. Contained within these contexts are the gendered roles of breadwinning husband and dependent wife, but also seemingly gender neutral concepts of the citizen and the 'consumer'. Conservative political thinkers, I have argued, have manipulated concepts of competitive individualism and equal opportunities for their own purposes, thus hiding both their own ideological confusion, and also their continued support for patterns of male dominance (Arnot, 1992b).

Identifying the shape and the tensions within New Right educational discourses, still however, begs the question about how such ambivalent tendencies affect the new educational system and also the educational chances and careers of women and men from different social and ethnic origins. Such discourses of the New Right suggest but do not describe the specific educational policies which affect gender, race and class divisions.

The construction of Conservative education policy in the 1980s has been represented as an attempt at 'modernizing' gender relations (c.f. Weiner, 1989; Arnot, 1992b) in a way that belies its patriarchal basis. Despite the rhetoric, new distinctions are being made between the rights and responsibilities of male and female citizens in the public and familial spheres (Arnot, 1992a) and new forms of gender differentiation are being created within areas of knowledge[3]. The reassertion of male values is particularly evident in the hierarchical reordering of school knowledge, the styles of pedagogy and modes of assessment. State educational policy is being used to construct and regulate gender relations in new ways. And the reasons, I would want to argue can be found in what ten Tusscher (1986) called the 'crisis in patriarchy' by the 1980s.[4]

The focus of this chapter is to explore further the nature of that crisis in relation to state policy and practice. I begin my analysis by briefly outlining some of the debates within feminist theories of the state. These debates helped me reconsider the ways in which feminist critiques of social democratic education and state policy-making are not just interconnected but part of the same processes.

In the second section I will demonstrate how gender issues and women's struggles contributed to the 'crisis in patriarchy' which lay at the heart of contemporary educational reforms. I consider in more depth the ways in which feminists challenged the patriarchal relations constructed by social democracy and how such challenges encouraged particular state responses. I also very briefly explore in the final section the ways in which Conservative educational policies can be understood as attempts to retrieve and restructure male-female relations. I argue therefore, in conclusion, that feminist educational struggles cannot remain at the margins of our analyses of contemporary social reconstruction.

Theorizing Patriarchy and the State

Although it is now commonplace to talk about patriarchal relations as historically formed, nevertheless it is still very difficult to conceptualize the nature of the historical process which has shaped gender relations and theorize its significance. Walby's (1990) much debated theory of patriarchy,[5] suggests that we should look initially at the ways in which modern society has involved a transition from private forms of patriarchy where women were subordinated in the household by individual men to modern versions where women are now allowed access to the public spheres, yet subordinated to men by new forms of patriarchy.

The consequences of such a shift from private to public forms of patriarchy for education has not as yet been analyzed but it suggests an interesting line of thought for educationalists to pursue (c.f. Araujo, 1992). It implies that we should now view patriarchal relations within the occupational structures of teaching as part of this more general societal shift and focus our efforts on understanding the role which state educational provision played in the transformation of patriarchal relations over the last century. It suggests that we understand the changing nature of patriarchy and hence its modes of legitimation and modes of transmission.[6]

From such a perspective, we might begin to think therefore about the significance of opening up the public sphere of teaching to women and of allowing women access to 'male' forms of instrumental knowledge. Should such educational reforms now be understood as part of a broader pattern of encouraging women to enter the public sphere only to reinforce their subordinate status within new sets of patriarchal relations? Were we looking at the development of new more public forms of patriarchy, facilitated through mass secondary and higher education in the post-war period?

Walby's theory is useful in encouraging us to focus attention not upon the maintenance of the social order but rather the nature of educational change and the shifting relationship between schooling and its social context. It encourages us to consider the ways in which patriarchal relations are recontextualized by schooling in such a way as to prepare children, perhaps, for different forms of patriarchal control. It suggests that schools may have played a part in changing our assumptions about the nature of family life and marriage in society and in contributing to the shifting dissonances of modern society.

What Walby's theory does not do, however, is illuminate the operation of the state except insofar as she suggests a complexity of state agencies and approaches. In 1983 MacKinnon pointed out that 'feminism has no theory of the state' — a statement that was particularly pertinent to contemporary feminist educational theory. Many feminists especially those in social policy, political science and women's studies have since quoted this famous opening line as the starting point for a new theoretical project. As a result, there is a considerable amount of debate on the advisability or inadvisability of developing a unitary theory of the state. Can a theory of state cater for the complexity of women's experiences of state policies and practice (see Weedon, 1987; Allen, 1990; Phillips, 1991)?

This is not the place to rehearse the complexity of these discussions and analyses. Fortunately some excellent and highly accessible summaries are now available of the different feminist theories of the state (for example, Kenway, 1990; Franzway, Court and Connell, 1989; Watson, 1990). A reading of this literature allows us to discover the diversity of feminist interpretations of the relationship between the state and gender or sexual politics. Many of the summaries point, for example, to key distinctions between socialist, radical and liberal feminist interpretations of the impact of the state upon women. The result has been seen in the more sophisticated reinterpretations of the relationship between patriarchy as a political power structure and state formation. Few contemporary feminists today would see the state as either monolithic or simplistically 'patriarchal' or 'male'. Increasingly feminists have recognized that there are 'a series of *arenas* which constitute the state both discursively and through shifting interlocking connections and practices' (Watson, 1990, p. 7, my emphasis). As Watson observes,

> In the last decade recognition that the state is a category of abstraction which cannot simply be characterized as a unified entity has increasingly informed feminist work on the subject. There are many different varieties of state, spatially and historically. Each of these has its own combination of institutions, apparatuses, and arenas, which have their own histories, contradictions, relations and connections, internally and externally. (*ibid*)

Such statements are not unfamiliar to any student of educational policy, especially those working within Marxist or Foucauldian traditions.[7] What may be less familiar, however, for many educationalists are the hard hitting critiques of the liberal democratic state developed by feminist theorists concerned to describe the ways in which women are positioned through political discourses and practices. Carol Pateman's (1980) challenge to the tenets of liberal democracy as patriarchal in conception and in practice has reverberated around feminist social science. She has posited the existence of a 'fraternal social contract' as the central component of liberal democracy and identified gendered concepts of citizenship and male defined notions of democracy. She has encouraged others to reassess, in light of patriarchal relations, the significance of the philosophies of 'master thinkers' such as Hegel, Rousseau and Kant (for example, Lloyd, 1986).

Such feminist political theory encourages us to move, as Connell (1990) does, to the proposition that:

> The state is constituted within gender relations as the central institutionalisation of gendered power. Conversely, gender dynamics are a major force constructing the state, both in the historical creation of state structures and in contemporary policy. (p. 519)

This new sensitivity to the structuring influence of gender dynamics on state apparatuses, bureaucracies and discourses has encouraged new conceptual understandings about the relationship between patriarchy and the state. For example, Franzway, Court and Connell (1989) and Connell (1990) stress the capacity (although not unlimited) of the state to 'regulate' gender categories, relations and practices. The state is conceived now as 'an active player in gender politics'. It is represented as a 'significant vehicle' of both 'sexual and gender oppression and regulation' (Connell, 1990).

A key line of argument focuses on the role which the state has played in constructing the division between public and private relations, between predominantly male and female spheres. State maintenance of these allegedly complementary but separate spheres, which are key to so many social policies including education, shapes women's oppression but also becomes (as a result) a site of 'contention and struggle' (Franzway, Court and Connell, 1989).

Such a view of the state also allows a different perspective on the internal dynamics of state itself, its policies and practices. Men and women are to be found in different locations, and at different levels within the hierarchies of state bureaucracies and within the echelons of political power. Struggles for the right to control and shape a new 'gender regime'[8] could affect the nature of public feminist campaigns and also internal struggles within the political structures to increase women's representation and power sharing. 'The control of the machinery of government can be tactically decisive' (Connell, 1990).

Looking at the machinery of government in the United Kingdom it is difficult to contest the view that men have long controlled the policy-making process and implementation structures. A political system where women constitute only 60 out of 651 (9.2 per cent) democratically elected Members of Parliament is hard to describe as anything other than a men's club. Connell outlines the consequences well:

> State structures in recent history institutionalise the European equation between authority and a dominating masculinity: they are effectively controlled by men; and they operate a massive bias towards heterosexual men's interests. (*ibid*, p. 535)

Within the state, men's interests therefore, like those of capital are 'actively constructed'. But even more critically so too are feminist demands upon by the state. As Watson (1990) argues, feminist struggles have been constructed not in isolation from the state, nor necessarily external to it. Women's demands are a product of the process in which some demands have been acceded to and not others. Feminist struggles, therefore, are integral to the purposes and action of the state within modern society.

From this perspective it becomes politically important for our understanding of social change that we are able to interpret the ways in which feminist demands have been 'diluted' or even 'coopted' through 'engagement with the institutions and discourses which constitute the state' (*ibid*, p. 6). It is also vital to our analysis, that the state is viewed, not as a static entity but as constantly undergoing change — the contradictions and inconsistencies, the forms of contention and struggle create crisis tendencies but they also allow new political possibilities (Connell, 1990, p. 532).

In light of these strictures, let us briefly look at the role which feminist educational politics has played in the United Kingdom in the last two decades. We can consider the ways in which feminist campaigns and research have created one of the 'arenas' which constituted the 'Conservative educational revolution' (c.f. Jones, 1989) of the 1990s.

Feminism, Patriarchy and Social Democratic Education

One way of comprehending the relationship between state educational policy and gender politics is to reassess the post-war period when the social democratic principles underpinned educational reforms were challenged by feminist educationalists. In the first decades after the Second World War, principles such as equality of opportunity (equal access) and universalism (equal or comparable provision) seemed to favour the removal of biological discourses which had shaped educational processes and outcomes since the nineteenth century. Any support for the notion of biological differences between the sexes increasingly was hidden in the new rhetoric of promoting equal educational for all. The emphasis initially became one of assimilating women into mainstream male culture and educational values at a time when the economy required their labour.

For the purposes of promoting a meritocratic society, educational policy-makers hid behind psychological discourses of differential pupil abilities. References to biological differences between the sexes were being replaced by an increasing reliance upon male-female differences in personalities, interests and above all 'educational needs' (Wolpe, 1976). Differences between male and female pupils, particularly in relation to their interest in marriage and parenthood, were discussed by policy-makers as naturally part of the different psychological make up of girls and boys. It seemed appropriate therefore to work on the design of appropriate female and male subjects and curricular routes which would also suit the needs of young men and women in the post-war economy (CCCS, 1981). The organization of the school curriculum and its timetabling, assessment and teaching styles, the culture of the school constructed and regulated such assumed differences between male and female approaches to learning, skills and abilities; all this at the same time as concern was expressed about the failure of girls to seize post-war educational opportunities (c.f. Finch, 1984). In effect, the processes of gender differentiation were being built into the warp and weft of the conventions of school life (DES, 1975; Arnot, 1983).

By the early 1970s the contradictions between social democratic principles and such gendered curricula, teaching and learning were increasingly evident, especially in a context where stronger and more critical versions of egalitarianism were developing.[9] The impetus for a resolution of such conflicting influences came from the women's movement, a movement which (ironically) had been nourished by welfarism and state education. Contained within the groundbreaking 1944 Education Act with its promise of 'education for all' was the possibility of women's liberation from their domestic destinies (Burton and Weiner, 1990). Yet when the ensuing expansion of education (particularly secondary and tertiary education) 'hurtled a generation (of women) beyond the confines of their mothers' world into the male sphere of public affairs and work', they found to their cost that no provision had been made to care for their children (Rowbotham, 1986) and that male dominance through occupational hierarchies restricted and contained their advancement. For many, particularly white middle class women, individual experiences of private forms of patriarchy were being supplemented (some for the first time) by the collective experience of public forms of male domination. The liberalism which framed social policy had, it seems, remained committed to the division between public and private domestic spheres. Also traditional and unequal gender relations within the family, even if reconstructed by new social policies, were hardly being challenged by other forms of provision in the welfare state (Pascall, 1986; Dale and Foster, 1986; Williams, 1989).

By the late 1960s such tensions between women's position in the home and in the labour force, not surprisingly, were to surface and explode in the second wave of the women's liberation movement. This movement took as its project the removal of the shackles of male dominance in all spheres. At a deeper level it exposed the male-female power relations which underlay economic and political structures and which shaped state policies and practice. As Rowbotham (1986) comments in retrospect, the feminist project became one of extending the definitions of political or economic democracy to ever more diverse and intimate spheres. If the liberal democratic state shaped the notion of rights in relation to the public sphere, feminists demanded that they be extended into the personal sphere. On the new agenda were:

> . . . domestic inequality, identity, control over sexuality, challenge to cultural representation, community control over state welfare and more equal access to public resources. (p. 86)

In the educational world, this political awakening took various forms. By the late 1960s, women were becoming increasingly disillusioned with the failure of educational policy-makers to deliver equality of opportunity. The ideals of collectivism behind the post-war settlement appeared to have failed to support women or their particular concerns in the development of educational provision. And the gap between rhetoric and reality was becoming increasingly evident to those educational researchers who had looked at the educational outcomes and experiences of girls within the educational system. Early attempts at feminist policy analysis (for example, Byrne, 1978) suggested that greater and more committed state intervention was needed if inequalities between men and women were to be ironed out and if the principle of equality of opportunity was to be upheld.

A range of perspectives in feminist educational thought were developed in the ensuing decades which had much in common with the political philosophies that had shaped the women's movement since the 1960s (Eisenstein, 1984). Indeed in recent years it has become common practice for feminist educationalists to identify the various tendencies of liberal feminism on the one hand, and radical, socialist and black feminism on the other (Middleton, 1987; Acker, 1987; Weiner and Arnot, 1987). Lesbian feminism, more developed in the United States, had a twilight existence in the context of British educational work (see recent contributions in Jones and Mahony, 1989), especially since sexuality was such a studiously avoided aspect of British school life (Kelly, 1992).

Liberal feminism, in particular, assumed pride of place within educational research traditions, teachers' initiatives and national policy-making bodies. Its success seemed initially to result from the compromises it reached between feminist principles of improving women's position in society and offering suggestions for reforms from within male dominated structures. It asked for political commitment and goodwill rather than resources and strong state intervention; it required educating rather than constraining individuals: it was encouraging rather than punitive in approach (Arnot, 1991).

What gave liberal feminism its strength was its commitment to the principle of sustained economic growth, to alleviating the shortage of skilled 'manpower' through a process of 'upskilling' (Deem, 1981). It offered a way forward by proposing that women adapt to changing economic opportunities and men are helped to come to terms with increased family responsibilities. In some respects it attempted to tie the two ends of the chain and bring the modes of teaching and learning into line with the original intentions of the post-war policy-makers of equality of educational opportunity.

Yet, despite such apparent conformity with the goals of the post-war economy, liberal feminists in their own way struck at the heart of the liberal democratic state. They challenged the versions of male meritocracy which had dominated post-war thinking (Arnot, 1983). They objected publicly and often to the ways in which as Sullivan (1990) put it, 'gender' was arbitrarily assigned to social characteristics and roles. Liberal feminism suggested instead the need to 'degender' the public sphere.

Within that approach were the seeds of a particularly devastating attack on the dominant concept of public policy-making and system of male representation within the state. Eisenstein (1987), Kenway (1990) and Connell (1990), for example, have argued that liberal feminists, by fighting for the principle of equal rights of citizenship to be extended to women, exposed and challenged the gendered discourses and structures of government. As Connell argued, 'Liberal feminists took the concept of rights and turned it against the patriarchal model of citizenship' (p. 513). They protested at the control which men had over the political, judicial, military and cultural life of the country. Some feminists went even further by revealing the procedures and processes within the state which frame a masculine discourse of 'need' (Fraser, 1989). Recognition of the gendered nature of the state allowed liberal feminists to 'inspire a formidable and sustained politics of access . . .' (Connell, 1990, p. 513).

The new project was to transform the world of politics, industry, culture and education by 'degendering' it.[10] Gender would no longer be ascribed and utilized as a principle of social organization in the public sphere. Women would be encouraged to use their freedom to choose between a wider range of life styles, (even if still inevitably responsible for childrearing and the home). The Sex Discrimination Act (1975) and the equal opportunities policies (implemented in its aftermath) attempted to neutralize the consequences of capitalist economic restructuring for women by protecting their conditions of service, their rights to fair employment practice and a fair wage. In contrast little was done to tackle the dilemmas women faced in their dual roles, nor to promote greater equality in the home. Social and family policy significantly was not included in Sex Discrimination Act. Paradoxically, such legislation, like comparable anti-discrimination legislation developed in Australia and the United States, could also be described as signally the moment described by Sullivan (1990) when the distinction between public and private spheres is reconfirmed and women are 'relocated' in the private sphere. Degendering strategies, she argues, have a tendency to both 'privatise and depoliticise issues of particular relevance to women' (for example, abortion, maternity, childcare).

Much mainstream feminist educational thought in the 1970s and 1980s had in fact encapsulated the principles of social democracy which it sought to challenge. Even when, by the 1980s, feminist educational analyses became more sophisticated and attempted to identify the class and racial diversity of female experiences within education and to remove the more subtle cultural processes affecting individual advancement, one can still find a strong commitment to defending the privacy of the family, the tenets of individualism, teacher autonomy and the use of education as the means of social reform (for example, Spender, 1981a; Acker and Warren Piper, 1984; Thompson, 1983; Whyte, 1986).

Most feminist teachers and educationalists have been ambiguous about the role which the state performs in relation to patriarchy. If anything, much of the Western literature on gender and education, in fact, has tended to ignore the role of the state. This was particularly evident in the 1970s and 80s when sex role socialization theories dominated. Education writing seemed to suffer which I called (Arnot, 1981) following Bourdieu (1973) a 'misrecognition of the action of the state'. Benevolent or enlightened action was demanded of central government by liberal feminists in order, paradoxically, to transform precisely those gendered relationships which the state had historically helped to construct.

By the late 1970s it was becoming apparent that the politics of equal access were not sufficient. The egalitarian and libertarian philosophies of the women's movement had begun to have an effect upon educational debates and research. Increasingly feminist critiques of education within social democracy bit deeper and deeper, suggesting the inability of liberalism to create social equality or social justice. Liberal philosophy at the heart of educational policy and also the specific sets of relations constructed within the liberal democratic state and its institutional arrangements would have to be transformed if social justice was to be achieved.[11] The concept of equal rights was being exchanged for a demand for 'equality of power' (Rowbotham, 1986).

More 'egalitarian' campaigns called for democratic 'freedoms' and for the full economic, political and social rights of citizenship to be extended to all subordinate groups. Apple (1989), for example, argues that in the United States, the black and women's movements threatened the legitimacy of the dominant groups, especially in so far as the legitimacy of the social order was founded upon notions of property rights. These rights were held on the basis of ownership of property, such as economic contracts, political rights of participation and the rights of access to knowledge. In contrast egalitarian campaigns celebrated the notion of person rights which invested individuals with the power to enter into those social relationships on the basis of being simply members in the social collectivity (rights which ensured equal treatment of citizenship, freedom of expression, and equal access to participation in decision making).

The feminist challenge undermined the dominance of men who, on the whole, hold those property rights and legitimate their power through their ownership of cultural capital, their access to 'legitimate' knowledge and their access to high status academic qualifications. It is appropriate perhaps to reconsider in the context of male power, Bourdieu's insightful comment about the role which education plays in the legitimation of class privilege:

> . . . among all the solutions put forward throughout history to the problem of the transmission of power and privilege, there surely does not exist one that is better concealed, and therefore better adapted to societies which tend to refuse the most patent forms of the hereditary transmission of power and privileges, than that solution which the educational system provides by contributing to the reproduction of the structure of class relations and by concealing, by an apparently neutral attitude, the fact that it fills this function. (Bourdieu, 1973, p. 72)

Significantly, in the post-war period, the concept of male and female 'needs' and interests offered a much weaker base from which to legitimate patriarchal relations in comparison with the biological discourses of the nineteenth century. Increasingly male economic and political power, like that of the dominant social classes, had had to be justified in terms of 'proven' (i.e. certified) academic merit. By attempting to reform or even replace the principles and practice of male academia, feminists mounted a deeply threatening attack on the legitimacy of male economic, political and social privilege. By uncovering, for example, the 'patriarchal paradigm' of mass schooling (c.f. Spender, 1981b), the 'malestream' curricula and male oriented teaching and assessment styles, radical, socialist and black feminists, each in their own way, debunked the myth of education's gender neutrality.

Another critical aspect of the increasingly confident egalitarian tradition was the challenge it presented to the liberal principles of individual rational autonomy and freedom. Male dominance of educational policy-making, the control of education and access to higher education had been premised upon the notion of freedom of choice — men had chosen such positions and careers and women, although given the chance, had chosen alternative paths. Increasingly however the falsity of that claim was being revealed. Even if the formal opportunity existed, a combination of informal discriminatory practices, the construction of a 'gender order'[12] and women's not unrealistic assessment of their objective possibilities in employment militated against them taking full advantage of whatever opportunities were provided.

But female and male pupils were being shaped not just by the unofficial hidden discourses of the school curriculum, or the looming constraints of a gendered world of employment. They were also being moulded by their struggles within what Wood (1987) and Lees (1986) revealed as the sexual underworld of schooling. This underworld, so controlled by male sexuality, found expression in the 'spaces' created by the ideologies of individualism and personal autonomy. Within such 'freedoms' constructed through liberal discourses were to be found, for example, sexually and racially abusive language and harassment, the neglect or marginalization of young women, patronizing behaviour towards female students and reinforcement of traditional class and race-laden notions of femininity and masculinity. Those prejudices, whether sexual, racial or class-based, were often even permitted to find expression by teachers who supported the concept of 'free speech', 'privacy' and freedom of individual action. Teachers were often unaware of the extent to which their failure to intervene in the sexual and racial conflicts of schooling constituted in itself 'a significant political act' in favour of a specific form of gender order.[13]

Teacher sexism, ethnocentrism or classism therefore were only ever part of a much wider process by which large number of children were 'denied access' to their rights. Many of the problems faced by pupils in schools arose as a result of a range of incompatible principles. In the name of equality of opportunity, schools were encouraged to 'treat all alike' in order to overcome social disadvantages — even though those disadvantages were built into the social fabric. The development of a child's potential and their personal fulfilment were to take place within a hierarchically structured and cultural defined arena — one which was alien to the majority of children in the state system. At the same time, parents and communities who might have been able to help promote their children's welfare were disenfranchized from school participation by the strong commitment to teacher and school autonomy. What egalitarian educationalists increasingly made public were the consequences of this confused project for large groups of pupils.

Further they asked critical questions about even those progressive ideologies born in the expansionist days of the 1960s. Co-education and child-centred pedagogies, for example, were increasingly being revealed as deeply problematic by feminist educationalists. Feminists asked whether co-education, in the state secondary sector genuinely promoted a 'relaxed normality' between the sexes (c.f. Arnot, 1983). Had the principle of 'proximity equals equality' really worked in the case of gender? Or were co-educational schools in effect just a different way of constructing gender relations so that young women were assimilated into the world of male educational values and brought into closer contact with the opposite sex? Were mixed schools genuinely a means of reducing the differentiation between the sexes and or were they a more effective way of providing the conditions for female entry into a sex segregated labour market? Were the values of mixed comprehensive schools constructed with sex equality in mind?

Such were the questions asked of secondary education by feminist researchers. Interestingly their research revealed not just the limitations of the comprehensive ideal but also far more about the nature of adolescent masculinity and the ambiguity of male youth in facing a class-divided education system than had been recognized by male cultural theorists (for example, Willis, 1977). In the picture of contemporary school life which such feminist research offers, we see the increasing confidence of young women but also the effects of an uncertain adolescent masculinity, struggling to define male gender identity in the context of economic recession and an ever more violent world.

Coping with absent fathers who are positioned and controlled by their work within the public sphere, experiencing contradictory class and racially specific versions of masculinity, male pupils were shown to respond by colonizing the world of secondary schools. They set, through their actions and their public forms of resistance, the terms under which female pupils defined their identities (Lees, 1986).

By the 1960s, male and female pupils were being prepared for a restructured labour force in which each sex would still have differentiated roles but where they were treated in more equal fashion (Deem, 1981). In the new world of a mixed comprehensive secondary school in the state sector, all children would be encouraged to fulfil their academic potential. Yet what policy-makers had clearly not anticipated were the effects of subjecting the developing sexual identities of young people to the scrutiny of the opposite sex in such an apparently unprotected environment. The positive and the negative aspects of the gender relations being constructed through state secondary schools were now being revealed.

At the same time child-centred philosophy in primary education was also subjected to feminist critique, especially that of Walkerdine (1981). Here the 'spaces' for the free expression of a child's personality were encouraged by developmental psychology and psychoanalytic discourses which constructed male and female sexuality in particular ways. Pupils, especially male pupils, were encouraged to express their needs, whilst teachers were encouraged to develop their pupils' personalities through child-centred pedagogies. Yet despite the apparent freedom to be found in early education, the conflictual and contested nature of gender relations revealed itself, often without the teacher being aware of such undercurrents in her classroom. In Walkerdine's view, male dominance was legitimated through the psychological discourses which shaped teachers' understandings of male sexuality. The imperative of providing for the early 'natural' expression of male heterosexuality led not only to the uninterrupted displays of male aggression but also to the particular forms of girls' resistance, which involved the exploitation of women's domestic identities. The effects of such child centredness were not, it seems, liberatory for either sex.

What I have tried to show is that such feminist research, although often not intended as policy analysis, represented a sustained attack on post-war educational philosophies and practice. It made explicit some of the ways in which gender relations were regulated by the state, through various educational institutions. Further such research articulated women's educational needs and values, and by so doing attacked the legitimacy of centring educational provision upon male lifestyles and values.

The Gendering of Educational Politics

These critiques might not of themselves have been as effective a threat to the *status quo* had not many teachers, particularly within state primary and secondary education been attracted to feminist politics. Many women teachers have been active in setting up initiatives, campaigning for change in teacher employment, curricula content and in modes of teaching and assessment. Feminist academics and teachers have added their voices to debates about identifying pupils' special needs and targeting provision, and to democratize access into further and higher education, open and distance education. They have encouraged whole school policy development and introduced new concerns about child abuse and sexual harassment into the language and policies of schooling (see Weiner and Arnot, 1987).

Although British teachers seem to find it difficult to articulate a feminist pedagogy especially in the context of compulsory schooling, many of the strategies developed in the 'freer air' of adult and higher education and especially in women's studies were adapted to school classrooms (Thompson, 1983). Feminist teachers, through their practice, have recommended various teaching methods to try and improve female pupils' subject choice and performance. Many such strategies have been similar to progressive teaching practices and notions of critical pedagogy. They have given support to educational styles which emphasized the quality of the learning experience and encouraged more 'democratic' forms of work (for example, pupil participation and control of their own learning through mixed ability teaching, group work, course work, self-assessment, independent study and participation in school policy-making).

The different discourses of radical, socialist and black feminism by the 1980s had the effect of 'gendering' (i.e., making gender an explicit dimension) of educational policy-making. Some schools and local education authorities, particularly in metropolitan areas, adopted explicit sex equality or anti-sexist policies which focussed attention on female education and male centred education (Arnot, 1987). Such policies moved away from the limited projects of improving girls' curriculum choices in science and mathematics. They focussed attention on the need to 'empower' women, to discover and promote female values in education and to challenge male dominance in schools. At the same time socialist feminists added to the exposure of continuing class differentiation in education and black feminists (as part of the anti-racist movement) contributed to the 'racialization' of educational policy-making (Troyna, 1992).

The egalitarian feminist project called for the substantial democratization of education, through full participation and equal control of education by both sexes. It was a project, ironically, which called for more rather than less central government control, for more use of disciplinary powers and fewer 'freedoms' for sexism to exploit (Arnot, 1991).

The articulation of socialist feminism and black feminism to other arenas of struggle also strengthened the demands made on the state for equality to be extended to other subordinate groups. As I have argued elsewhere (*ibid*) feminist struggles were a major force in the attempts being made to restructure social democracy itself.

Radical feminist, socialist and black feminist discourses added their weight to the critiques of liberal philosophy in the late 1970s and 1980s. Not only, as Bowles and Gintis (1976) argued, was schooling shown to be affected by 'the long shadow of work' — the requirements of an advanced capitalist economy but the contradictions between capitalism and liberalism they identified were being reconsidered from a woman's perspective. Despite the considerable success of the education system in encouraging white middle class women into higher education, feminist educationalists revealed how working class and black girls remained at a considerable disadvantage. They dispelled the myth that one 'successful' woman like one 'clever' working class child vindicated the educational system and attested to the extent of equality of opportunity (Payne, 1980). Despite the promise of the post-war period, state policies in education had effectively regulated gender relations. They had not liberated women from their domestic destinies, instead they had created new conditions under which young women could not avoid the effects of patriarchal relations in a sex segregated labour market. Women were even more exposed to the impact of male control.

Increasingly too egalitarian feminists' attention was being focussed not just on the contradictions between schooling and the ideals of equality of opportunity in the public sphere but upon the model of the heterosexual monogamous nuclear family being assumed through the discourses and practices of schooling (Phoenix, 1987; Kelly, 1992). The construction of such families as the 'norm' began to be seen not merely as unrepresentative of the reality of family life in the modern Western societies, but also as inappropriate and oppressive. Sex education could begin to be used to teach pupils about a diversity of life styles, sexualities and moral values.

Yet in Britain, whilst the idea of pluralism is acceptable within the framework of cultural diversity, it seems to be unacceptable as a concept in the sexual context. Alternative sets of gender relations (a new 'gender regime') were represented by the Right as destabilizing the social order. It threatened the central function of the family as the key site for the socialization of each new generation into dominant values. Was there a fear perhaps that feminists were not just attempting to democratize contemporary relations between husbands and wives, male and female partners, but more importantly, they might be undermining the ways in which future generations would view patriarchal relations in the private and the public spheres?

One could argue, therefore, that feminism had begun to be effective in undermining in a very serious way the legitimacy of the patriarchal social order. Eisenstein (1987) put it well when she argued, 'Feminism has uncovered the truth that capitalist patriarchal society cannot deliver on its liberal promises of equality or even equal rights without destabilizing itself' (p. 239). Patriarchal structures, especially the family and the educational system were threatened by the egalitarianism of the women's movement. Feminist campaigns threatened the version of democracy and its failure to provide rights of citizenship to women (Heater, 1990), questioned the distinction between public and private spheres, the appropriation of the educational system by men, the criteria for the selection of knowledge and its modes of transmission, the gender regimes of schooling, the nature and values of family life and the promotion of heterosexuality as norm.

Thus if capitalism was in crisis by the 1980s, so too were patriarchal relations. The ways in which a social democratic state had regulated gender had been exposed as contradictory, especially the more the state utilized degendering discourses and strategies for the public sphere. Further, and not insignificantly, 'the myth of female classlessness' (Arnot, 1983) which had allowed for the homogenizing of all girls in the post-war period was now dispelled. Women, like men, were clearly situated within class and race structures. Further feminists had introduced a new agenda of sexual politics around normative notions of heterosexuality which were likely to be deeply worrying to those committed to traditional family life.

The New Right and the Modernizing of Gender

It is naive to imagine, therefore, that feminist demands for sexual equality had no political impact. The developments were regarded, along with comparable projects in the area of 'race', as subversive by a central government influenced by the radical right (Klein, 1989; Davies *et al*, 1990). Feminist campaigns were portrayed by members of the New Right as 'ideological extravagances' and as part of the 'forces in contemporary society which are deeply inimical' to the family (Centre for Policy Studies, quoted in Campbell, 1987, p. 170). Demands for sex equality were blamed for the rise in the divorce rate and single parenthood. Ten Tusscher (1986) observed that Thatcherism and the New Right managed to occupy the vacuum created by the breakdown of social democracy combined with the opening stemming from the perceived threat to patriarchy. This determined the nature of the New Right. It embraced the twin goals of restoring class forces in favour of capital and of restoring gender relations in favour of men (*ibid*, p. 76).

In the space of this chapter it is only possible to hint at the complexity of this response. I have argued elsewhere (Arnot, 1992b) that the Conservative approach put together a confused alliance between those who wish to maintain the public-private division and women's position within the family, and those who supported greater employment opportunities for women.

The family occupied a privileged place in New Right discourses but there was little attempt in the 1980s to reconcile the confusion of conservative and liberal functions being assigned to the family or to develop any deep understanding about the actual shifts in contemporary family life (David, 1983a; Campbell, 1987). The family was held responsible for the 'defence of the individual against socialism and excessive state power'; on the other hand, it was the basis of private property and the location of the consumer responsible for the management of his/her financial affairs. Then again, the family was the 'centre of affections', 'the transmitter of traditions' and the necessary condition of authority. Such functions transcended all allegiances of class and had no historical specificity — they were essentially universal (Campbell, 1987).

Parenthood represented, for neo-conservatives such as Scruton, the political and moral values of hierarchy, authority and loyalty (Williams, 1989). For neo-liberals, parenthood represented the symbol of the economic values of consumerism and a means of social stability in an aggressively competitive economy. Paradoxically, 'the family had to be maximized in order to minimize the state'. By rehabilitating the family, arguably the government could break down the 'scrounger welfare state' and through a 'moral crusade' counter the effects of sexual permissiveness that grew out of the 1960s (Campbell, 1987, p. 166).

Needless to say such patriarchal discourses were not easily applied to policy. On the one hand, the impact of the women's movement in the country — even if disorganized — had changed public opinion sufficiently to be able to curtail the extent to which the New Right could promote traditional values, especially surrounding women's domesticity. Segal (1983) argues that the Conservative government was held back by the 'continual vigour and success of feminism in mobilising support for women's rights and equality'. Change in women's employment since the Second World War had encouraged middle class career women, some of whom could be found as female Conservative party members fighting against any simple equation between women and motherhood.

It has become increasingly clear from recent feminist analyses that despite the desire to re-establish traditional family structures and 'remoralize' the nation's children, the Conservative government still wished to be seen as committed, at least in rhetoric, to a version of equality of opportunity and equal rights. Conservative women sustained notions of themselves as equal to men 'in the sight of God' (Campbell, 1987). Neo-liberals encouraged the notion of individual liberty, particularly economic freedom in the market place as consumers and political freedom from coercion and excessive state control (even if they assumed such liberties would only apply to men (Segal, 1983, p. 119)). The solution to this contradiction could not be found by expelling women from the market place especially since capital still required female waged labour. Instead the notion of competitive individualism could be selectively applied to men and women who had no family responsibilities (David, 1983a & b) or alternatively to women who had already fulfilled one of their roles, as home makers, and could now re-enter the market. Such 'solutions', as Wilson (1980) argued, allowed the Conservative government to represent itself as 'the modern party'.

> the theme of the Conservative party under Mrs Thatcher as the modern party, the party that welcomes and harnesses change and is committed to an attack on the 'old fashioned' dogmas of trades unions and an assortment of blinkered ideologues — Fabians, Marxists, feminists and the like — whose time is past and who have got fatally out of step with the world we live in. (Wilson, 1980, p. 205)

Such 'modernizing tendencies' within Conservative party policy were to find somewhat confused expression within the various education reforms of the 1980s. We can find a cacophony of different voices which demanded initially an education for all children in moral values and in parental responsibilities, and the cutting back of state funds even if it has deleterious effects on women's opportunities (David, 1983b). Although not openly 'anti-feminist' (in comparison with the Reagan administration in the USA) Mrs Thatcher's government encouraged the view that it would restore patriarchal values. It was surprising therefore her educational policies actually made little reference to traditional biological discourses.

Instead the Conservative government sustained the degendering liberal strategies of the last two decades, depoliticizing and neutralizing the effects of feminist educational demands. The 'new vocationalism' it promoted in the early 1980s rather than replace equality of opportunity as the dominant ideology, recontextualized it within the framework of a highly technological society. It suggested strategies to 'modernise gender relations and the female workforce' (Weiner, 1989) even if the evidence suggested that gender inequalities in training and educational routes were just as prevalent (Arnot, 1991 and 1992b). Feminist demands rather than feminists themselves were incorporated into the reconstructed politics of access, later to be called 'active citizenship' (Arnot, 1992a).

Another Conservative party strategy has been to neutralize feminist educational campaigns through new forms of assimilation. The National Curriculum, whilst apparently offering equal entitlement, re-established male cultural priorities and values. It reasserted male hierarchies of knowledge, selected subjects in which men excelled, disposed of subjects traditionally the preserve of working class girls (Arnot, 1989) and is currently revaluing modes of teaching, learning and assessment which privilege middle class male students.

Conclusion

Not surprisingly feminist educationalists have been confused in their response to Conservative government education reforms. Discontent over curricular choices has been reduced by the introduction of a compulsory common curriculum, even if differentiated options and levels within subjects are reemerging. Teacher autonomy has again been used to justify the refusal to offer political commitment to sex equality in the new reforms. Teachers have again been given the responsibility to initiate social reform. Emphasis upon democratizing higher education has diffused public concern about the disadvantages experienced by working class, black and female students.

Clearly a new agenda is being set. New sets of gender relations are being constructed through education which are likely to work in favour of white middle class girls. The state is actively engaged in restoring patriarchal relations, but in different form and with different consequences to that of the post-war period. Without an understanding of that project, it is unlikely that we can adequately read the significance of shifts in contemporary society.

Notes

1 Mr Kenneth Baker, then Secretary of State for Education and Science, in 1988 was quoted as saying that the age of egalitarianism is now over (c.f. Arnot, 1991).

2 See for example, Eisenstein (1990) and Yeatman (1990).

3 National Curriculum subjects as technology has various options within it, and science can be studied for a single or a double award (reflecting the time given to the subject on the timetable). In these subjects, girls are likely to continue with their existing patterns of opting for design and for the reduced science course.

4 Public debates about the decline of marriage, the extent of illegitimacy and teenage motherhood, single parenthood, divorce rates, increase in youth crime etc. often blame women and also the women's liberation movement. This is discussed in the chapters by Miriam David and Heidi Safia Mirza in this volume.

5 Acker's (1989) response reveals the continuing concern over the concept of patriarchy and the importance of not diverting attention away from the significance of gender as part of the fundamental constitution of all social life, by suggesting that patriarchy is a separate structure operating alongside that of the economy.

6 Elsewhere (Arnot, 1983) I posited the notion of different modes of transmission of gender relations through schooling, drawing upon the Basil Bernstein's theory of educational codes. The value of this concept is that it highlights the fact that gender relations can be transmitted through different forms of social control and different curricular arrangements.

7 A number of writers have outlined theories of the state in relation to education. A good early summary was that by Dale (1986). More recent discussion can be found in Ball (1990) and Dale (1989).

8 In my earlier work I discussed schooling in terms of constructing particular gender order or a gender code. These concepts had many similarities with the concept of gender regime discussed by Connell, Ashenden, Kessler and Dowsett (1982). The emphasis here is upon the production of gender difference through school structures and culture.

9 The development of egalitarian thought in the post-war period was analyzed by the Centre for Contemporary Cultural Studies (1981). Gaby Weiner and I attempted to document the egalitarian tradition among feminists in the last two decades — Weiner and Arnot (1987).

10 I have drawn the concept of 'degendering' discourses from the insightful analysis by Sullivan (1990) of Australian equal opportunities legislation. It ties in well with contemporary discussion in the UK about 'deracialization' and 'racialization' of educational policy (Troyna, 1992) in the same period.

11 Gaby Weiner and I argued that egalitarian approaches, such as those of radical, lesbian, socialist and black feminism 'each in their own way, wished for no less than the transformation of the educational system. They had no wish to ameliorate the existing inadequate education system; they wanted to transform its power base' (Weiner and Arnot, 1987, p. 357).

12 See note 8 (op cit).
13 Walkerdine (1981) and Stanworth (1983) make such points.

References

ACKER, J. (1989) 'The problem with patriarchy', *Sociology*, **23**, 2, pp. 235–40.

ACKER, S. (1987) 'Feminist theory and the study of gender and education', *International Review of Education*, **33**, 4, pp. 419–35.

ACKER, S. and WARREN PIPER, D.W. (Eds) (1984) *Is Higher Education Fair to Women?*, London, SRHE-Nelson.

ALLEN, J. (1990) 'Does feminism need a theory of the state?' in WATSON, S. (Ed.) *Playing the State: Australian Feminist Interventions*, London, Verso Press.

APPLE, M.W. (1989) 'How equality has been redefined in the Conservative Restoration' in SECADA, W.G. (Ed.) *Equity in Education*, Lewes, Falmer Press.

ARAUJO, H.C. (1992) 'The emergence of a New Orthodoxy: Public debates on women's capacities and education in Portugal (1880–1910)', *Gender and Education*, **4**, 1–2, pp. 7–24.

ARNOT, M. (1981) 'Culture and political economy: Dual perspectives in the sociology of women's education', *Educational Analysis*, **3**, 1, pp. 97–116.

ARNOT, M. (1983) 'A cloud over coeducation: An analysis of the forms of transmission of class and gender relations' in WALKER, S. and BARTON, L. (Eds) *Gender, Class and Education*, Lewes, Falmer Press.

ARNOT, M. (1986) *Race, Gender and Education Policy Making*, Milton Keynes, Open University, Course unit E333, Module 4.

ARNOT, M. (1987) 'Political lip service or radical education reform? Central government responses to sex equality as a policy issue' in ARNOT, M. and WEINER, G. (Eds) *Gender and the Politics of Schooling*, London, Hutchinson.

ARNOT, M. (1989) 'Crisis of challenge: Equal opportunities and the National Curriculum', *NUT Education Review*, **3**, 2, pp. 7–13.

ARNOT, M. (1991) 'Equality and democracy: A decade of struggle over education', *British Journal of Sociology of Education*, **12**, 4, pp. 447–66.

ARNOT, M. (1992a) 'Feminist perspectives on education for citizenship', paper presented at the International Sociology of Education Conference, Citizenship, Democracy and the Role of the Teacher, Westhill College Birmingham England.

ARNOT, M. (1992b) 'Feminism, education and the New Right' in ARNOT, M. and BARTON, L. (Eds) *Voicing Concerns: Sociological Perspectives on Contemporary Education Reforms*, Oxford, Triangle Books.

BALL, S.J. (1990) *Politics and Policy Making in Education*, London, Routledge.

BOURDIEU, P. (1973) 'Cultural reproduction and social reproduction' in BROWN, R. (Ed.) *Knowledge, Education and Cultural Change*, London, Tavistock Publications Ltd.

BURTON, L. and WEINER, G. (1990) 'Social justice and the National Curriculum', *Research Papers in Education*, **5**, pp. 203–27.

BOWLES, S. and GINTIS, H. (1976) *Schooling in Capitalist America*, New York, Basic Books.

BYRNE, E. (1978) *Women in Education*, London, Tavistock.

CAMPBELL, B. (1987) *The Iron Ladies: Why Do Women Vote Tory?*, London, Virago.

CENTRE FOR CONTEMPORARY CULTURAL STUDIES (CCCS) (1981) *Unpopular Education: Schooling for Social Democracy in England Since 1944*, London, Hutchinson.

CONNELL, R.W. (1990) 'The state, gender and sexual politics', *Theory and Society*, **19**, pp. 507–44.

CONNELL, R.W., ASHENDEN, D.J., KESSLER, S. and DOWSETT, G.W. (1982) *Making the Difference; Schools, Families and Social Division*, Sydney, Allen and Unwin.

DALE, J. and FOSTER, P. (1986) *Feminists and State Welfare*, London, Routledge and Kegan Paul.

DALE, R. (1986) 'Perspectives on Policy Making' Part 2 E333 Course Module 1 *Introducing Education Policy: Principles and Perspectives*, Milton Keynes, Open University.

DALE, R. (1989) *The State and Education Policy*, Milton Keynes, Open University Press.

DAVID, M. (1983a) 'Sex education and social policy: New moral economy?' in WALKER, S. and BARTON, L. (Eds) *Gender, Class and Education*, Lewes, Falmer Press.

DAVID, M. (1983b) 'Teaching and preaching sexual morality: The New Right's anti-feminism in Britain and the USA', *Journal of Education*, **166**, 1, pp. 63–76.

DAVIES, A.M., HOLLAND, J. and MINHAS, R. (1990) *Equal Opportunities in the New Era*, London, Hillcole Group, Paper 2.

DEEM, R. (1981) 'State policy and ideology in the education of women, 1944–1980', *British Journal of Sociology of Education*, **2**, 2, pp. 131–44.

DES (1975) *Curricular Differences for Boys and Girls* (Education Survey 21), London, HMSO.

EISENSTEIN, H. (1984) *Contemporary Feminist Thought*, London, Counterpoint Unwin Paperback.

EISENSTEIN, H. (1990) 'Femocrats, official feminism and the uses of power' in WATSON, S. (Ed.) *Playing the State: Australian Feminist Interventions*, London, Verso Press.

EISENSTEIN, Z. (1987) 'Liberalism, feminism and the Reagan state: The neoconservative assault on (sexual) equality', in MILIBAND, R., PANITCH, L. and SAVILLE, J. (Eds) *Socialist Register*, London, Merlin Press.

FINCH, J. (1984) *Education and Social Policy*, London, Longman.

FRANZWAY, S., COURT, D., CONNELL, R.W. (1989) *Staking a Claim: Feminism, Bureaucracy and the State*, Cambridge, Polity Press.

FRASER, N. (1989) *Unruly Practices: Power, Discourse and Gender in Contemporary Social Theory*, Cambridge, Polity Press.

HEATER, D. (1990) *Citizenship: The Civic Ideal in World History, Policies and Education*, London, Longman.

JONES, C. and MAHONY, P. (Eds) (1989) *Learning Our Lines: Sexuality and Social Control in Education*, London, Women's Press.

JONES, K. (1989) *Right Turn: The Conservative Revolution in Education*, Hutchinson, Radius.

KELLY, L. (1992) 'Not in front of the children: Responding to right wing agendas on sexuality and education' in ARNOT, M. and BARTON, L. (Eds) *Voicing Concerns: Sociological Perspectives on Contemporary Education Reforms*, Oxford, Triangle Books.

KENWAY, J. (1990) *Gender and Education Policy: A Call for New Directions*, Victoria, Australia, Deakin University.

KESSLER, S. *et al* (1987) 'Gender relations in secondary schooling' in ARNOT, M. and WEINER, G. (Eds) *Gender and the Politics of Schooling*, London, Hutchinson.

KLEIN, G. (1989) 'New Right-new era', *NUT Education Review*, autumn, **3**, 2, pp. 14–19.

LEES, S. (1986) *Losing Out: Sexuality and Adolescent Girls*, London, Hutchinson.

LLOYD, G. (1986) 'Selfhood, war and masculinity' in PATEMAN, C. and GROSS, E. (Eds) *Feminist Challenges: Social and Political Theory*, Sydney Australia, Allen and Unwin.

MacKinnon, C. (1983) 'Feminism, Marxism, method and the state: Toward feminist jurisprudence', *Signs*, **8**, pp. 635–8.
Middleton, S. (1987) 'The sociology of women's education' in Arnot, M. and Weiner, G. (Eds) *Gender and the Politics of Schooling*, London, Hutchinson.
Pascall, G. (1986) *Social Policy: A Feminist Analysis*, London, Tavistock.
Pateman, C. (1980) *The Disorder of Women*, Cambridge, Polity Press.
Payne, I. (1980) 'A working class girl in a grammar school' in Sarah, E. and Spender, D. (Ed.) *Learning to Lose*, London, The Women's Press.
Phillips, A. (1991) *Engendering Democracy*, Cambridge, Polity Press.
Phoenix, A. (1987) 'Theories of gender and black families' in Weiner, G. and Arnot, M. (Eds) *Gender Under Scrutiny: New Inquiries in Education*, London, Hutchinson
Rowbotham, S. (1986) 'Feminism and democracy' in Held, D. and Pollitt, C. (Eds) *New Forms of Democracy*, London, Sage.
Segal, L. (1983) 'The heat in the kitchen' in Hall, S. and Jacques, P. (Eds) *The Politics of Thatcherism*, London, Lawrence and Wishart.
Spender, D. (1981b) *Men's Studies Modified*, Oxford, Pergamon Press.
Spender, D. (Ed.) (1981a) 'Education: The patriarchal paradigm and the response to feminism' in *Men's Studies Modified*, Oxford, Pergamon Press.
Stanworth, M. (1983) *Gender and Schooling*, London, Hutchinson.
Sullivan, B. (1990) 'Sex equality and the Australian body politic' in Watson, S. (Ed.) *Playing the State: Australian Feminist Interventions*, London, Verso.
Thompson, J. (1983) *Learning Liberation: Women's Response to Men's Education*, London, Croom Helm.
Troyna, B. (1992) 'Can you see the join? An historical analysis of multicultural and anti-racist education policies' in Gill, D., Mayor, B. and Blair, M. (Eds) *Racism and Education: Structures and Strategies*, London, Sage.
ten Tusscher, T. (1986) 'Patriarchy, capitalism and the New Right' in Evans, J. *et al* (Eds) *Feminism and Political Theory*, London, Sage.
Walby, S. (1990) *Theorizing Patriarchy*, Oxford, Basil Blackwell.
Walkerdine, V. (1981) 'Sex, power and pedagogy', *Screen Education*, **38**, pp. 14–23.
Watson, S. (1990) 'The state of play: An introduction' in Watson, S. (Ed.) *Playing the State: Australian Feminist Interventions*, London, Verso Press.
Weedon, C. (1987) *Feminist Practice and Post-structuralist Theory*, Oxford, Basil Blackwell.
Weiner, G. (1989) 'Feminism, equal opportunities and vocationalism: The changing context' in Burchell, H. and Millman, V. (Eds) *Changing Perspectives on Gender*, Milton Keynes, Open University Press.
Weiner, G. and Arnot, M. (1987) 'Teachers and gender politics' in Arnot, M. and Weiner, G. (Eds) *Gender and the Politics of Schooling*, London, Hutchinson.
Whitty, G. (1989) 'The New Right and the National Curriculum', *Journal of Educational Policy*, **4**, 4.
Whyte, J. *et al* (Eds) (1986) *Girl Friendly Schooling*, London, Methuen.
Williams, F. (1989) *Social Policy: A Critical Introduction*, Cambridge, Polity Press.
Willis, P. (1977) *Learning to Labour*, Farnborough, Saxon House.
Wilson, E. (1980) *Only Halfway to Paradise*, London, Tavistock.
Wolpe, A.M. (1976) 'The official ideology of education for girls' in Flude, M. and Ahier, J. (Eds) *Educability, Schools and Ideology*, London, Croom Helm.
Wood, J. (1987) 'Groping towards sexism: Boys' sex talk' in Weiner, G. and Arnot, M. (Eds) *Gender Under Scrutiny: New Inquiries in Education*, London, Hutchinson.
Yeatman, A. (1990) *Bureaucrats and Technocrats and Femocrats*, Sydney, Allen and Unwin.

Chapter 10

Feminism and the Struggle for a Democratic Education: A View from the United States

Kathleen Weiler

Feminist educators in the 1990s throughout the industrialized world face similar problems and issues. Despite national differences, they share a concern about the future of education for women in societies marked by the resurgence of right-wing ideology and the conservative control of the state. The chapters in this volume reflect differences in national circumstances, but all share a commitment to social justice and see education as a key arena of struggle for women and other excluded and oppressed groups. Like other progressive theorists in the 1990s, these writers have been faced with both theoretical and material challenges to left analysis in the rapidly changing circumstances of the late twentieth century. First, they have been affected by critiques of what is broadly identified as post-modernist and postcolonial theory. These theories have challenged the 'master narratives' of Western thought in general and the truth claims of Marxism and feminism in particular. Second, they have been faced with the realignment of politics following the success of neo-conservative forces in the 1980s, the ever more rapid growth of a world wide corporate capitalist economic system and the seeming collapse and 'failure' of socialism in Eastern Europe and Russia. It is possible to argue, as Madeleine Arnot has, that these developments have in a sense 'freed' the left from the legacy of social democracy, with its acceptance of capitalism and its strategy of reform from within (Arnot, 1991). But it is not at all clear what sort of politics will emerge to mobilize groups around a progressive agenda in this new world. In this chapter I would like to consider these questions with particular reference to recent developments in the United States.

The struggle over the meaning of education and democracy in the post-modern world continues a long battle between those who would restrict access to knowledge and power to elites and those who seek a more equal and participatory society. Education in the United States, for example, has been an area of contestation since the common school movement of the mid-nineteenth century first proposed public supported free schools for all children as a means to control and discipline 'dangerous' groups in a rapidly urbanizing and industrializing society. It was contested when public schools were first conceived on the model of factories, in the large urban schools for the first great wave of immigrants to the United States around the turn of the the twentieth century. In these schools, as in urban schools today, self-proclaimed educational 'experts' envisioned an education for the masses which would provide the mechanics of reading and writing, and would teach obedience to authority and acceptance of work discipline. This image of public education was shaped by business imperatives for skilled and compliant workers. As Ellwood Cubberley, a leading educator of the time, put it:

> Our schools are, in a sense, factories in which the raw products (children) are to be shaped and fashioned into products to meet the various demands of life. The specifications for manufacturing come from the demands of twentieth-century civilization, and it is the business of the school to build its pupils according to the specifications laid down. (quoted in Callahan, 1962, p. 152)

This definition of education was not uncontested at the time. The great Chicago educator and labor leader Margaret Haley, speaking before the National Education Association in 1904, identified the contradictory and contested nature of schooling in capitalism:

> Two ideals are struggling for supremacy in American life today: one the industrial ideal, dominating through the supremacy of commercialism, which subordinates the worker to the product and the machine; the other, the ideal of democracy, the ideal of the educators, which places humanity above all machines; and demands that all activity shall be the expression of human life. (cited in Hoffman, 1981)

Margaret Haley was an elementary school teacher and organizer for the Chicago Teachers Federation, a powerful early teachers' union composed of women elementary school teachers. The CTF was organized not only around issues of teachers' wages and working conditions, but also around the political and philosophical questions of what education should be in a democracy. Haley and other militant women educators like Ella Flagg Young, the first woman superintendent of schools in Chicago, and university educators such as John Dewey challenged the vision of education put forth by the 'efficiency experts' and 'scientific managers' whose greatest concern was cost efficiency and the provision of a standardized minimum education for the poor. They argued for the vital role of educators in encouraging a critical education both for individual growth and for the achievement of a more generous and inclusive democracy. The struggle between those who want to define education to the demands of business and corporate elites and those who want to expand education to build a more participatory democracy has been repeated over and over again in the present century. The writers in this collection continue to argue for the possibilities of a feminist and counter-hegemonic education, but in the context of a rapidly changing world and through the lens of both post-colonial and post-modernist theories.

Theory and Practice

Writing in the early 1990s, the feminist scholars included in this collection have been influenced in varying degrees by the challenges of post-modernist feminist theory and by post-colonial critiques of racist and Eurocentric ideology and forms of domination.[1] These theories have raised serious questions about the unexamined voice of authority in Western modernist theory, claims of universal truths set forth by a small and privileged group of theorists, and the possibility of formulating theory or policy around concepts such as freedom, social justice, or truth. Theorists writing in this tradition have suggested instead what Cornell West (1990) has called a 'new cultural politics of difference' which attempts to embrace 'diversity, multiplicity, and heterogeneity':

> to reject the abstract, general and universal in light of the concrete, specific and particular; and to historicize, contexualize and pluralize by highlighting the contingent, provisional, variable, tentative, shifting and changing. (p. 19)

As West points out, while this cultural politics of difference rejects a politics and philosophy based on the white male Eurocentric tradition, it does not reject the ideal of social justice. Certain versions of post-modern theory have raised fears of the abandonment of progressive and activist politics, that these challenges to the European rationalist tradition lead to a spinning into nihilistic abstraction.[2] These concerns are shared by the writers in this collection, but at the same time, these writers take seriously the critique of the universalizing tendency of white Western feminist analysis that post-modernist and post-colonial writers like Cornel West have raised. In her article in this collection, Sue Middleton argues that the realities of the post-colonial, integrated world of electronic meanings and corporate images creates a need for

> theories which could accommodate people's multiple and simultaneous positionings in complex, changing, and often contradictory patterns of power-relations — between races or cultures within countries, between the Anglo-American-European nations and those of the 'third world', between indigenous populations and those descended from former colonists, between those of different sexual orientations, those of different religions, the differently abled, etc.

The writers in this collection are thus trying to theorize a more just education for women while moving beyond a one dimensional theoretical perspective that focusses only on gender. Of course this is not to assume that the feminist project of recognizing gender as a significant category of social analysis has been achieved. As several writers in this collection — Sandra Acker, Miriam David, Gaby Weiner and Madeleine Arnot in particular — make clear, all too often male theorists continue to ignore gender in their analysis and it is still a major part of the feminist project to point out these gaps and silences. But it is also clear that focussing on gender alone will not capture the realities of women's education. The challenge for feminist theorists is to try to take account of and comprehend the complexity of all forces of identity formation acting upon women in relation to educational institutions and policies in a rapidly changing world.

Speaking in another context, Catherine Hall has commented that national identities are 'continually contested terrains in which meaning is not given but discursively constructed and reconstructed in conditions of historical specificity' (Hall, 1992, p. 240). The chapters in this collection explicitly or implicitly suggest that the same is true of the identities of 'gender', 'race', and 'sexuality' The construction of hegemonic meanings of these identities is a constant process of denying alternative meanings; as Hall comments in terms of the construction of 'Englishness', the celebration of a dominant identity hides the 'dependencies, inequalities, and oppressions' that mark contemporary societies. The maintenance of hegemonic meanings — of gender or race, for example — requires the erasure of what Foucault calls 'dangerous memories', the subjugated knowledges of the past and I would add the possibilities of pleasure and desire of those who are 'not meant to survive', in Audre Lorde's words. What the chapters in this collection are seeking to create is a theoretical opening to begin to analyze the construction of identities in a society defined by relationships of inequality and oppression. This implies theorizing the processes of reification and the fixing of identities in place (a tendency not only of the dominant apparatus, but of oppressed groups themselves, who celebrate such identities as a means of coalescing and forging political alliances and practice) but also theorizing oppression and resistance in a way that can encompass and acknowledge the shifting quality of our lives. Such an approach underlies Heidi Safia Mirza's careful analysis of the reification of the black family in this collection. As she argues, the ideology of the 'strong black woman', while apparently positive, too often serves to divert attention away from the larger social forces of racism and class privilege.

The influence of post-modernist and post-colonial theory can be seen in these chapters in their attention to the construction of difference and otherness in terms of race and ethnicity as well as gender and in their recognition of the complex interrelationship of overlapping modes of oppression. The neo-conservative agenda for education in all of the countries discussed in this collection is deeply retrogressive in terms of race, attacking the limited gains that have been made since the 1960s both by independent periphery nations and by internally colonized peoples of color in the central nations such as those represented in this collection. With the increasing integration of world economies and cultures through the hegemony of electronic images and modes of consumption, previously subordinated groups have been included into a world market as consumers as well as producers of products. At the level of education and knowledge, this incorporation of all peoples into a world consumer economy has led to new configurations of racist categories on the part of dominant groups, privileging the traditional forms of knowledge and loci of power of the center and maintaining on the margins those who have been oppressed and exploited. Women as well as people of color are thus constructed and reconstructed as marginal 'others'. As Russell Ferguson (1990) comments:

> When we say marginal, we must always ask, marginal to what? But this question is difficult to answer. The place from which power is exercised is often a hidden place. When we try to pin it down, the center always seems to be somewhere else. Yet we know that this phantom center, elusive as it is, exerts a real, undeniable power over the whole social framework of our culture, and over the ways in which we think about it. (p. 9)

This tendency to envision society in terms of the oppositions of 'center' and 'margins' thus leaves the underlying problematic of power relations untouched — and this is true in terms of sexuality, race, ethnicity, as well as gender.

But the post-war period has also seen demands for cultural autonomy and the assertion of the value of non-white and non-Western culture and knowledge. In education, the voices of women of color and subordinated and colonized women have challenged the racial hegemony of white feminist analyses of education. The chapters in this collection point to the need to theorize race and racism in any educational analysis as racial and post-colonial relationships play themselves out historically in each local setting. Linda

Tuhiwai Smith, for example, uses the Maori struggle to develop the traditional Maori institution of the whare in a state supported school for girls to illuminate the challenges to white knowledge and institutional authority when Maori women are given voice. This New Zealand example echoes Michèle Foster's discussion of the lives of African American teachers in the United States, who, she argues, have been working against racist institutions and ideologies both before and after desegregation efforts of the 1960s and 1970s. These challenges to the underlying assumptions of white and Western feminism have revealed the workings of privilege and power at the level of feminist analysis itself and have resulted in a call for a more reflexive theory that can address the realities of women in different sites and with different histories.

Women and Educational Policy

Post-modern and post-colonial theory clearly has influenced the feminist critiques presented here. But as feminist educators, these writers are also deeply concerned with issues of the state and public policy that shape the lives of women in each national setting and throughout the world. This concern with the 'real world' makes concrete questions of oppression and power, and the ways women's (and men's) everyday lives are shaped through both discourse and policy. The contribution of feminist scholarship in education is to raise gender as a major focus in the analysis of neo-conservative movements, corporate hegemony, and the fusing of state and elite interests world wide. By providing examples in different national settings, the chapters in this collection focus our attention on the question of the world in which we try to intervene and engage in practice. These chapters all ask us to reflect upon what a feminist analysis of education in this world can entail and in so doing they move between theory and policy in focussing on the effect of state and institutional practices on the lives of women.

Feminist critics, like other educational theorists on the left, have increasingly been influenced by Gramsci (1971), and in particular his formulation of hegemony and the ways in which powerful groups constantly struggle to control and dominate discourse and set the parameters of political understanding and action. A Gramscian perspective seems particularly appropriate to the world of the 1990s, in which the line between the 'real' and the image of the real is more and more blurred and in which public discourse has in a Gramscian sense been captured by the powerful. This hegemonic vision glorifies competition and privatization, not only of social services and space, but of feeling as well. At the same time, terms such as education and democracy have been redefined and placed outside the realm of public debate. Education in this discourse becomes a means to defend privilege and to exclude most people from the possibilities of full participation in a democratic society while the underlying assumptions about both human capabilities and the nature of society that justify these deeply political policies are treated as self-evident truths beyond criticism or public debate. But underlying the struggles over resources and the restructuring of education is a struggle over ideas and the meaning of ideas. With their almost total domination of public discourse about education, corporate and politically conservative leaders have attempted to define and fix meanings of such terms as education and democracy and to retain meanings of 'race' and 'gender' that perpetuate white male control and positions of power.

All of the countries represented by the writers in this collection have been affected by the resurgence of right-wing ideologies and policies, as the ideology of *laissez-faire* has been applied to education, emphasizing parental choice and the competition of schools in a kind of open market of children. These tendencies have of course been mediated and shaped by local histories and power configurations. Lyn Yates points out, for example, that the involvement of feminists in educational policy has been stronger in Australia than in other English-speaking countries. Nonetheless, as her analysis of Australian state curriculum policy around issues of gender makes clear, the relationship between the state and feminists is by no means simple. In other settings, the power of the right is much stronger and in a sense easier to analyze in terms of women's concerns. In the United States, progressive theorists and activists have been increasingly on the defensive in the 1980s, in part because of the historic weakness of the organized left. But Britain, New Zealand and Canada, while including stronger left and progressive political traditions, have experienced similar neo-conservative attacks on the ideals of equality and justice. The impact of Thatcherism in Britain described by Madeleine Arnot and Gaby Weiner, for example, is different yet very familiar to those of us in Canada, New Zealand and the United States. Madeleine Arnot points to the need to analyze both the economic policies of the New Right in Britain upon women, and the ideological contradictions of those policies as well. As she points out, 'the range of strategies adopted by the Conservative government in the 1980s had the effect of incorporating women into the labor force under the worst possible terms — by reducing their protection, raising unemployment rates, failing to provide child care provision, adding to their domestic burden, etc.' (Wilson, quoted in Arnot, 1992, p. 60). In her analysis of conservative education reforms in Britain in the 1980s, she argues that gender and women's struggles 'contributed to a "crisis in patriarchy" which lay at the heart of contemporary educational reforms' (see Arnot's chapter in this volume). This is similar to Miriam David's argument that contemporary Conservative educational policies cannot be understood without reference to gender and the family. The same dynamic is clear in other nations as well, as the political agenda increasingly is determined by powerful conservative interests, expressed in state policies and in the economic moves of powerful corporations. And all of these countries are affected by a complex and intertwined world economy dominated by multinational corporations. All are marked by a 'color line' of white privilege and the oppression and struggles of people of color both internationally and internally within nations. All rest upon conceptions of the family which assume women's unpaid labor in child care and housework in addition to their participation in the work force. The educational policies put forth by neo-conservative groups in these countries show striking similarities, calling for educational policies to meet the needs of business, increasing standardization and control over teachers' work, and encouraging moves toward two-tiered educational systems which would protect the interests of the groups who hold power, and legitimate the educational 'failure' of a growing class of low paid service workers composed largely of white women and men and women of color.

Neo-Conservative Educational Theory in the United States

In the United States, the conservative agenda for education can be clearly seen in the educational 'crisis' that emerged as an issue in the 1980s. Beginning with *A Nation at Risk* in 1983, a series of privately and publicly funded commissions have issued studies defining and suggesting remedies for this 'crisis'. In virtually all of these accounts, the crisis in education has been tied to the crisis of the economic position of the United States in the world. Inadequate education at all levels has been blamed, for example, for the inability of US auto manufacturers to compete with the Japanese; for growing poverty and the declining standard of living of US workers; for the increase of teen pregnancy; for increasing rates of murder and violence. And the reforms of education that have been proposed by these private and public commissions are again framed in terms of a model of competition and efficiency taken from the corporate world (ignoring in an interesting twist the failures and state of crisis of many of these same corporations). US educational institutions are expected to be 'lean and mean', with a new competitive rigor that will somehow rescue a society that is increasingly and openly inequitable and divided by a widening gulf between those who have and those who have not. But of course it is also possible to view the 'crisis' in education not so much as the cause of economic and social phenomena, but as the *result* of political decisions about the allocation of resources and of the social and ethical values of those who define public educational policy in this country.

The growing social inequality in the United States in the last two decades is well documented. As numerous studies have documented, the period between

1977 and the present has seen a marked increase in the income of the wealthy, while the income of the middle class and particularly the poor has declined sharply, with women, and particularly women of color, hardest hit. Fiscal restructuring at the federal as well as the local level has reduced corporate taxation and support of education. In exactly the same period, of course, corporate and business involvement with education at the level of rhetoric has greatly increased. Thus corporations increasingly claim the expertise and right to define the content and nature of education, while at the same time, their actual material support of education declines. In his recent book, *Savage Inequalities*, (1991) Jonathan Kozol documents the glaring inequities of public schooling in the United States, particularly in areas dependent almost exclusively on property taxes. But even when the most glaring disparities between districts are judged illegal, the tax structure itself denies adequate support for public education for all children, leaving those who can afford it to buy the private advantages of well-equipped classrooms, small class size, and a critical and challenging education for their children. As was true in the early twentieth century, educational debate and policy in the United States is dominated by ideas of social efficiency and human capital, which advocate the increase of testing and control over the work of teachers, an acceptance of an education for working class children that will prepare them for low level jobs, and in essence simply the abandonment of the poorest and most needy children to schools that are unable to provide even the most basic conditions for learning and teaching. For most women, and particularly for women of color, these policies have led to the elimination of the small gains achieved by the social reform programs of the 1960s.

The decline of public support and growing inequality of public education reflects the move toward the privatization of education and the increasing turn to the corporate sector for an agenda for education. This educational free market based on the inadequate and inequitable allocation of resources would guarantee the present movement toward an even more inequitable society, one structurally organized to maintain and extend the power of those who benefit from this political and economic system. In the United States, for example, the acceptance of what is essentially a two-tiered system of education underlay the educational policies of the Reagan and Bush administrations in the 1980s and early 1990s. An example of these underlying goals can be seen in the 1991 Bush administration's version of conservative educational reform, called America 2000. This plan entailed three main features for public education: (i) parental choice, which would include both public and private schools; (ii) the promise of $150 million dollars from private corporate sources to design 535 innovative new schools, one for each congressional district; and (iii) the introduction of national standardized tests for all children at fourth, eighth, and twelfth grades. These tests would initially be voluntary, but could easily become required. Even a brief examination of these proposals reveals the trend toward privatization and the absence of a commitment to an equal education as the right of all children in this country. The introduction of 'choice', in which children take their tax dollars with them to the schools of their choice, is based on a model of a free market. In this scheme, children were envisioned not so much as little workers as little consumers, who would compete for the best educational product. The commitment to a decent and well supported education as the right of every child was thus replaced by a privatized and competitive vision of education in which schools would compete to be attractive to students. Those children who were not able to work the system to get into the best schools would apparently be left to attend the worst schools. Not only would the most disadvantaged children be left in the most disadvantaged schools in this conception, but the ideal of a common, democratic education in which children of different backgrounds would go to school together, was completely absent. What was proposed instead was a model of a competitive free market, in which the strong win out and the less fortunate lose in a zero sum game that recalls the Social Darwinism of the nineteenth century. The idea that a good education in well-equipped and well-maintained schools is the right of *every* child was completely absent in these schemes.

The second aspect of the America 2000 plan called for the creation of experimental 'lab' schools, which would be models for improved education; this plan contained no provision for public support, but rested on the promises of corporations to find the money to support these new schools. Once again, this was a turning to the private, corporate sector for financial support, a questionable practice in purely practical terms, and a political retreat from the idea of tax supported public education as every child's right. Moreover, it was one more move toward the privatization of education, in which corporate interests (who are supposedly putting up the money, after all) attempt to influence the content and shape of education. It is ironic but instructive that the third element of the America 2000 plan called for the introduction of nationwide standardized testing. For all the talk of choice, innovation, and freedom as goals, the real vision of education that underlay these proposals was a narrow vision of fragmented knowledge that could be measured by multiple-choice tests. These tests do not measure the quality of critical thought and the ability to articulate ideas, but the ability to reduce knowledge to measurable bits of data. Moreover, the tests, to be used to compare students and schools nationwide, would not be accompanied by any greater resources to provide equal educational opportunity for all students. So once again the advantaged would be competing with the disadvantaged, with almost certainly predictable results. Such mass testing would not alleviate the real crisis in US education, but the results could be used to justify differences in achievement of both children and schools, by imposing ideals of competition and hierarchy while accepting and exacerbating a divided and unequal society. America 2000 rather eerily echoes the proposals of the National Curriculum in Britain, in which the 'Ground Rules' set programmes of study, attainment targets and statements of attainment for teachers in a mechanistic fashion that envisions teachers as facilitators rather than engaged intellectuals (see Weiner's chapter in this volume). In the language of these conservative reform proposals, not only realities of class, but of race and gender are absent. There is no recognition of the effects of history, no conception of culture or ideology, and a tacit acceptance of the structural inequities faced by women and people of color. Narratives such as Michèle Foster's account of the lives and work of African-American women teachers in this volume are completely ignored in the neo-conservative language of competition and measurement.

We can see the same politically conservative educational discourse when we look more closely at the institutions of public higher education to which women and students of color are trying to gain access. The two-tiered quality of the higher education system is exacerbated by the nature of the educational cuts that are being made in the United States, for example, when community colleges are disproportionately affected compared to the flagship elite state Universities. The students who suffer from these cuts, of course, are the same students who attended the underfunded and inadequate public elementary and high schools. Moreover, these cuts disproportionately affect both women and 'minority' groups, who have traditionally been excluded from access and power in higher education. This reduction of possibilities for women and other disempowered groups is repeated in the other countries represented in this collection. As Sandra Acker makes clear in her analysis of women in British higher education, women have made relatively few inroads into the higher levels of British universities, and continue to be faced with discriminatory practices and attitudes. Cuts in education thus disproportionately affect women, who are clustered in less prestigious and less secure positions.

Despite continuing patterns of inequity, higher education has in fact become more democratic in the period since the Second World War, both in terms of curriculum and students. It is not that long ago that institutions of higher education were essentially closed to women, 'minorities', and to a large extent, to poor or working class students. While we may recognize that patterns of privilege have hardly disappeared in higher education, we should also remember that fifty years ago, the opportunities that are now under attack by the Right simply did not exist and that scholarships and grants were essentially based on limited private charity. Moreover, the curriculum itself, what is defined as valuable knowledge, has begun to be transformed, as the voices and histories of those who had been excluded are now acknowledged. Women's studies, for example, despite continuing resistance from conservatives, has become an established field of scholarship and a growing presence in US universities. And women students are moving (if still very slowly in some cases) into fields that have traditionally been the exclusive province of men. Both of these developments — the more inclusive group of students, and the richer and more diverse conception of culture and knowledge as reflected in the curriculum — are moves toward democracy in higher education.

This democratization, however we may recognize its limits and the need to progress further, has nonetheless called forth a vitriolic response, particularly in relation to curriculum, which has become the site of an ideological battle in all of these countries. In England, the introduction of the National Curriculum demonstrates the importance of the framing of knowledge in the formal school curriculum. By gaining control over the state, Conservative forces in Britain have been able to dictate the grounds of the ideological struggle over educational content as well as access. And the energies of left and feminist educators must be expended on fighting these retrograde reforms, rather than working toward more constructive goals. As Gaby Weiner comments, 'The proposed framework for assessing and monitoring the National Curriculum is so bureaucratic, bulky and time-consuming, and that there has been little opportunity for subversion or the pursuit of alternatives' (*ibid*). In New Zealand, as Sue Middleton points out, one of the platforms of the conservative National Party in the 1990 elections was to attack the need for anti-racist charters and a commitment to racial equality in schooling, what they called an 'Orwellian social agenda'. One of the first actions of the National government after its electoral victory was to abolish the requirement for an articulated anti-racist policy by schools. Education was to be seen as a free competition among individuals for the good of the 'enterprise culture' of the National agenda. This neo-conservative attack on progressive curriculum has also focused on women's issues. The contradictions between individualism and ruthless competition have led to the glorification of the family as the source of morality and nurturance. One obvious solution to this contradiction is to emphasize gender difference, to glorify the 'natural role' of women as nurturers and domestic workers who support their men as they battle in the heartless world. This neo-conservative vision underlies struggles over curricular knowledge and the absence of women or women's histories in school texts.

The rhetoric and the not so hidden goals of neo-conservatives are also clearly revealed in the panic over multicultural education, feminism, and (rather amazingly) post-modernist theory that made up the attack on 'political correctness' in the United States in the early 1990s. This concerted right-wing campaign included cover stories in the major news magazines, the publication of several books funded by conservative institutes, and coverage on the public and major television networks; it claimed the alarming collapse of higher education because of the infiltration of students and professors of color (assumed to be students or scholars only because of preferential admissions or hiring policies, not because of their own abilities), the fearsome power of feminists, and the abandonment of the classics of Western thought (the best of all that has been written) by inferior works by women and people of color (inferior by definition, since they aren't included in collections of the classics of Western thought — the best that has been written, etc.) In this nightmare vision, teachers and students were said to have been silenced and intimidated by the powerful cabal of African Americans, Latinos, feminists, gays, lesbians and who knows what other undesirables who supposedly controlled US higher education. While these attacks may be hysterical and overwrought, it is important not to discount their seriousness, first, because 'political correctness' may very well reappear as a 'crisis' and convenient focus of racist and neofascist politics, and second, because I think this campaign reflects the fear and anger about the moves toward the democratization of education that have occurred. The attack on political correctness serves as a convenient excuse to silence dissent or criticism of the *status quo* and to reassert the traditional social hierarchy.

Nonetheless, I think very important issues about knowledge and the shape of higher education have been raised in the discussions surrounding this campaign. Questions, for example, about such issues as who has the right to speak and interpret various people's histories are serious and important to consider. The extent to which separate cultural groups, particularly those who have been exploited and oppressed, are self-contained, with a culture and art accessible only to their own members, is a serious issue for debate. Can only an African American teach about African American novels? What obligation do we as educators have to include the histories and cultures of those not only different from ourselves, but about whom we may ourselves be miseducated or ignorant? How can we as teachers acknowledge our own histories and privileges without taking a position of interpreter and expert about the words and lives of those whose experience are very different from our own? How do we judge what of all the possibilities of human history should be taught? These are all serious and important questions. But debating the nature of knowledge from a recognition of the rich diversity of culture and language in this society and with the acknowledgment of present conflicts and the scars of past oppression is a very different perspective from the demand to return to the supposed purity and eternal verities of a canon of academic knowledge established by a privileged elite in early twentieth-century Europe and the United States.

Important questions were raised in the 1991 panic over 'political correctness' in the United States and in the curricular debates in the other nations represented in this volume. But what is striking is the way in which these issues have been so quickly dismissed and closed for discussion by the very conservative critics who first raised them. It seems obvious that underlying many of these attacks is a fear of the changes that have occurred in higher education in the last thirty years, changes in the composition of student bodies, in faculties, and in the curriculum itself. These changes have been in the direction of greater inclusiveness and greater democracy. And in a society dominated by manipulated media images and sound bites, schools and colleges, along with churches and unions, are among the few institutions where public discussion and debate of political and social issues can take place or be encouraged. And it certainly is worth considering that the cuts and continued failure to support education have particularly hit institutions that serve the less affluent and powerful students in this society with women of color most severely affected, and thus directly attack greater participation and a more democratic education.

Conclusion

The chapters in this collection view contemporary education in a variety of national settings from feminist perspectives. Social inequities in these countries differ, reflecting the separate histories and conflicts in each country, the extent to which post-war social democratic social welfare policies have remained in place, and to some extent the strength of organized labor and other progressive forces. But despite these differences, the division of these societies by class, race, and gender is fundamental. In all of these settings, education is contested terrain, between those who seek to use state supported schools as a means to discipline, control, and exclude subordinate groups, and those who see education as a means to an engaged democracy.

A democratic education rests on the ideal of a society that is inclusive and celebrates the rich diversity of human beings, not as 'capital', but as creative, intelligent, and feeling beings open to the rich possibilities of human life. This view of democracy as encompassing the inclusion and participation of all groups and individuals is at the heart of struggles over education. It is the potential of educational institutions to be sites for critique and open and heated discussion that makes them dangerous and feared by those who want acquiescence and ignorance about the the realities of power and privilege. Repeatedly (and certainly in the present political climate) elites have attempted to narrow democracy to a limited sphere of individual interests, while leaving political discussion and power to the few. Thus women's concerns and women's lives have been excluded from neo-conservative discourse about education. But over and over again women and others who have been excluded by this narrow definition of democracy have organized and demanded inclusion in the political process and redefined what it means to be an active member of civil society. They have argued for a conception of democracy that is more than simply individual freedom for private choices, but implies as well the participation of all members of the society in the rights and responsibilities of citizenship. Vincent Harding has spoken of the need for 'advanced ideas of democracy'; these 'advanced ideas' entail the participation of all members of the society in making the decisions that affect their lives, and this, of course, implies the recognition of the diversity of culture that marks the post-modern world, and the memory of the struggles for social, economic, and civil rights that have shaped its history (Harding, 1990). It also implies a conception of the social good, a commitment to the well-being and decent lives for all citizens.

The problems facing education reflect decisions and choices that have been made about the use of resources, the distribution of wealth and concentration of power, and the value of human lives. As these chapters make clear, policy matters. The authors in this volume point to the need for feminists to theorize the state as an arena of struggle, not as a monolith. Underlying all of these papers is a recognition that the world we live in and the ways in which we understand it are not fixed and are not inevitable. To formulate a strategy to counter the trends of the last decade and the escalating crisis in education, to intervene to create a gender fair education, they argue that we need to analyze the nature of this crisis and the choices and policies that have brought it about. And all share a conviction that just as exploitation and oppression are human acts that both are grounded in and create identities of center and margin, so political resistance and a demand for transformation are human acts grounded not in essential identities but in the political imagination and in collective work in the world.

Notes

1 Feminist theory influenced by post-modernist thought has burgeoned in the last decade and now studies are constantly appearing. See, as representative collection, de Lauretis (1986), Nicolson (1990) and Butler and Scott (1992). For feminst critiques of colonialism and racism, see, for example, Spivak (1990) and Anzaldua (1987).

2 For a thoughtful analysis of the potential political dangers of post-modernist thought, see Hartsock (1987).

References

ANZALDUA, G. (1987) *Borderlands\La Trontera*, San Fransciso, CA, Spinsters.

ARNOT, M. (1991) 'Equality and democracy: A decade of struggle over education', *British Journal of Sociology of Education*, **12**, 4, pp. 447–67.

ARNOT, M. (1992) 'Feminism, education and the New Right' in ARNOT, M. and BARTON, L. (Eds) *Voicing Concerns: Sociological Perspectives on Contemporary Education Reforms*, Oxford, Triangle Books.

BUTLER, J. and SCOTT, J. (Eds) (1992) *Feminist Theorize the Political*, New York, Routledge.

CALLAHAN, R. (1962) *Education and the Cult of Efficiency*, Chicago, IL, University of Chicago Press.

DE LAURETIS, T. (Ed.) (1986) *Feminist Studies/Critical Studies*, Bloomington, IN, Indiana University Press.

FERGUSON, R. (1990) 'Introduction: Invisible center' in FERGUSON, R.M., GEVER, M., MINH-HA, T. and WEST, C. (Eds) *Out There*, Cambridge, MA, MIT Press.

GRAMSCI, A. (1971) *Selections from the Prison Notebooks*, New York, International Publishers.

HALL, C. (1992) 'Missionary stories: Gender and ethnicity in England in the 1830s and 1840s' in GROSSBERG, L., TREICHLER, P. and NELSON, C. (Eds) *Cultural Studies*, London and New York, Routledge.

HARDING, V. (1990) *Hope and History*, Maryknoll, NY, Orbis Books.

HARTSOCK, N. (1987) 'Rethinking modernism: Minority vs. Majority theories', *Cultural Critique*, **7**, pp. 197–206.

HOFFMAN, N. (Ed.) (1981) *Woman's True Profession*, Old Westbury, NY, The Feminist Press.

KOZOL, J. (1991) *Savage Inequalities*, New York, Crown Publishers.

LORDE, A. (1984) *Sister Outsider*, Trumansburg New York, Crossing Press.

NICOLSON, L. (Ed.) (1990) *Feminism\Postmodernism*, New York, Routledge.

SPIVAK, G. (1990) *The Post-Colonial Critic*, New York, Routledge.

UNITED STATES NATIONAL COMMISSION ON EXCELLENGE IN EDUCATION (1983) *A Nation at Risk*, Washington, D.C., The Commission.

WEST, C. (1990) 'The new cultural politics of difference' in FERGUSON, R., GEVER, M., MINH-HA, T. and WEST, C. (Eds) *Out There: Marginalization and Contemporary Cultures*, Cambridge, MA, MIT Press.

Notes on Contributors

Sandra Acker is an Associate Professor in the Department of Sociology in Education, Ontario Institute for Studies in Education, Canada. Before moving to Canada, she taught for a number of years at the University of Bristol in England. She has published widely on gender issues, higher education, and teachers, and edited *Teachers, Gender and Careers* (Falmer Press, 1989). Her research interests include primary teachers' workplace cultures and thesis supervision of graduate students.

Madeleine Arnot is a University Lecturer in Sociology of Education in the Department of Education at Cambridge University, and Fellow of Jesus College England having taught the Open University for many years. She has published widely on class and gender relations in education and equal opportunities policies on race and gender. She co-edited with Gaby Weiner *Gender Under Scrutiny* and *Gender and the Politics of Schooling* (Hutchinson, 1987) and is currently writing a book on *Feminist Politics and Education Reform* (Falmer Press).

Miriam E. David is Head of Research in Legal, Political and Social Sciences at the Business School, South Bank University London, England. Prior to that she taught social policy and women's studies at the University of Bristol for 12 years. She has an international reputation for her research and scholarly work in families, gender and education and social policies. Her publications include *For the Children's Sake*, with Caroline New, 1985. *Parents, Gender and Education Reform*, Oxford, Polity Press.

Michèle Foster is an Associate Professor of Education and African-American and African Studies at the University of California-Davis (USA). In 1992 she received the Distinguished Scholar Award (Early Career Achievement Level) from the Standing Committee on the Role and Status of Minorities in Educational Research and Development of the American Educational Research

Association. She has published extensively on the social and cultural context of learning, sociolinguistic analyses of classrooms, and ethnographic and qualitative studies of African-American families, communities and teachers.

Sue Middleton taught in schools at elementary, junior high, and high school levels. She is a Senior Lecturer in the Department of Education at the University of Waikato, Hamilton, New Zealand. Her most recent work is *Educating Feminists; Life histories and pedogogy* (Teachers' College Press, 1993). Her research interests include teachers' life-histories and the implications for women of educational restructuring.

Heidi Safia Mirza is a Senior Lecturer in Social Science at South Bank University, London, England. She has taught Afro-American studies at Brown University, USA and Sociology at the University of London. She is the author of *Young, Female and Black* (Routledge, 1992).

Linda Tuhiwai Smith is a Senior Lecturer in Maori Education at the University of Auckland, New Zealand. She belongs to two Maori tribes, Ngati Awa and Ngati Porou, she also teaches in the Maori Studies Department and coordinates a group of Maori women who produce the journal *Te Pua* which focuses on Maori women's issues.

Kathleen Weiler is an Associate Professor in the Education Department at Tufts University, Massachusetts, USA. She is the author of *Women and Teaching for Change* (Bergin and Garvey, 1988) and has written on various aspects of women and education. She is currently engaged on an historical study of rural women teachers in California.

Gaby Weiner is currently Director of Studies in the School of Education and Health Studies at South Bank University, London, England. She has edited a number of collections including *Just a Bunch of Girls* (Open University Press, 1985) and *The Primary School and Equal Opportunities* (Cassell, 1990) and more recently co-edited with Madeleine Arnot, *Women's Education in Europe* (Carfax, 1992). She has written widely on equal opportunities in education, women's history and feminist theory and is also director of a research project on equity and staffing in higher education.

Lyn Yates is a Senior Lecturer in the School of Education of La Trobe University in Australia. She has written extensively on gender, curriculum theory and educational policy. She is the author of *Theory/Practice Dilemmas* (Deakin University, 1990) and *Education for Girls: Policy, Research and the Question of Gender* (Australian Council for Education Research, 1993).

Index